Six Television Plays

BY REGINALD ROSE

SIMON AND SCHUSTER : NEW YORK
1956

The plays included in this volume all appeared on "Studio One," except for *Crime in the Streets*, which appeared on "The Elgin Hour."

FIRST PRINTING

LIBRARY OF CONGRESS CATALOG CARD NUMBER: 56-6676
MANUFACTURED IN THE UNITED STATES OF AMERICA
H. WOLFF BOOK MFG. CO., INC., NEW YORK

FOR BARBARA—who is as much a part of these plays as if she had written every word—with love and gratitude.

Contents

Foreword

IT HAS ALWAYS been my impression that forewords written for collections such as this one usually contain a great deal of deeply introspective comment by the author concerning the subject matter included and what it means to him artistically and emotionally. I intend to make some comments (how deeply introspective they will be I cannot say) and some additional observations which may prove interesting to those readers whose ambition it is to become writers, but I feel that this type of addenda, in order to be explicit, should take the form of short essays appearing after each play in this book.

This still leaves a foreword to be written, and all I have left for it is a carefully weeded-out selection of unrelated trivia and personal notes. If you care to bear with this kind of doodling, fine. If not, the first play begins on page 1 and is highly recommended by the publishers of this volume.

First, should anyone be interested in the history of a relatively brief career in television and how it came about, I submit the following. My first television play, which was performed in December 1951, was a half-hour original, written in sheer desperation as a protest against the nightly agonies television had to offer. Those of you who had television sets in 1951 will know what I mean. As I look at it now, what I had written merely added more agony to the pile. But it did pay me $650, and open my eyes to a brand-new method for keeping the pot boiling (the only problem at the time being the ability to afford a pot). That play shall remain nameless, as shall the next dozen plays I turned out, all of which were written between January 1952 and November 1953, and all of which were uniformly mediocre. During this period I worked as a copywriter for a small advertising agency specializing in men's and women's wear, and all of my television writing was done at night and on week ends. I realized that these sixteen-hour days were becoming ridiculous when I found myself referring to my oldest boy, then four years of age, as "what's-his-name."

(The happy solution to this dilemma should appear here, I believe. I now work a four-hour day and know all four boys' names at all times.)

Finally, in November of 1953, with considerable urging on the part of Florence Britton, "Studio One's" story editor, I wrote my first hour-long original drama, The Remarkable Incident at Carson Corners. Not long after that the advertising business and I parted ways, both of us immeasurably brightened, and both probably the richer for it. Since then I have written some fourteen one-hour original plays for television, six of which are included here. I have enjoyed myself thoroughly, spent a great deal of leisure time with my wife and family, and managed to pay most of my bills by the tenth of the month.

This kind of creative and financial fulfillment was beyond my reach before I began writing for television, although I had earned my living as a writer for five years previous to my television debut. As an advertising copywriter I must admit that the work I did was creative, though a bit stifling perhaps. Sample: "This lovely wisp of a girdle effortlessly tucks you in at the tummy, as it flattens you at the derrière!" For five years I had wanted to call a spade a spade, and a derrière a behind. Television finally allowed me this pleasure (Act III of The Remarkable Incident at Carson Corners). For an ex-advertising writer this was the rarest of ambrosia. End of history.

To be serious, I am sincerely grateful to the medium which has presented my work to huge audiences and paid me well for it. I am constantly stunned by the complexities of television production and amazed that this infant medium has managed to achieve, at least in its dramatic offerings, a maturity which, in general, surpasses the standards set by motion pictures over the past forty-odd years. During an average week a viewer can see perhaps fourteen live one-hour plays, at least several of which will offer skillfully written, expertly staged dramas with an intelligent and mature point of view. The search for adult entertainment in motion pictures is more difficult and the rewards come less frequently. Hollywood has of course produced its share of fine films, but its self-imposed standard of what the average motion picture should be is considerably below that of live television.

For the playwright, television has much to offer. It offers him an area of work which provides much of the immediacy of the theater, plus all of the intimacy of the motion picture. It offers him an opportunity to produce dramas which, if he avoids certain regrettable taboos, can be as adult and revealing as much of our finest theater. But most important, television gives the serious playwright the opportunity to earn a living while learning his craft. I know of no other medium for the written word which can do the same.

A new school of serious writers has sprung up in the past few years, writers with much that is important and revealing to say about the social patterns of our times. Were there no television, with its endless demands for material, most of these writers would be scrambling to compete in overcrowded markets and turning out work unrepresentative of their talents, or, faced with meeting the economic needs of their families, they would be forced into other fields.

I can't help going back to reminiscences about my singularly drab advertising career in making this point, and I suddenly remember with great clarity three sterile days spent trying to name a new brassiere developed by one of our clients. Toward the close of the third day I leaped to my feet with what I felt to be divine inspiration. I had the name! Into the office of the agency president I raced (this is possible in small agencies) and stood proudly before him. "The name of the new brassiere is . . . Upsa-Daisy," I said. He looked at me for a moment. Then he spoke. "By God, boy, you have got a flair for this business," he said. It developed later that the client hated the name. Thought it was vulgar. To this day I still consider it quite titillating.

The point I wish to make is this: Were it not for the advent of television I might still be trying to think of a name for that brassiere.

Writing for television has been, for me, an exciting and rewarding experience. I have met, worked with and learned a great deal from brilliant, imaginative directors like Franklin Schaffner, Sidney Lumet and Paul Nickell. And I have been helped inestimably in my development as a writer by Felix Jackson, producer of "Studio One" for the past three seasons. I am indebted to these people and extremely grateful for their assistance and encouragement.

All of the plays in this book were written during the period January 1954–April 1955. I am proud of some of them, and would give much for the opportunity of rewriting others. These others (and they shall be nameless here) are presented, however, exactly as they were aired. The only apologies I have to make for them have already been made to my wife. I hope you may enjoy reading them as much as I've enjoyed writing them.

REGINALD ROSE

February 1956

The Remarkable Incident at Carson Corners

―― JANUARY 11, 1954 ――――

PRODUCER	Felix Jackson
DIRECTOR	Paul Nickell
SET DESIGNER	Kim Swados
ASSISTANT TO PRODUCER	William Markham Altman
STORY EDITOR	Florence Britton
ASSOCIATE DIRECTOR	Paul Stanley
PROGRAM ASSISTANT	Joan Pilkington

CAST

MR. ROGERS
  Harry Townes
MR. PRINCE
  John C. Becher
MRS. PRINCE
  Doreen Lang
MRS. CALDWELL
  Priscilla Gillette
DR. CALDWELL
  Hugh Reilly
MISS FRANK
  Frances Fuller
MRS. WRIGHT
  Sarah Seeger
MR. WRIGHT
  Robert P. Lieb
MR. WOODBRIDGE
  John Shellie
MRS. WOODBRIDGE
  Lois Holmes
MR. KOVALESKY
  O. Z. Whitehead

MRS. MCGINNIS
  Ruth White
MR. MCGINNIS
  Frank Overton
BOBBY MCGINNIS
  Stefan Olsen
ALICE WOODBRIDGE
  Jane Alexander
BERT HENDRICKS
  Glen Walken
BILLY MCGINNIS
  Pud Flanagan
TOMMY PRINCE
  Charles Taylor
HAROLD WRIGHT
  Stanley Martin
SUSAN CALDWELL
  Susan Halloran
JOEY ROGERS
  John Connaughton
PAINTER
  Jack Ragotzy

—— ACT I ——————————————

Fade in on the outside of the schoolhouse. A sign over the entrance reads "Carson Corners Public School." It is nearly six o'clock in the evening. The schoolhouse is a large, two-story frame building which is at least fifty years old. The entrance leads directly into the ground-floor classroom. Next to entrance is a door which leads into the basement. Directly in front of this is the bottom of an iron fire escape which leads up to a landing on the second floor and into another class-

room which we do not see. The children use the fire escape as a stairway in good weather. It is a fairly recent addition to the building, having been built about eight years ago. Through a window we see the lighted classroom. There are several adults there already and others are arriving, but nowhere do we see any children. Hold on long shot of scene as several adults, all extras, arrive. Mr. and Mrs. Prince stand in front of the school, having arrived early. They are both fortyish, middle-aged people. They nod and bow to several of the extras as they enter the school. Camera moves in on them slowly. A man and woman pass them. Mrs. Prince smiles.

MRS. PRINCE: Hello, Emily.

The woman nods and couple enters school.

MRS. PRINCE (To Mr. Prince): Did you see how Emily Hendricks looked?

MR. PRINCE: I didn't notice.

MRS. PRINCE: I'll bet she's put on ten pounds. That woman hasn't got the sense she was born with, letting herself go like that.

MR. PRINCE: She should have eaten at our house tonight. That was a great little supper you put together. I'm starving.

MRS. PRINCE: We're going over to the Caldwells' later for a snack. Now stop fussing. The invitation said six o'clock sharp. I couldn't help it.

MR. PRINCE: Six sharp! Now there's a dandy time for you. You'd think the kids'd have sense enough to let a man eat his supper in peace. And talking about kids, where's Tommy? I haven't seen that boy for three days.

MRS. PRINCE: Oh, he's probably inside. He's really worked hard to prepare for tonight.

MR. PRINCE: To prepare what? What are these kids cooking up anyway? I've seen them whispering to each other on the streets all week now. Every time you walk by them they shut up like little clams.

MRS. PRINCE (*Smiling*): I know. I've never seen anything so cute. Oh, they're probably going to put on a play or a pageant—something like that. I'm dying to see it. I think the whole idea of the children surprising us is just cunning.

> *Mr. Rogers, a mild-mannered, quiet little man of forty-five or so, comes hurrying by, obviously worried about being late. He doesn't notice the Princes.*

MR. PRINCE: Well, why don't they surprise us at seven o'clock? (*Grinning*) Look at him. (*Calling*) Hey . . . slow down, Mr. Rogers.

> *Mr. Rogers stops, distracted. He looks around absent-mindedly and sees the Princes.*

MR. PRINCE: You're not gonna run a four-minute mile at your age, are you?

> *Mr. Rogers smiles and walks over to them.*

MR. ROGERS: Evening, Mr. Prince. Hello, Mrs. Prince. I guess I was going pretty fast. Joey said to be sure I wasn't late. What time is it?

MR. PRINCE: Ten of six. Plenty of time.

MR. ROGERS: Oh. I was rushing to close the store early and naturally Essie Loomis had to come in to browse among the patent medicines. I couldn't get her out of the place. You know how she reads every label. I was sure I'd be late. Guess I was a little snappy with her. Well, that woman drives me—

MRS. PRINCE: Shhhh.

> *An elderly woman walks by, carrying a small package. She glares at Mr. Rogers and walks haughtily to the door.*

MR. ROGERS (*Low*): Liver extract. See you inside. (*He hurries after Miss Loomis, calling*) Miss Loomis . . .

> *He catches up with her at the door and follows her in as the Princes smile.*

MRS. PRINCE: Oh, look, dear. There are the Caldwells. (*Calling*) Cecily . . .

> *Cut to Dr. and Mrs. Caldwell as they look at the Princes and smile. The Princes walk to them. Mrs. Prince takes Mrs. Caldwell's hand.*

MRS. CALDWELL: Hello, Helen. Is that your new coat? Lovely . . .

> *The women ad-lib as we cut to men.*

MR. PRINCE: Hello, Doc. How goes it?

DR. CALDWELL: Fine, Harry. How's that cough?

MR. PRINCE: Well, it was killing me, but I got your bill this morning and—phfft—it disappeared just like that.

> *Mr. Prince laughs heartily and is joined by the doctor. They turn to the women.*

MRS. PRINCE: . . . at Harding's in Centerville. They've got the most wonderful sale. You ought to run down.

DR. CALDWELL: She ought not to run down. Let's get inside before I go broke.

MRS. CALDWELL: Fred . . .

> *They start to walk inside.*

DR. CALDWELL: Say, does anyone know what these pipsqueaks are up to? Susie's been looking like a little spy all week. What's the mystery?

MRS. PRINCE: Nobody knows. Isn't it the cutest thing? The children haven't even told Miss Frank what it is. She told me she asked them point-blank in geography class yesterday. They made her go back to the lesson. Can you imagine?

DR. CALDWELL (*Laughing*): I can not. Poor Miss Frank.

> *They are at the door. Mr. Prince opens it. Cut to shot of Mr. and Mrs. Wright, well-dressed people in their forties, obviously among the more influential people in town. They are standing at side of building. Mr. Wright is smoking a last cigarette before going in. Mrs. Wright*

waves at *the Princes and Caldwells, and turns to Mr.
Wright.*

MRS. WRIGHT: Mervin, do you have to smoke that down to the
last quarter of an inch? I'm cold.

MR. WRIGHT: Be finished in a minute, dear. (*Calling to someone off*) Hello, Bill. (*Low to Mrs. Wright as he nudges
her*) Bill and Henny Woodbridge.

*She squints as the Woodbridges enter. They are an
older couple. Mr. Woodbridge is the school principal.*

MR. WRIGHT: How are you, Bill?

MR. WOODBRIDGE: Just fine, Merv. Well, Mrs. Wright, you
look all spruced up. Ready for the show?

MRS. WRIGHT (*To Merv*): There. You see? I told you it was
a show.

*Mrs. Wright and Mrs. Woodbridge move off to one
side. Cut to shot of them.*

MRS. WRIGHT: Henrietta, it's been ages.

MRS. WOODBRIDGE: Hello, Julia. How are the children?

MRS. WRIGHT: Just fine. Phyllis lost her first tooth yesterday.
It would be right here in front.

She demonstrates. Cut to shot of two men.

MR. WRIGHT: What kind of a show is it, Bill?

MR. WOODBRIDGE: Well, to tell you the truth, I don't know if
it's a show or not. I'm only the principal of this school. I'm
not supposed to know anything. (*Chuckling*) I don't dare
ask the kids about it. They'd have my head.

MR. WRIGHT: They're really something. Harold won't tell me
a thing. Changes the subject every time I ask him about it.

MR. WOODBRIDGE: That's a smart boy you've got there, Merv.
Top student. Wish I had more like him.

*Cut to shot of two women as Mr. Wright ad-libs his
thanks for this praise.*

MRS. WRIGHT: . . . these kids have made me so curious . . .

MRS. WOODBRIDGE: I know what you mean. Julia, if you could
see the way Alice has been acting lately. Well, Alice just
loves being mysterious anyway.

MRS. WRIGHT: Girls do.

MRS. WOODBRIDGE: Yesterday I told her I was surprised they let
her in on it with her being only ten, and she just looked
at me.

MRS. WRIGHT (*Laughing*): I know the look.

The men walk over to them.

MR. WRIGHT: Come on, let's go in. It must be about ready to
start.

> *He takes Mrs. Wright's arm and leads her to the door.
> They start to walk in. As they reach the doorway, the
> door to the basement opens and Mr. Kovalesky, the
> janitor, walks out. He is old, but with the agelessness of
> people who have spent all their lives around children.
> He is a mild little man who speaks with an accent. He
> has served the school for over thirty years and of course
> the children call him Kovey. He smiles humbly at Mr.
> Woodbridge.*

MR. KOVALESKY: Good evening, Mr. Woodbridge, Mrs. Woodbridge.

MR. WOODBRIDGE: Hello, Kovey. Are you invited too?

MR. KOVALESKY: Yes, sir. Special invitation.

> *He smiles.*

MR. WOODBRIDGE: Well, that's fine.

MR. KOVALESKY: I just fix the furnace to be sure we got plenty
heat.

MR. WOODBRIDGE: Good.

> *Mr. Kovalesky begins to lock the basement door. Mrs.
> Wright looks into schoolroom.*

MRS. WRIGHT: Well, now, isn't that darling. They've got reserved seats . . . and an usher!

> *Cut to inside of schoolroom. It is a large room with the*

flavor of a real old-fashioned school. Along the front
wall is a blackboard on which is laboriously lettered,
"Welcome to Carson Corners Public School." There
are seven or eight rows of old desks, complete with
inkwells, etc. In front of room is the teacher's desk.
On either side of it is a small table and two chairs
which face the children's desks. Directly in front of
the teacher's desk is another small table and chair. Off
to one side are two rows of three chairs, placed as a
jury box would be. Along one wall are three windows
on which are pasted the usual decorative cut-outs.
There is a door at front of room which leads into another room, a room we never see. This door is closed.
At the children's desks are seated Mr. Rogers, Mr. and
Mrs. Prince, Dr. and Mrs. Caldwell, Miss Loomis,
and all of the adult extras to be used. The room hums
with conversation. The mood is festive, joyous. The
air is electric with excitement. The Wrights and
Woodbridges stand in the doorway beaming. The only
child we see is the usher, Bobby McGinnis. He is
twelve years old, but acts years older now. He is un-
smiling, reserved, and reacts to the good-natured kidding he receives from the adults with a cold reserve.
He carries a piece of paper to which he refers when
seating the parents. He walks toward the Wrights and
Woodbridges as Mrs. Wright waves to Miss Loomis,
the spinster. Bobby looks at his list.

BOBBY: Mr. and Mrs. Wright. Seats nine and ten. This way,
please.

MR. WRIGHT: Hello, Bobby-boy. You the usher?

BOBBY: Yes, sir.

They start to walk toward the seats. The Woodbridges
follow.

MR. WRIGHT: Hope you've got a pair of front-row seats for us.

BOBBY: Second row, Mr. Wright. (*Bobby turns to Mr. Woodbridge. Brusquely*): Please wait at the door, Mr. Woodbridge.

MR. WOODBRIDGE: Wait at the door? All right. Anything you say, Bobby.

MRS. WOODBRIDGE (*Low*): You know, he sounded downright rude.

MR. WOODBRIDGE: Nonsense.

MRS. WOODBRIDGE: Well, he did.

We pick up the Wrights going to their seats as Bobby stands by.

MRS. WRIGHT: Will you look at Dr. Caldwell trying to stuff those long legs of his under that little desk. Mervin, look.

MR. WRIGHT: Never mind his. I'm worried about mine.

They start to sit down. Bobby goes back to the door to get the Woodbridges. Cut to shot of the Caldwells. Dr. Caldwell is trying hard to get comfortable.

MRS. CALDWELL: What's the matter?

DR. CALDWELL: I'm all tangled up in this thing.

MRS. CALDWELL (*Smiling*): Your stomach is growling.

DR. CALDWELL: Any reason why it shouldn't?

MRS. CALDWELL (*Calling*): Hello, Julia . . . (*Mrs. Wright turns and waves at her*) How are you? (*Mrs. Wright nods comme-ci, comme-ca*) Don't forget, you're coming over later for a bite.

Mrs. Wright nods and mouths the following.

MRS. WRIGHT (*soundlessly*): See you later.

Cut to the Woodbridges being seated by Bobby McGinnis. Mr. Rogers is seated directly behind them. He leans forward to Mr. Woodbridge.

MR. ROGERS: Good evening, Mr. Woodbridge. This is a very nice thing your children are doing.

MR. WOODBRIDGE: Oh . . . thank you, Mr. Rogers.

MR. ROGERS: Very nice. Good evening, Mrs. Woodbridge.

She nods pleasantly at him and he leans back in his seat and smiles. Bobby walks back up the aisle to the door, passing the seats in which the Princes sit. As he passes, Mr. Prince raises his hand and waves it frantically at Bobby as if he were a child in school.

MR. PRINCE: Teacher! Teacher!

The entire room bursts into laughter. But Bobby merely walks by him to the door.

MR. PRINCE: Hey, Bobby . . . what's the matter?

MRS. PRINCE: Harry, stop it, will you please!

The laughter dies down to consistent buzzing as we cut to doorway. Mr. and Mrs. McGinnis stand there. Mr. McGinnis is a big, rough-looking man who seems ill-at-ease in his go-to-meeting suit. Mrs. McGinnis is small and quiet, a mousy woman, but a woman who can be firm when firmness is called for. Both of them are somewhat silent in contrast to the boisterous behavior of the others. Bobby comes up to them. He scans the list.

BOBBY: Mr. and Mrs. McGinnis. Seats seventeen and eighteen. This way, please.

MR. MC GINNIS: (*Low*): Hello, son.

BOBBY (*Quietly*): Hello, Dad.

Mrs. McGinnis smiles at Bobby.

MR. MC GINNIS: What is this?

BOBBY: I can't tell you.

MRS. MC GINNIS: Now you promised not to ask the boy again, Ralph. Take us to our seats, Bobby.

MR. MC GINNIS: I said, what is this? Your mother and I didn't want to come here now. All these people. I asked you if there was gonna be a lot of people.

BOBBY (*Low*): Dad, please . . .

MRS. MC GINNIS (*Firmly*): Take us to our seats, son.

She takes Mr. McGinnis' arm and they walk down the

aisle, *Bobby leading them. Cut to the Woodbridges.
Mrs. Woodbridge turns to her husband.*

MRS. WOODBRIDGE: There's Mrs. McGinnis. I believe I'll just
go over and say hello to her.

*Mr. Woodbridge nods. Mrs. Woodbridge gets up and
edges her way out to where the McGinnises are just
being seated. We see her take Mrs. McGinnis' hand
and smile at her. Mrs. McGinnis smiles back and says
something we do not hear. Now there is a slight scattering of applause which centers about Mr. Wright.
Cut to him as he grins and claps his hands.*

MR. WRIGHT (*Calling*): Start the show!

*He claps his hands lustily and continues even after the
rest of the applause has died down.*

MRS. WRIGHT: Mervin, for Heaven's sake, act your age.

*He stops applauding and turns to her, grinning like a
child.*

*Cut to Bobby now as he walks back up the aisle. As he
passes Mr. Prince, Mr. Prince catches his arm.*

MR. PRINCE: Hey, Bobby, when's it gonna start? Nobody's
absent or tardy. Let's go. (*He laughs*)

*Bobby pulls his arm away and goes to the door. Mr.
Kovalesky stands there uncertainly, grinning and looking uncomfortable.*

BOBBY: Kovey . . . I mean Mr. Kovalesky. This way, please.

MR. KOVALESKY: It's all right you call me Kovey, Bobby.

*He follows Bobby down the aisle. Bobby takes him to
the front of the room to the table at left of the
teacher's desk and pulls out one of the two chairs for
him.*

MR. KOVALESKY: Here you want me to sit?

*He starts to walk away, embarrassed, pointing to the
rows of children's desks.*

MR. KOVALESKY: I sit over there. Is good enough.

But Bobby takes his arm firmly and turns him to the table.

BOBBY: This is where you're supposed to sit, Mr. Kovalesky. You have to.

MR. KOVALESKY: I have to. (*Shrugging*) All right. Here.

He sits down sheepishly, facing the audience. Bobby walks away.

MR. WRIGHT (*Calling, off camera*): Hey . . . are you the guest of honor, Kovey?

Mr. Kovalesky grins and shrugs. Scattered applause greets his action. Ridiculously, he performs the prize-fighter's routine of shaking hands with himself.

MR. PRINCE (*Calling*): Atta-boy, Kovey.

Cut to Bobby at the door. He scans his list, notes that everyone is there, and firmly closes the door. He remains standing in front of it. Now the people are restless as they wait. The applause starts again, rhythmic, demanding. This time it continues as Mr. Wright calls out.

MR. WRIGHT: Let's have the show!

As if in answer, the door at front of room opens and six children file out. The applause loses its rhythm and becomes enthusiastic. The six children very solemnly move to the jury chairs and sit down. They do not acknowledge the presence of the audience in any way. Included among them are Alice Woodbridge, aged ten, Bert Hendricks, aged nine, and two girls and two boys of varying ages between eight and twelve. These last four are extras.

Cut to Mrs. Woodbridge. She leans over to her husband, delighted.

MRS. WOODBRIDGE (*Whispering*): Just look at Alice. If that isn't the best-looking dress. That Parker girl doesn't show up at all next to her.

MR. WOODBRIDGE: Shh.

> *Cut to close shot of Alice Woodbridge to identify her. Then cut to doorway as Tommy Prince, aged thirteen, comes out stiffly, solemnly, and goes to table at right of teacher's desk. Cut to show Mr. Prince smiling broadly and nudging his wife. She waves to Tommy and blows him a kiss. Tommy sits down at the table, poker-faced. Now Harold Wright, aged eleven, comes out of the door and is greeted by violent applause from Mr. Wright alone. Mrs. Wright stops him angrily. Harold ignores this and goes to the table at which sits Mr. Kovalesky. He shakes hands with Mr. Kovalesky stiffly.*

MR. KOVALESKY: Hello, Harold. You gonna sit with me?

> *Harold nods and sits down. Mr. Kovalesky claps him on the back. Harold remains coldly aloof. Out of the door now comes Susan Caldwell, aged ten. Cut to the Caldwells.*

MRS. CALDWELL: Will you look at Susie's face! Sarah Bernhardt. I'm going to giggle.

MR. CALDWELL: Be quiet, Cess.

> *Susan goes to the table in front of the teacher's desk and stands there facing the audience. There is a long, tense silence. Then, as loudly as she can, she speaks.*

SUSAN: The court will rise!

> *It is too loud. Someone laughs. Someone else hushes the crowd. Everyone looks at each other questioningly and then good-naturedly they rise amidst a sudden buzzing of conversation.*

SUSAN: His honor, Judge Joseph Rogers.

> *Everyone looks at the door as we cut quickly to Mr. Rogers' blissfully proud face. Cut back to door as Joey comes out. He is a serious-faced boy of twelve or thirteen. He carries a gavel. He walks slowly to the*

teacher's desk, stands behind it solemnly and raps the gavel on it.

JOEY: This court is now in session.

He sits down. Again the loud buzzing starts in the room. Cut to Mrs. Woodbridge as she leans over to her husband.

MRS. WOODBRIDGE (*Delighted*): Bill, if this isn't the most original idea! I never . . .

But the sharp rapping of the gavel silences her and stops the hum of conversation. Cut to Joey. He leans over to Susan, who is sitting at her table.

JOEY: Clerk . . .

Susan looks back at him, a bit nervously.

JOEY (*Low*): Go ahead, Susie.

Susan stands up, holding a sheet of paper. In a loud, strained voice she reads from it.

SUSAN: This court will now try the case of the people of Carson Corners against . . . (*She looks at Mr. Kovalesky, who smiles*) Mr. Peter Kovalesky.

Excited buzzing fills the room. Joey raps the gavel. The room quiets. Susan looks for her place.

SUSAN: Against Mr. Peter Kovalesky . . . for murder!

There is a startled gasp from the audience, and then stunned silence. Mr. Kovalesky begins to rise, shocked suddenly, and confused.

Fade out.

—— *ACT II* ——————————————

Fade in on schoolroom, no time lapse. The parents are as bewildered as Mr. Kovalesky. He is standing. Susan sits down and looks away from him. The children, suddenly children again, are frightened at what they have done. Then, suddenly, there is a loud babble of talk in the room. Everyone speaks at once as Mr. Kovalesky struggles for words. We catch snatches of sentences.

MR. WRIGHT (Loud): What do you kids think you are doing? Getting every one down here to listen to nonsense like that. . . .

MRS. WRIGHT: Why, I never heard of such a thing! Harold Wright, you just wait till . . .

MR. PRINCE: Hey! What's the idea? I suppose you kids think that's funny. . . .

MRS. WOODBRIDGE: Did you hear that, Bill? Did you ever . . .

MRS. CALDWELL (Rising): Susie! Susie Caldwell, you come over here this minute. . . .

> Doctor Caldwell pulls her down. Cut to Mr. Kovalesky. Amidst the confusion he speaks softly, standing facing the children.

MR. KOVALESKY: No. No. What kind of a thing to say? You make a joke. Susie! (He walks over to her. She looks away, frightened) You make a joke.

> He gets closer to her as the noise from the room continues. Joey raps the gavel. Mr. Kovalesky shakes his finger at Susan.

MR. KOVALESKY: That's not a good joke. Murder. Not good.

> He takes Susan's arm. Dr. Caldwell stands.

DR. CALDWELL (Shouting): Get your hands off her!

> He begins to stride to the front of the room.

MR. WOODBRIDGE (Shouting): Quiet! Quiet! (The hubbub begins to subside) Kovey, sit down! Now be quiet—all of you!

> The noise dies out completely. Dr. Caldwell, finding himself standing, sits down sheepishly. Mr. Kovalesky sits down. Mr. Woodbridge looks around the room.

MR. WOODBRIDGE: I know as little about what's going on here as any of you. But whatever it is, we're going to have order.

There's no sense in getting these kids any more frightened than they are right now. Now let's talk one at a time.

MR. WRIGHT (*Loudly*): Right!

MRS. WRIGHT: Well . . . I'd certainly like to know why . . .

MR. WOODBRIDGE: Julia . . . just a minute . . . please . . . (*He turns to Joey*) Joey, are you in charge of this?

JOEY: No, sir. We all are. All the kids.

MR. WOODBRIDGE: Do you know it's not very funny to accuse a man of murder . . . even in a joke?

JOEY: Yes, sir. Mr. Wood—

MR. WOODBRIDGE: I think you'd better apologize to Mr. Kovalesky.

JOEY: Sir . . .

> But Mr. Kovalesky, having recovered his composure, turns to Mr. Woodbridge, smiling.

MR. KOVALESKY: No. Is all right. Just kids. I know kids for thirty years. They have a joke. Is all right.

MR. WOODBRIDGE: All right, Kovey. Now I think we can call an end to this. (*To his wife*) Henny . . .

MR. ROGERS (*Standing*): Mr. Woodbridge . . . pardon me. I was thinking. The children . . . they worked all week to surprise us. All the whispering . . . the preparations. My boy Joey made me give him two weeks' allowance in advance. Now I see it was to buy that thing . . . that gavel.

> Someone laughs and the tension is broken. Mr. Rogers laughs, too.

MR. ROGERS: Well . . . maybe it's not such a good idea, but if Mr. Kovalesky wouldn't mind . . . it would be a shame to disappoint the children. Maybe no one agrees with me. I don't know. Thank you.

> Mr. Rogers sits down, a bit embarrassed.

MR. PRINCE (*Calling*): Sure. Let 'em go ahead. It's their party.

> The buzzing starts in the room.

MR. WOODBRIDGE: Kovey?

Mr. Kovalesky looks around and grins as everyone seems to relax once again.

MR. KOVALESKY: Sure. They good kids.

MR. WOODBRIDGE: All right. Does anyone else want to say something?

MR. WRIGHT: Order in the court!

Everyone laughs and Mr. Woodbridge sits down. The children have watched all of this impassively, seeming to be above it. Joey raps the gavel and the room quiets down.

JOEY (*To Mr. Kovalesky*): The court has appointed Harold Wright as your lawyer, Mr. Kovalesky. Any objections?

MR. KOVALESKY (*Grinning*): No, your honor. (*To Harold*) I got a good lawyer, eh, Harold?

JOEY: Counsel for the prosecution.

Tommy Prince stands up and looks at the parents, then at the kids. Slowly he walks over to the jury as we hear Mrs. Prince titter. Mr. Prince hushes her.

TOMMY (*Strained*): Ladies and gentlemen of the jury. We're going to prove that the man sitting over there in that chair, Mr. Peter Kovalesky, is a murderer. We're going to prove that the murder he did was pre— (*He looks at a slip of paper in his hand*)—was premeditated. That he probly had it all figured out before he did it . . . and that all the time he's been laughing and kidding around he knew he did it!

Mr. Kovalesky watches, amused, as Tommy paces up and down now.

TOMMY: Five months and six days ago, something happened that maybe most people in Carson Corners don't think about much any more.

Cut to Mr. and Mrs. Prince. Mr. Prince, hanging on every word, nudges his wife proudly.

TOMMY: But I'm thinking about it and so is every kid who goes to this school.

Tommy pauses, catches his breath nervously.

TOMMY (Very fast): I'm talking about the time Billy Mc-
Ginnis fell off the fire escape right outside this door and
was killed.

*Mr. McGinnis gets to his feet, shouting, as Bobby
McGinnis runs down the aisle.*

MR. MC GINNIS: No! What are you trying to do?

*Bobby runs in front of him as he strides into the aisle,
furious.*

BOBBY (Screaming): Dad! Don't—

MR. MC GINNIS: Get away from me!

BOBBY: Please . . . please, Dad. You've got to listen!

Bobby tries to hold him back.

MR. MC GINNIS: You ought to be whipped! Letting them make
a game out of your own brother's death.

He raises his arm.

BOBBY: Dad! Please . . . it's not a game!

*Mr. McGinnis looks closely at Bobby and then at
Tommy Prince, and then at the others in the room who
stare at him silently. Then he sits down and covers his
face with his hands. Bobby sits next to him. Mrs.
McGinnis stares straight ahead. Mr. Kovalesky looks
strangely at Tommy now as he continues.*

TOMMY: It was an accident. That's what everyone said. The
railing was busted . . . broken . . . and Billy fell through
it. Well, we don't think he fell. We think he was pushed
through the railing and killed . . . by Mr. Kovalesky!

*The room explodes with excitement. Mr. Kovalesky,
enraged, gets up and goes for Tommy. Mr. Prince
comes down the aisle fast. Others in the room stand
and shout. Mr. Woodbridge bellows for order. Joey
raps the gavel.*

MR. KOVALESKY (Roaring): What do you say? What do you
say about me? That's a lie! I take you and give you good!

He grabs Tommy, but Mr. Prince gets there and pulls him away violently.

MR. PRINCE: Stop it! You touch him and I'll break your head open!

He shoves Mr. Kovalesky aside and grabs Tommy by both shoulders.

MR. PRINCE (*Furiously*): Now listen to me! Do you know what you just said?

Calmly, Tommy nods that he does.

MR. PRINCE: Do you know what it means, Tommy? Answer me.

TOMMY: Yes, I do.

MR. PRINCE: You're not playing with kid stuff, Tommy. This isn't a cute little idea any more.

TOMMY (*Strongly*): We never said it was!

Mr. Prince looks at him closely and sees that Tommy means it. He steps back. Tommy looks at him steadily.

MR. PRINCE: Have you got anything more to say?

TOMMY: Yes.

MR. PRINCE (*Loud*): Well then, say it! I'm listening.

He goes back to his seat. There is a great silence in the room. Mr. Kovalesky looks around at everyone, then he turns to Mr. Woodbridge, frightened now.

MR. KOVALESKY: Mr. Woodbridge . . .

MR. WOODBRIDGE: Maybe you'd better sit down, Kovey.

Mr. Kovalesky sits down. Everyone waits silently. Tommy sits down. Joey turns to Harold Wright and nods.

JOEY: Counsel for the defense.

Harold gets up and goes to the jury.

HAROLD: Ladies and gentlemen of the jury, we all know Mr. Kovalesky . . . Kovey. Kovey has been janitor of our school for over thirty years. We see him every day. He's always been good to the kids, and . . .

MR. WOODBRIDGE (*Standing*): I think we ought to get to the point. All this nonsense . . .

MR. WRIGHT (*Angrily*): Let him talk!

> *Mr. Woodbridge sits down.*

HAROLD: Well, the idea is, Kovey is our friend. He's always been friends with the kids in school, even when they play jokes on him. You know, jokes like the water bucket we put on top of the basement door. He never even got sore. Kovey likes kids, and a man who likes kids the way Kovey does could never have pushed Billy McGinnis off the fire escape. He never could. Everybody knows that about Kovey.

> *Harold sits down next to Mr. Kovalesky. Tommy stands up.*

TOMMY (*To Susan*): Call the first witness.

SUSAN (*Standing*): Bert Hendricks.

> *Bert Hendricks, a boy of about nine, is sitting in the jury box. He gets up and walks across to Susan. She stands up and takes a Bible from the teacher's desk. Bert puts his hand on it and raises his other hand.*

SUSAN: Swear to tell the truth, the whole truth and nothing but the truth, so help you God?

BERT: Yop.

SUSAN: What's your name?

BERT: Bertram Frank Hendricks, Jr.

> *Bert sits in the witness chair at right of teacher's desk. Susan sits down. Tommy goes over to Bert, stands next to him.*

BERT: Hi.

TOMMY: Bert, did you know Billy McGinnis?

BERT: Sure. He was my best friend in the whole school.

TOMMY: Did you see him the day he died?

BERT: Sure. I saw him every day. He sat right next to me in geography and arithmetic. Size place. You know. He was the same size as me.

JOEY: Just answer the questions.

BERT: Okay.

TOMMY: Tell us what happened when you saw Billy McGinnis that day.

BERT: Okay. Well it was about eleven o'clock because Mr. Woodbridge's class was just having recess. Most of the kids were playing games and stuff in the yard. I was going upstairs to finish my history homework before the class started. You know how Mr. Woodbridge gets sore . . .

We are close on Bert as the image starts to distort slowly, indicating a flashback. As image clears, we see the fire escape in broad daylight. Mr. Kovalesky comes out of upstairs doorway carrying a broom. He puts it down, takes out a pipe, fills it with tobacco and lights it. Then he begins to sweep the steps. When he is halfway down, he pauses to mop his brow and then grins when he sees someone coming upstairs, off camera.

MR. KOVALESKY: Hey, not so fast, mister. Where are you going?

He bars the way with the broom. Now we see Bert in a jacket and wool hat, carrying a load of books up the stairs. He squirms under the broom. Mr. Kovalesky pulls his hat down over his eyes, and laughs heartily.

BERT: Ah, cut it out, Kovey!

Indignantly he goes up to the landing as Mr. Kovalesky chuckles. Then he turns, and, leaning against the railing, he makes a face at Mr. Kovalesky. The railing sags.

MR. KOVALESKY (*Shouting*): Look out!

Bert leaps to safety as Mr. Kovalesky comes up to the landing in a hurry.

BERT: Gee! Did you see that? Holy cow!

Mr. Kovalesky tests the loose railing. It sways precariously.

BERT: Look at it wiggle!

MR. KOVALESKY: Yes. This gets fixed right now. You want to help me with the tools, Bert?

BERT: No, I can't. I gotta go in.

> *Mr. Kovalesky starts down the stairs. Bert stands on the landing, still amazed.*

BERT: Holy cow! (*Then Bert looks down and waves to someone*) Hi, Bill.

> *We see Billy McGinnis, a boy of eight or nine years old, at the bottom of stairs. He carries books. Mr. Kovalesky reaches him.*

BILLY: Hi.

> *Mr. Kovalesky puts his arm on Billy's shoulder and starts to say something to him, but we only hear Bert calling.*

BERT: Wait till you hear what happened to me!

> *Bert watches as Billy nods to Mr. Kovalesky. They go toward the cellar door, pausing in front of it as Mr. Kovalesky gets his key and opens it. They go in. The image distorts slowly now and when it becomes clear again we see a full shot of the parents in the school-room, listening. Camera pans room slowly as we hear, but do not see, Bert Hendricks. The faces of the parents are intent. Camera pan ends on Mr. and Mrs. McGinnis as Bert talks. Mrs. McGinnis is sobbing softly. The face of Mr. McGinnis is hard.*

BERT: Well, anyway, in the middle of history class I had to go . . . well, I had to go downstairs. It was maybe about quarter of twelve. I don't know. I tried the railing again. You know, I gave it a shove. It was still busted. When I got downstairs I saw Billy McGinnis coming out of Miss Frank's room. We used to meet like that sometimes downstairs. He looked . . . scared.

> *The image distorts, indicating a flashback. When it*

clears we see Bert reaching the bottom of stairs as Billy comes out of downstairs schoolroom.

BILLY: Hey . . . Bert . . .

Bert goes over to him, grinning.

BERT: You wanta trade socks on the arm? You first. Come on, Bill.

BILLY: No. Listen, I gotta tell you something important. Honest.

BERT: What?

BILLY: You know when I went in the basement with Kovey before? (*Bert nods impatiently*) Guess what I saw.

BERT: How do I know?

He jabs Billy on the arm.

BILLY: Quit it. You know the Community Fund cans we filled up at the collection the other day? Kovey has 'em hidden down there. I think he stole 'em.

BERT (*Breathless*): No kiddin'!

BILLY: Honest. There must be fifteen dollars in 'em. He had 'em stuck behind the boiler. He saw me looking at 'em, so I ran out. I tried to tell Miss Frank, but she said I was innarupting the class. I'm scared, Bert. He's probably after me.

BERT: Holy cow! (*Bert looks nervously at the basement door*) Listen, I gotta go back. So long.

He starts running up the stairs. Billy looks around nervously as Bert disappears into the room upstairs. Then Billy starts to run up the stairs as we hear the children from the downstairs classroom faintly begin to sing "America."

BILLY (*Shouting*): Hey, Bert! Wait a minute. Wait . . .

The image begins to distort. When it clears, we are back in the schoolroom, close on Tommy Prince. There is an angry grumbling in the room.

TOMMY (*Loud and clear*): We think that Mr. Kovalesky

pushed Billy off the fire escape because Billy saw the Community Fund money he stole!

Instantly the room becomes alive with excitement. Mr. Kovalesky stands up in anger.

MR. PRINCE (*Shouting*): What about that? You heard what he said! Open your mouth. What about it?

MR. KOVALESKY: No! No! I didn't. He don't tell the truth. . . .

MR. PRINCE (*Shouting*): Then what is the truth? Let's hear!

MR. WRIGHT (*Shouting*): Look at him! Look at his face!

The rumbling continues as Mr. Kovalesky looks around him, frightened now.

MR. KOVALESKY: No! No! I never pushed him. Never. . . .

MR. PRINCE: Who did?

DR. CALDWELL (*Shouting*): What about the money . . .

MRS. CALDWELL (*Shocked*): Fred!

DR. CALDWELL (*Ignoring her*): I said what about that Community Fund money?

MR. KOVALESKY (*Shouting*): It's a lie! A lie! I don't steal money! (*He walks up to the front row of seats*) They lie! Children! They lie to you!

His shouting quiets the room. He stops. He looks around the room. The faces are ugly, all but the children's. They watch quietly, impassively.

MR. KOVALESKY (*Quietly*): Miss Frank, she give me cans to hold. So nobody should steal. I don't steal! Ask her. You ask Miss Frank. (*Calling*) Miss Frank . . . (*Everyone looks around the room. Miss Frank is not there*) Miss Frank!

MRS. CALDWELL: She's not here. She had to go over to Centerville.

MR. KOVALESKY: Miss Frank! Ask Miss Frank!

Tommy has come up behind Mr. Kovalesky with a large paper bag which he has taken from behind the teacher's desk. He reaches into it now, pulls out a can, puts it on the desk in front of Mr. Kovalesky. Then he takes out another, and another, puts them down. Then he picks one up and shakes it. The coins jingle in it. Everyone watches silently. Mr. Kovalesky stares, afraid.

TOMMY: This is exhibit A. Joey Rogers found them behind the boiler in the basement last Friday. He sneaked in there when—

MR. WRIGHT (*Calling*): Last Friday! That's five months later. Five months! Do you hear that? He stole 'em. . . .

MR. PRINCE (*Shouting*): That's enough for me! Listen, everybody—(*The room is bursting with noise*) Listen! There's a boy dead. . . .

MR. KOVALESKY: No! You don't understand. . . .

Cut to Mr. McGinnis. He starts to rise, murder in his eyes. Mrs. McGinnis, sobbing, grabs him, pulls him down. He lets her.

MR. KOVALESKY: Miss Frank forgot. She forgot. I never steal. Never in my life. And I don't kill a child. How could I kill a child? No! I don't. I swear!

Mr. Prince comes down the aisle, enraged.

MR. PRINCE: You swear. I'll show you how to swear!

Several other men, extras, follow him down the aisle. Mr. Wright gets up. He grabs one of the cans and shakes it under Mr. Kovalesky's nose.

MR. WRIGHT: Listen to it! There's the proof!

Mr. Kovalesky backs away, terrified. Mr. Prince grabs Mr. Kovalesky's arm, yanks him to the teacher's desk.

MR. WOODBRIDGE (*Frightened*): What are you doing? They're only children!

But they push him away. Mr. Wright and several other men follow Mr. Kovalesky, angry, hard, ready for violence. Mr. Prince grabs the Bible, forces Mr. Kovalesky's hand onto it. Mr. Wright grabs his other hand, raises it.

MR. PRINCE (*Violently*): Now swear! Swear!

>*Mr. Kovalesky, terrified, looks around at them. They stare angrily back, waiting. He licks his lips.*

MR. KOVALESKY (*Hoarsely*): I swear!

>*Mr. Prince rips the Bible away from him, puts it on the desk and grabs him by the front of his jacket.*

MR. PRINCE: You're a liar!

MR. KOVALESKY: No!

MR. WRIGHT: Let's get him! Come on!

>*Mr. Rogers bursts into the group.*

MR. ROGERS: What are you doing to this man? Who gave you the right—

MR. PRINCE: Get out of my way.

MR. ROGERS: I will not get out of the way. Are you the law in this room?

>*The crowd moves back at this. They look at each other, and then look away. Their rage is diminished somewhat. Mr. Kovalesky straightens up, seeming to find strength in Mr. Rogers' words.*

MR. ROGERS: I'm ashamed that our sons and daughters have seen us behaving like animals. What are they thinking of us? (*He steps up to Mr. Prince*) The avenger. You're so ready to punish. Did you see this man commit a crime? (*To Mr. Wright*) Did you? (*To everyone*) Did any of you actually see him? (*No one answers. He steps to Mr. Kovalesky's side and looks at him*) Maybe it was as the children say. Maybe it was . . . but this is not the way.

MR. KOVALESKY: No! It was not as they say! I tell the truth!

MR. PRINCE (*Roaring*): Shut up! We've had enough talk. Let's do something about it now.

>*The men surge forward again, but a sharp voice roars out, stopping them.*

MR. MC GINNIS: Let him talk!

>*Cut to him. He stands on his feet. The room silences*

*instantly. Everyone looks at him. He continues to
stand, stonily. They back away from Mr. Kovalesky.
Cut to Mr. Kovalesky as he tries to collect his thoughts.
He doesn't know what to say, where to begin.*

MRS. WRIGHT (*Shrilly*): Why didn't you fix the railing?

*We hear a rumble of agreement from the crowd.
Trembling, frightened, he begins to talk in answer to
Mrs. Wright.*

MR. KOVALESKY: I was going to fix. (*Camera pans the crowd
as they listen*) I was going to. I went into my basement. I ask
Billy he should help me carry the tools. They get sometimes
a little heavy for an old man. . . .

*The image distorts to signify flashback. When it clears,
we see a small, dark, neat-looking basement, complete
with the usual basement equipment, workbench, furnace, etc. No one is in it, but the door opens now and
Billy McGinnis comes hopping down the few steps. He
turns at the bottom.*

BILLY: Hey, Kovey, what do you want the tools for? Something busted?

*Billy waits at the bottom of steps for Mr. Kovalesky.
We hear door at top of steps rattling and being pulled.*

BILLY: Huh, Kovey?

Finally Mr. Kovalesky comes down the steps.

MR. KOVALESKY: That door. I gotta fix it sometime. You ask
me something, Billy?

*But Billy has gone over to the workbench, where he
has a drill which he is working and at the same time
he is making a noise with his mouth like grinding gears.
Mr. Kovalesky grins at him and starts to rummage
among some tools in a hanging tool rack on wall.*

BILLY: Kovey, how do you work this thing?

MR. KOVALESKY: You wait a minute. I show you.

He takes a wrench from the rack, and goes over to

Billy, laying the wrench on a table next to his lunch box. But Billy has by now spotted the Community Fund cans behind the boiler. He looks at them, and then looks at Mr. Kovalesky fearfully. He begins to back away toward the steps. Mr. Kovalesky has not noticed that Billy saw the cans.

MR. KOVALESKY: What's the matter, Billy?

BILLY: Nothing.

He runs up the steps and out. Mr. Kovalesky scratches his head, shrugs, and goes back to the tool rack. Absently, he begins to look for the wrench, sees that it is missing and then turns and sees it on the table. He smiles, goes over to it. He picks it up, and then sees a newspaper lying on the table next to his lunchbox. He glances at it, gets interested in it, then picks it up and starts to read. He sits down in a chair, still reading, and reaches for his lunch box. He opens the box, takes out a sandwich and gets comfortable.

Image distorts to signify end of flashback. When it clears we see the parents in the schoolroom. We hear Mr. Kovalesky's voice but do not see him.

MR. KOVALESKY: I sat down and had my lunch then. Liverwurst. Pie. Coffee. An apple. The railing was broke and I was hungry. I didn't know—I didn't know—

Image distorts to signify flashback. When it clears we see the basement again. Mr. Kovalesky is just finishing his lunch. We hear the children begin to sing "America," and then we hear Billy, calling.

BILLY: Hey, Bert. Wait a minute. Wait . . .

Mr. Kovalesky munches his apple peacefully. Suddenly we hear a terrible scream from outside. He listens. We hear the sound of running feet and a great commotion. He gets up quickly and goes to the door and out. Billy McGinnis lies on the ground. Four or five kids are grouped around him, afraid to touch him. Other children run toward him. The only child not there is Susan Caldwell. Mr. Kovalesky looks up. The railing is hanging loosely. He closes his eyes in horror, then opens them and begins to go to Billy. Mr. Woodbridge now runs toward Billy. Mr. Kovalesky stops, stands back, afraid to become involved now. No one looks at him or sees him through this entire scene.

MR. WOODBRIDGE: Look out! Stand back! (He elbows his way into the group) Get out of the way, children. Who is it?

TOMMY: It's Billy McGinnis, Mr. Woodbridge.

BERT: Yeah, It's Billy. Gee!

Mr. Woodbridge kneels down next to Billy. Billy moans. Mr. Woodbridge examines him briefly as the children watch in shocked silence. Then Mr. Woodbridge gets up, carrying Billy in his arms. Mr. Kovalesky watches from the sidelines. As Mr. Woodbridge starts to walk, carrying Billy, Bert Hendricks pulls at his coat tails.

BERT: You shouldn't pick him up, Mr. Woodbridge.

But no one pays attention. Bert follows Mr. Woodbridge and the silent children.

BERT: You're not supposed to move the body. (Mr. Woodbridge doesn't listen) But, Mr. Woodbridge, you taught us yourself in First Aid, we should never move the body.

Mr. Woodbridge reaches the door to the downstairs schoolroom and goes in. The children follow, all but Bert.

BERT (Wonderingly): You told us yourself. Don't you remember?

Then Bert goes inside. The image distorts to signify end of flashback. When image clears, we are back in classroom, close on Dr. Caldwell's face. He had not been one of the crowd of men who surrounded Mr.

Kovalesky. *He stands up angrily now as the crowd be-gins to talk all at once, ad-libbing to each other about Mr. Kovalesky's story.*

DR. CALDWELL: Quiet! (*Shouting*) Quiet, all of you! I've got something to say here!

He begins to walk slowly over to Mr. Woodbridge, who sits looking at him openmouthed. Everyone watches him silently.

DR. CALDWELL: I don't know whether the boy was pushed, or whether he fell . . . but I know this. The man who lifted Billy up and carried him inside is as much a murderer as if he had taken a gun and shot the boy. (*The crowd gasps*) That's right, Mr. Woodbridge. A murderer!

Dr. Caldwell stands over Mr. Woodbridge.

DR. CALDWELL (*Angrily*): An eight-year-old boy knew better than you what to do. And you're the beloved principal of our school . . . the man who teaches First Aid to our kids. Isn't that so, Mr. Woodbridge?

Mr. Woodbridge stands up, angry and bewildered.

MR. WOODBRIDGE: What do you mean, talking to me like that? You have no right—

DR. CALDWELL: I have no right! Let me tell you something. I'm a doctor. They bring me broken bodies and they say "Fix 'em up, Doc" after they've lifted 'em and moved 'em and lugged 'em around so that no one can fix 'em any more. They kill my patients with kindness. Maybe you did that, Mr. Woodbridge. Maybe you killed Billy. Think about it.

He walks away from Mr. Woodbridge, leaving him standing there horrified. Everyone looks at Mr. Woodbridge, waiting.

MR. WOODBRIDGE (*Softly*): But the boy was lying on the ground.

The people continue to stare hostilely at Mr. Woodbridge for a long minute. He looks around him. Then he seems to gather anger within himself. He turns and walks over to Mr. Kovalesky.

MR. WOODBRIDGE: What about him? Who saw him come up out of the basement? I was right there and I never saw him. How do we know he's telling the truth? Maybe he was up on the fire escape. Maybe he pushed the boy. Nobody saw him. All we know is what he tells us in his idiotic broken English. (*He turns quickly to Harold Wright*) Did you see him? (*Harold stares at him. He runs to Tommy*) Did you? (*Tommy looks at him silently. He runs to the jury box, near hysteria*) Did anyone see him coming up out of the basement? (*To Alice*) You? (*To Bert*) Did you?

The children look at him quietly. He walks away from them. Mr. Rogers takes his arm and begins to lead him back to his seat.

MR. WOODBRIDGE (*Softly*): But the boy was lying on the ground. . . . He shouldn't be left to lie on . . . the . . . ground.

Everyone is stunned at the way Mr. Woodbridge has acted. He sits down in a daze. Then he bends over to his wife and she comes and stands next to him and puts her arms around him. In the quiet room now, Mr. Rogers finds it easy to take over. The crowd, confused, doesn't know which way to turn. He goes to Tommy.

MR. ROGERS: Is there anything else, Tommy?

TOMMY: Well . . . the defense attorney is supposed to cross-examine . . .

MR. ROGERS: No. I mean any more facts.

TOMMY: Well . . . no, sir. It wasn't supposed to be like this, Mr. Rogers . . . all this yelling! It was supposed to . . . be a *trial.*

He turns and looks at Joey for guidance, but as he does, Susan Caldwell stands up in front of Joey. She is frightened, aware of all the eyes upon her, and not liking it.

SUSAN: Please . . . I . . . want to say something.

MRS. CALDWELL (*Shouting*): Susie! You sit down!

SUSAN (*Close to tears*): No! I have to. I can't help it. I have to.

MR. ROGERS: (*Gently*): Go ahead, Susie.

MRS. CALDWELL: I will not let that child make a fool of us. Fred, stop her!

SUSAN (*Determined*): You can't stop me!

MRS. CALDWELL: Fred!

DR. CALDWELL: Let her be, Cess.

> *Susan is near tears, and shakily she begins. Camera is close on her face.*

SUSAN: I wasn't in school the day of the accident. Mommy wouldn't let me go 'cause I had a cold. It was about twelve-thirty. I was lying on the couch making a horsetail when Daddy came in from lunch. . . .

> *Image starts to distort, signifying a flashback. When it clears, we see the Caldwell living room. We do not see the couch yet. Dr. Caldwell walks in from the kitchen. It is obvious that he is exhausted. He rubs his eyes as if they ache. He goes over to the television set and turns it on. Then he turns and sees Susan lying on the couch in her robe. She is making a horsetail with some yarn and a wooden spool with brads in it. Next to her is a box of tissues. Dr. Caldwell goes over to her.*

DR. CALDWELL: Well, how's my girl?

SUSAN: Sniffly. You look awful tired, Daddy.

DR. CALDWELL (*Smiling*): I'm dead. Maybe if you'd tell your friends to stop having the measles I could get some sleep. (*He pinches her cheek*) What are you making?

SUSAN: A horsetail.

DR. CALDWELL: Well, that's fine.

> *He pats her on the cheek and sits down in the armchair as we see an old-time silent movie come on the TV set.*

With it we hear the silly, choppy music with which old
silents are usually scored. He watches it for a moment,
relaxing. Then he begins to chuckle. The phone rings.
He turns.

SUSAN: I'll get it.

She gets up, goes to the phone in the foyer. Dr. Caldwell continues to chuckle.

SUSAN: Hello.

She listens while Dr. Caldwell explodes with laughter.
He never takes his eyes off the set through rest of scene.

SUSAN (*Calling*): Daddy, it's the hospital.

DR. CALDWELL: I'll call them back.

Susan talks into the phone as he breaks up with laughter
again. Then she turns to him.

SUSAN: It's Miss Phillips, Daddy. She wants you to come over
there right away.

DR. CALDWELL (*Laughing*): I said I'll call them back.

SUSAN (*Shocked*): Daddy! She says its urgent! Something
about a fall or something. I can't hear her so well on account
of the TV.

DR. CALDWELL: One of these days that woman will drive me
nuts. Every time someone skins a knee it's an emergency
with her. Tell her I'm finishing my lunch. I'll be there in a
half hour.

He laughs lustily again as Susan slowly hangs up. She
turns, upset, bewildered at his callousness. Close in on
him now as he snickers, then roars with laughter. Image
distorts to signify end of flashback. When it clears we
see Susan, back in the schoolroom. She is in tears,
standing behind her table. Everyone watches her in
silence. She looks up, sobbing.

SUSAN: I'm sorry, Daddy. I had to . . . I had to . . .

Cut now to Dr. Caldwell. He had forgotten about this
incident, but now is shocked, almost destroyed at hav-

ing it brought back to him. He looks at Susan, and the only sound we hear is her sobbing. He tries to say something to the people, but can't. He stands there alone. Then he turns to Mr. McGinnis across the room. Mr. McGinnis, too, is standing, looking at Dr. Caldwell. The two men face each other. Then Mr. McGinnis turns away and sits down. Dr. Caldwell stands alone. He lowers his head. Fade out.

——— *ACT III* ———————————————

Fade in on school, no time lapse. Dr. Caldwell sits down, his head lowered. He turns to his wife amidst a great silence. She looks at him strangely. We still hear Susan's sobbing faintly.

DR. CALDWELL (*Low*): Cess. I didn't know. How do you know? It was a half hour. That's all. Cess, I was exhausted. *She looks straight ahead at Susan, who sits watching now with tear-stained face.*

DR. CALDWELL: It was Buster Keaton. Funny man, he never smiles. I was watching Buster Keaton. Cess . . . (*He stands up and thunders out*) The boy was dead when I got there! I never could have saved him! Never! (*He looks around at the silent crowd, roaring*) It happens! Do you think it never happens? People make mistakes! *They listen in silence. He stares around helplessly. Then he sits down.*

DR. CALDWELL (*Low*): I'm sorry. . . .

MR. WRIGHT (*Jumping up*): Good! You're sorry. Did you hear that, everybody? Our doctor is sorry! (*He goes angrily to Dr. Caldwell*) I've been in your house . . . had your cold little instruments all over my chest and back. What were you listening to, Buster Keaton?

MRS. CALDWELL: Stop it!

MR. WRIGHT: Stop it? We ought to ride him out of town on a rail!

MRS. CALDWELL (*Rising*): Let him alone! He said he couldn't have saved him! What more can he do now?

MR. WRIGHT: Do you think what he says makes any difference? We're not doctors. Maybe he's lying. . . .

> Dr. Caldwell gets up out of his seat and lunges at Mr. Wright amidst a sudden chorus of screams and shouting.

MRS. CALDWELL: Fred! Fred!

MR. WRIGHT (*Screaming*): No! Stop him!

> A man grabs Dr. Caldwell from behind and pins his arms.

DR. CALDWELL (*Loud*): You rotten little—

> Mr. Prince moves between the two men. Dr. Caldwell struggles to break free.

MR. WRIGHT: The man's a maniac!

SUSAN (*Sobbing*): Daddy . . . don't . . .

> He stops and looks at Susan.

DR. CALDWELL (*Suddenly quiet*): Let me go.

MR. WRIGHT: Let you go! You ought to be handcuffed!

MR. PRINCE: Let him go.

MR. WRIGHT: What are you doing?

MR. PRINCE: Let him go.

> The man behind Dr. Caldwell lets him go. The doctor stands there. Mr. Prince watches him closely. Then Dr. Caldwell pushes Mr. Prince out of the way and goes to Susan, who still stands behind her table. She looks up at him, tears on her cheeks. He wipes them off.

DR. CALDWELL (*Quietly*): It's all right, Susie. It's all right.

> She looks at him steadily. He waits, then turns and walks through the little knot of men at the front of the room to his wife. Cut to Mr. Prince. He goes over to

Mr. Kovalesky. Mr. Rogers stands next to Mr. Kovalesky.

MR. PRINCE (*Loud*): Listen to me! We're going off in all directions here. This is the man we're trying. Let's not forget it. He's as guilty as Cain! I know it and so do most of the good people in this room!

MR. ROGERS: Do they? Does Mr. Woodbridge know it? Does Dr. Caldwell know it? Does Mr. Wright know it?

Cut to Mr. Wright, who looks questioningly and a bit fearfully at Mr. Rogers. Mr. Rogers goes to him.

MR. ROGERS: Do you know who the guilty man is, Mr. Wright? *Mr. Rogers turns to Joey as Mr. Wright tries to make an answer.*

MR. ROGERS: Joey, come here.

Mr. Rogers walks to the witness chair. Joey slowly follows him, stands in front of the chair. Mr. Rogers smiles at him.

MR. ROGERS: Hello, son.

JOEY (*Low*): Hello, pop.

MR. ROGERS: Sit down, Joey. I want you to tell Mr. Wright a story.

JOEY: A story?

MR. ROGERS: It happened in the store one night about six months ago. There was a discussion with Mr. Wright. An angry discussion. Do you remember it?

JOEY: Yes, I do.

MR. ROGERS: Tell it. Every word.

JOEY: All right, pop. (*We are close on Joey as he starts his story*) Well, like my father said, we were in the store. It was a Friday night. I remember that because I was s'posed to go to the basketball game. Anyway, I was cleaning up in back when I heard the door open. Mr. and Mrs. Wright came in. They were in a hurry. . . .

Image distorts to signify flashback. When it clears we

see the door of Mr. Rogers' drugstore opening. Mr. and Mrs. Wright enter and go to the counter. Mr. Rogers is behind it. He looks up pleasantly.

MR. ROGERS: Good evening, Mrs. Wright. Mr. Wright. How are you?

MRS. WRIGHT: Just fair, thank you. I'd like a small iodine and a box of Band-Aids, please.

MR. ROGERS: Large or small Band-Aids?

MRS. WRIGHT: Large, I think. Harold runs through them like wildfire. I never saw such a boy for cuts and bruises. Why, only today in school he ran a splinter this long into his hand.

Mr. Rogers gets the Band-Aids and Joey comes into the front of store, gets the iodine, hands it to him.

MR. ROGERS: Well, that's too bad. You have to be careful of infection with splinters.

MRS. WRIGHT: If I worried about infections every time Harold picked up a splinter in school, I'd have been in my grave long ago. Those rickety old desks are just full of splinters.

MR. WRIGHT (*Impatiently*): Julia . . . we're late. Come on.

MR. ROGERS: Will that be all, Mrs. Wright?

MRS. WRIGHT: I think so. How much is that?

MR. ROGERS: Fifty-nine and two. Sixty-one cents.

She begins to fish through her purse as he begins to wrap the package.

MR. ROGERS: You know, it's a shame, the condition of our school. Have you been inside it lately, Mr. Wright?

MR. WRIGHT: No.

MR. ROGERS: I was there last week. I saw the children trying to study in their classrooms. It's hard to study when the room you're in is overcrowded, badly lighted. It even smells bad in there, Mr. Wright. You know how buildings smell when the wood has been absorbing dust for fifty years? It's not nice. You ought to go there and see it for yourself.

MR. WRIGHT (*Annoyed*): I don't know why you bother to sell

drugs, Mr. Rogers. You could make more money lecturing.

MRS. WRIGHT: Mervin!

MR. ROGERS (*To Mrs. Wright*): That's all right. (*To Mr. Wright*) My son goes to that school, Mr. Wright, and so does your son. It's a dirty old building that should have been condemned a long time ago. It's not a place where our children can enjoy their education. And when you don't enjoy it, it's pretty hard to learn.

MR. WRIGHT: Listen here, Mr. Rogers, my son is getting enough learning out of that school to suit me! What are you trying to stir up around here?

MR. ROGERS: A better school maybe. You're the president of our Chamber of Commerce, Mr. Wright. Why don't you give us a school like the one they have in Centerville?

MR. WRIGHT: Centerville? You ought to be grateful there's a school at all in a little town like Carson Corners. Build a new school! Why, we hardly have the money to keep the old one going.

MR. ROGERS (*Quietly*): I've heard that the Chamber of Commerce is going to rebuild Main Street, with new sidewalks, new store fronts and even a statue. That must take a lot of money.

MR. WRIGHT (*Angry*): Rebuilding Main Street is good for business, and that's what I'm interested in.

MR. ROGERS: Well, who's interested in seeing that the school our kids go to doesn't fall down on their heads some day?

MR. WRIGHT: Now you've got it falling down, have you? Little children plunging to their death. You're a troublemaker, Rogers. Let me tell you something. If you don't like this school, why don't you go where there's one that suits you? Come on, Julia.

> He turns and heads for the door with Mrs. Wright following. Joey stares after them. Mr. Rogers puts his arm around Joey.

MR. ROGERS: Thank you very much, Mr. Wright.

Cut to close shot of Joey and his father as we hear the door close. Joey is visibly upset, but Mr. Rogers smiles at him and pats his hand. Image distorts to signify end of flashback. When it clears we see a shot of the crowd, listening. Then we cut to a shot of Mr. Wright standing angrily in front of the room.

MR. WRIGHT: Well, what does that prove? I suppose I'm a criminal, too? Cart me off to jail. Beautifying Main Street is the same as stealing money from the Community Fund. Right?

MR. ROGERS: No one said that, Mr. Wright.

MR. WRIGHT: Then what did you prove? Tell me!

MR. ROGERS (*Quietly*): That's for you to decide. (*To Joey*) All right, son.

Joey gets up and starts to leave the witness chair. Mr. Wright turns angrily.

MR. WRIGHT (*To crowd*): Who does this man think he is to get up here in front of everybody and make a fool out of me?

DR. CALDWELL: He's the same as any of us. He lives here.

MR. WRIGHT: You're a great one to speak up, Doctor!

MRS. CALDWELL (*Standing up*): Then I'll speak up! My husband isn't good enough to talk to you any more. I don't think it worries him, Mr. Wright. He's got something else to think about, and so have you. Mr. Rogers didn't make a fool out of you. Nobody can do that for you. You have to do it for yourself.

She sits down amidst a sudden hubbub.

MR. WRIGHT (*Furious*): You people! What do you know?

MRS. PRINCE (*Calling*): Why don't we have a new school?

MR. WRIGHT: If you think I'm going to stand here and listen to this . . . Get a bunch of people together and they all want to put their stupid two cents in. (*To his wife*) Get your coat!

The general noise continues as Mr. and Mrs. Wright get their coats. He takes his wife's arm and goes to the door. As he reaches for it, it opens and Miss Frank enters, breathless, but smiling expectantly.

MISS FRANK: Oh, now, don't tell me it's over. Why, I just this minute—

MR. WRIGHT: Here! Here's the proof we've been waiting for. Miss Frank, come with me.

He throws his coat on a seat and takes Miss Frank by the arm, hurries her down the aisle. She looks around, trying to orient herself.

MR. WRIGHT: Now we'll see who's telling the truth around here.

MISS FRANK: For heaven's sake, what's happening? Is this some kind of a joke?

They are at the front of the room now. Mr. Kovalesky jumps up, takes the bewildered Miss Frank by the arm.

MR. KOVALESKY: Miss Frank! You tell them . . . (*Mr. Wright pushes him back into his seat*) Tell them. They say crazy things. . . .

MISS FRANK: Tell them what? What are you talking about? (*To Mr. Wright*) Would you mind telling me?

MR. WRIGHT: We have some questions to ask you.

Miss Frank turns to Mr. Rogers.

MISS FRANK: What are they doing?

MR. ROGERS: Miss Frank . . .

MR. WRIGHT: Let's get this over with.

MR. ROGERS (*Gently*): Miss Frank, we would just like to question you.

MISS FRANK: Question me? What have I done?

MR. ROGERS: You've done nothing. Please, Miss Frank . . .

MR. PRINCE (*Calling*): Come on. What about the money? Ask her.

MISS FRANK: What is he talking about?

DR. CALDWELL (*Booming*): Tell the woman what's going on!

MISS FRANK (*To Mr. Rogers*): I don't understand. This isn't a joke, is it?

MR. ROGERS (*Gently*): No. It isn't a joke, Miss Frank. Come here and sit down, won't you?

> *Wonderingly, she goes to the witness chair and sits in it. She looks at Joey, then at the children sitting quietly, then at the angry faces of the men around her.*

MR. KOVALESKY: Please . . . Miss Frank . . .

MISS FRANK (*Wonderingly*): What have my children done?

MR. ROGERS: They've had a trial, Miss Frank. They've accused Mr. Kovalesky of pushing Billy McGinnis to his death.

MISS FRANK: They've what! Why, that's fantastic!

MR. ROGERS: They say Billy was killed because he discovered that Mr. Kovalesky had stolen some money. Some of the people here believe them, Miss Frank.

MISS FRANK: They don't! How could they? Kovey push Billy? Why, the railing was broken. Everyone knows that.

MR. PRINCE: Now look, let's stop all this talk. We want some answers here.

MR. WRIGHT: Right. Miss Frank, you made a collection—

MR. ROGERS: Just a minute. Let me finish. Then ask your questions! (*Quietly*) Miss Frank, did you know the railing was broken before Billy fell?

MISS FRANK: Before he fell? Well, how could I? I'm sure I would have—

> *Cut to Alice Woodbridge in the jury box as she stands up.*

ALICE: Miss Frank . . .

> *Everyone turns to her suddenly and she becomes frightened. She looks around her.*

ALICE: Nothing.

> *She sits down. Mr. Rogers comes over to her.*

MR. ROGERS: You mustn't be frightened, Alice. Anyone can

say whatever he wants to say. Even the children. Isn't that
why you came here tonight? (*Alice nods slowly, frightened*)
There. Now tell us what you wanted to say.

ALICE (*Low*): Well, I just remembered something before—

MRS. PRINCE (*Calling*): We can't hear her!

ALICE (*Louder*): I just remembered something before. (*She
looks around fearfully. Mr. Rogers smiles encouragingly at
her and nods*) Well, I'm in Miss Frank's class, and 'cause
I'm pretty good in spelling she lets me be the board-eraser
monitor. To clean the board erasers, I mean, when they
have spelling. (*We are close on Alice now*) The morning
Billy was killed . . . I went outside with the erasers about
quarter to eleven like I always did.

> *Image distorts to signify a flashback. When it clears we
> see the outside of the school, early morning. We hear
> Miss Frank chanting through the closed door.*

MISS FRANK: Constitution. C–o–n–s–t–i–t—(*The door opens
and Alice walks out carrying a half-dozen erasers*)—
u–t–i–o–n. Class?

THE CLASS (*Chanting*): C–o–n–s—

> *Alice closes the door, as we hear the class chant out
> the rest of the word in unison. Alice begins to pound
> the erasers together, creating a cloud of chalk dust. She
> keeps busily at it throughout the following scene. The
> basement door opens now and Mr. Kovalesky comes
> out of basement followed by Mr. Prince.*

MR. PRINCE: That furnace is in good shape, Kovey. I'll bet it
lasts another five years. Basement's not too damp either.

MR. KOVALESKY (*Proudly*): I try to keep good. Is very old.

MR. PRINCE: I know you do, Kovey. Smoke?

> *He offers a pack of cigarettes.*

MR. KOVALESKY: No, thanks.

> *Mr. Prince lights up.*

MR. PRINCE: Well . . . now I suppose we have to go over

the fire escape. I'm telling you, Kovey, sometimes this inspection business is for the birds. (*Mr. Kovalesky nods agreement*) I spent the whole day in the county hospital yesterday. Clean as a whistle. You could eat off the floor. I knew it before I went there.

> *Mr. Kovalesky smiles and nods. They walk to the fire escape. Mr. Prince takes the railing at the bottom and pushes it.*

MR. PRINCE: How's this thing holding up?

MR. KOVALESKY: Good.

MR. PRINCE: Well, it ought to. Let's see . . . when did they build the fire escape?

MR. KOVALESKY: I don't know. Maybe 1946, around there.

MR. PRINCE: Guess that's about right. Feels good and solid. (*They start walking up*) Say, you don't have to come up with me.

MR. KOVALESKY: I have to get my broom upstairs.

> *As they walk up, we see that Mr. Kovalesky is nervous. Laboriously he edges between Mr. Prince and the weakened part of the railing, trying to hide the railing with his body so that Mr. Prince will not see it. Mr. Prince, busy with the following lines, doesn't notice his awkward maneuvering. He watches Mr. Prince warily.*

MR. PRINCE: Y'know, Kovey, you'd think this county building inspector deal would be pretty good. Let me tell you I go nuts half the time just looking at things. I'd almost like to quit it, but the money is steady. You know how it is.

> *He walks up without testing the railing.*

MR. KOVALESKY: Steady is the most important.

MR. PRINCE (*Patting railing*): And how. Well, I suppose this is solid all the way up.

MR. KOVALESKY: Sure. I keep it good.

MR. PRINCE: Okay, Kovey. I'll give you an A for effort.

Mr. Prince laughs heartily. The door to the ground-floor schoolroom opens and Miss Frank comes out as Mr. Prince, standing on the second-floor landing, takes the last few puffs of his cigarette.

MISS FRANK (*To Alice*): Well, young lady, you've had enough time to clean a dozen erasers!

ALICE (*Startled*): Oh! Miss Frank, I'm sorry. They were awful chalky.

Miss Frank looks up and sees the two men on the landing. Now she speaks partially to herself and partially to Alice.

MISS FRANK: Oh, there's Mr. Prince. He must be inspecting the building. I wonder if Mr. Kovalesky told him about that loose railing. I noticed it this morning.

ALICE: I didn't hear him say anything.

MISS FRANK: No? Well that could be dangerous. I'd better mention it to him.

She starts for the fire escape as Mr. Kovalesky goes inside upstairs. Then she stops.

MISS FRANK: Well, now, here I go probably getting Mr. Kovalesky into all kinds of trouble. I believe I'll just wait till Mr. Prince leaves and then tell Mr. Kovalesky about it.

Mr. Prince is walking down the steps by now. He flings his cigarette away as he reaches the bottom. Miss Frank turns to Alice.

MISS FRANK: Aren't you finished yet?

ALICE: Just got one more to do.

MISS FRANK (*Sarcastically*): Well, any time you're ready . .

Mr. Prince passes her. She nods at him. He tips his hat and exits. Now she starts to go to the fire escape, but we suddenly hear a raucous shout from her room, and then a chorus of childish laughter. She throws up her hands, turns, goes into the room, Alice beats at the last eraser. Mr. Kovalesky comes out of the second-floor door with the broom and begins to sweep the steps. He looks down and grins as he sees someone coming up the steps.

MR. KOVALESKY: Hey, not so fast, mister. Where you going?

He bars the way with the broom. Now we see Bert Hendricks coming up. He squirms under the broom. Mr. Kovalesky pulls Bert's hat down over his ears, and laughs heartily.

BERT: Ah, cut it out, Kovey!

Image distorts to signify end of flashback. When it clears we are close on Miss Frank's face. She is horrified. She looks at Mr. Rogers, then at the crowd, trying to find words, then she almost whispers.

MISS FRANK: I was going to . . . I was going to say something. I really was. But . . . I didn't want to get anyone . . . into trouble. You understand. Don't you understand? (She begins to weep softly) It would have been so easy. He was right there, Mr. Prince was right there. . . .

She can't go on. She looks blankly around the room at the watching faces.

MISS FRANK (Softly): Why doesn't somebody say something? Camera stays on her as she breaks down, sobbing. Cut to Mr. Prince. He stands there, himself shattered, watching her. Then he turns and walks to the back of the room. He stands there alone, sick with what he has just heard. Faintly we hear Miss Frank sobbing. All else is quiet. He wants to say something to these people.

MR. PRINCE: Listen . . . I . . .

But there is nothing for him to say. He turns slowly to the wall and puts his face against it. Cut to Mr. Rogers. Only he and Mr. Wright are left standing in the room.

MR. ROGERS (Quietly): Sit down, Mr. Wright.

Mr. Wright quietly goes and sits in his seat. Miss Frank

wipes her eyes. Everyone sits waiting now as Mr. Rogers
goes to Miss Frank.

MR. ROGERS: Miss Frank, please . . . I would like to ask you
a question. (*She nods*) On the morning of Billy's death,
there was a collection taken in school for the Community
Fund. You were in charge of it. (*She nods*) What did you
do with the money?

MISS FRANK: The money? (*She thinks for a moment*) It was
in cans—cans like those. (*She points to cans on table*) I
gave it to Mr. Kovalesky to hold.

MR. ROGERS: Why?

MISS FRANK: Well, I had no place to keep it safe, and I wasn't
able to turn it in till the . . . next . . . day. Mr. Rogers
. . .

MR. ROGERS: Yes?

MISS FRANK: I never turned it in. I forgot about it completely.
I haven't thought about it from that moment to this. Those
cans. They must be . . . (*Suddenly she understands*) Oh,
no . . . they didn't think that! They didn't—

MR. ROGERS: Thank you, Miss Frank.

He turns away from her and faces the court. Mr. Kovalesky lowers his head, hides his face with his hands. No
one quite knows what to say to him. In the awkward
silence, Mr. Rogers goes to him, pats him gently on
the back. Then Tommy Prince walks over to Mr. Kovalesky.

TOMMY (*Softly*): We're sorry, Kovey. The kids. . . . We
didn't know. We're sorry. . . .

Mr. Kovalesky doesn't look up at him. Tommy walks
away sadly. The people sit stunned, unmoving. Mr.
Kovalesky never looks up. Mr. and Mrs. McGinnis are
rocklike, staring into space. The children wait patiently.
Now some of the people slowly begin to get up and
fumble for their coats. Finally Mr. Kovalesky gets up

and walks over to where Mr. and Mrs. McGinnis are sitting. The muffled sound of desks being raised is heard. The clumping of the feet is softer than it should be. Still no one has left the room. They are only going through the motions. They have to move, to do something with their bodies while they try to think of something, anything to say to the parents of the boy they all had a hand in killing.

MR. KOVALESKY: Mr. McGinnis . . . I was going to fix . . . (Mr. McGinnis doesn't move, doesn't look at him) Please, Mr. McGinnis. I like to say . . . how I feel. . . .

Mr. McGinnis turns to him. Then, slowly, he gets up. In the silence he turns to look at Mr. Kovalesky bitterly.

MR. MC GINNIS (Low): You feel dirty. Maybe you feel sick. Don't say it. I know how you feel. You want to break something. That's what I want to do, Mr. Kovalesky. I want to break your neck! I want to take some of these good people here and crush them like you crush a roach. But I won't.

He turns to everyone. They watch him and wait. He looks them over slowly.

MR. MC GINNIS: No. I won't touch you. I'm going home now with my wife and boy, and I'm going to get down on my knees and I'm going to raise these hands and I'm going to pray to God they forgive me for what you're going to hear right now. Listen to it. Don't miss a word. It's something I forgot a long time ago. Eight years ago.

Image distorts to signify a flashback. When it clears, we see the fire escape in daylight. A painter in white overalls is painting the bottom part of the railing and whistling cheerily. He looks at his watch and starts to work a bit faster. We see that he is putting the finishing touches on the fire escape. Now we see Mr. Mc-

     *Ginnis in overalls. He carries a large wrench up the
stairs.*

PAINTER: Better snap it up, Ralph. It's near quitting time.

MR. MC GINNIS: Right. I'm almost finished.

PAINTER: Brother, I'm beat. Not a bad job for two days.

MR. MC GINNIS: Yeah. Y'know, it's about time they had a fire
escape on the school. This dried-out old wood could really
go up in a hurry.

     *He begins working on top of the landing, tightening
the braces on the railing at the exact spot through
which Billy plunged.*

MR. MC GINNIS: Say, where we working tomorrow, Eddie?

PAINTER: Becker's place. We're due there first thing in the
morning.

MR. MC GINNIS: Oh, yeah, that roofing job.

     *He works on as the painter whistles. Then he stops
tightening a brace with the wrench and begins to look
for another brace. He goes through his pockets, looks
around the landing.*

MR. MC GINNIS: Now what the dickens did I do with that last
angle iron?

     *He tests the railing at the point where the brace be-
longs. It gives ever so slightly.*

MR. MC GINNIS: Hey, Eddie, are there any more angle irons
down there? I need one to finish this off.

PAINTER: Yeah, I think there's one around here, somewhere.

     *Mr. McGinnis comes down the steps. The painter has
finished and stands ready to leave, carrying paint,
brushes, etc.*

PAINTER: I'm taking off, kid. So long. I'll see you tomorrow.

MR. MC GINNIS: Right. So long, Eddie.

     *He begins to look around for the angle iron as Eddie
exits. He has not yet found it when we hear a voice off.*

MRS. MC GINNIS (*Calling*): Mr. McGinnis! (*He turns and she goes to him, smiling*) Surprise!

She kisses him. He smiles delightedly.

MR. MC GINNIS: Katie! What are you doing here?

MRS. MC GINNIS: I thought I'd come by to walk you home, dear. I think it's pretty darn nice of me.

MR. MC GINNIS (*Kidding her*): Oh you do, do you? (*Seriously*) Honey, I have to finish up first.

MRS. MC GINNIS: Oh, come on. It looks fine.

MR. MC GINNIS: I won't be long.

She kisses him again.

MRS. MC GINNIS: Let's go home now.

He looks up at the unfinished railing, then at her. Then he smiles.

MR. MC GINNIS: All right. Let me pack up my stuff.

He walks past her and we see a baby carriage now for the first time. He goes over to it, grinning as a new father grins and looks into it. He pokes his finger into it.

MR. MC GINNIS: Hiya, Billy. How's that big boy? Yes. What are you grinning at, you little monkey?

Cut to shot of Mrs. McGinnis as she smiles and smiles. Then cut to shot of the railing on landing, and hold. Image distorts slowly to signify end of flashback. When it clears we see the faces of the crowd in the room, filled with pain and pity. We hear the voice of Mr. McGinnis.

MR. MC GINNIS (*Loud*): Look at me, neighbors. I'm dying here! Dying! I helped to kill my son! D'ya hear me? His father! Turn your backs. Walk away from me. He was my kid! I put the wrench away and that was the end of it. It was like sinking it into his head! And he grinned at me! A nice, fat, happy kid. He was six months old. (*Wonderingly*) Then all of a sudden he was eight years old. So fast. On his birthday I gave him eight slaps on the behind . . . and one to grow on. Then he said, "Where's my present, Daddy?" and I had to tell him I forgot to get it. He cried. I went to the store next day and got it. But he didn't come home that day. I forgot. (*Thundering*) We forget too much! We forget or we're too lazy or too tired or too scared to do the things people have to do. They're only little things . . . things we yell at our kids to do. They shouldn't have to show us where we're wrong. We're supposed to show them! If we don't . . . who's going to save them from each other?

He stops now as if gathering strength. Then he continues.

MR. MC GINNIS (*Roaring*): Listen to me. Pay attention. We can't let it happen again. We're human beings. We live together . . . all of us . . . right next door! We've got to live for each other . . . or we're nothing! Hear me now. We've got to do better.

He turns away from them. Mr. Rogers goes to him, puts his hand on his arm, nods gently. Mr. McGinnis turns now and takes the hand. He looks at Mr. Rogers for a long time. Then he turns to the others who are grouped around him now, each child with his own parents. They wait.

MR. MC GINNIS (*Low*): I forgive you. (*They look at him, unable to answer him*) Someone forgive me. . . .

Then Mrs. McGinnis comes to him and gently puts her arms around him, drawing him close. He sinks his face into her neck, and she kisses him, holding him protectively. Then, slowly, the people and the children begin to file out.

Fade out.

The Remarkable Incident at Carson Corners

The Remarkable Incident at Carson Corners has a great deal of signficance for me, since it was the first hour-length original drama I ever attempted. Having reached a point in my career at which I felt reasonably safe writing half-hour original melo-dramas for shows such as "Danger," and hour-long adaptations of second-rate novels, I approached this relatively new problem with something less than absolute confidence. As a matter of fact, I put the half-developed Carson Corners outline aside twice in favor of half-hour cops-and-robbers dramas, which I knew were easily done and eminently salable.

But there was something intriguing about this story of the responsibilities of human beings toward each other which had been nagging me for two years, and I kept going back to it, looking for a method of telling it without being overbearingly pompous. It took a while for me to realize that the problem of telling the story of man's indifference to the needs of his fellow man had to be brought from the abstract, where it be-longs intellectually, to the specific, where it could be drama-tized effectively.

After a great many false starts, I finally decided to tell this story in a small-town setting where it would be relatively easy to show how the moves and attitudes of each inhabitant could directly affect each other inhabitant. It was necessary to reduce what was a pretty high-handed idea, I must admit, to a single incident which would shock the inhabitants of a small town into ultimately realizing their guilt. I felt that the incident had to be a tragedy—not an impending tragedy that could be prevented, but a near-forgotten tragedy in which a great many people had an unwitting hand. The death of a child was the tragedy I ultimately selected, since it offered great dramatic possibilities in the actual telling of the story, and also effectively symbolized the problem I was trying to comment on in the larger picture: that is, the destruction of the innocents by the indifferent.

The idea of using the children themselves as the instruments which begin the chain of events leading their elders inexorably to the acknowledgment of their own guilt came next. The selection of the schoolroom as the main setting and the mock trial as a suspense-generating device followed almost automatically. The problem then became the handling of an intricate web of flashbacks, each involving another adult in the death of the child until it finally became clear that all were guilty, from the falsely accused janitor to the child's own father.

In many ways, this play remains my favorite of all the television dramas I've written. I don't know whether this is because of the intense morality of the theme, the intricate handling of the mechanics, the emotional content of the play, or simply its very gratifying reception. Whatever it was, I've been trying to top it ever since.

That The Remarkable Incident at Carson Corners was well received was in much part due to director Paul Nickell's brilliant and sensitive handling of a very complex script, and to some fine performances in parts which were mainly brief sketches of real people.

Paul Nickell, who is one of television's most impressive talents, was able to manipulate some thirty actors in one room at one time with remarkable fluidity and grace, and still keep the action flowing without confusion. The device he used to heighten the drama of key moments in the play, the single hollow beat of a kettle drum, was shocking and effective, and has since been imitated many times.

The public response to Carson Corners was quite remarkable. Today, nearly two years later, public schools, parent-teacher groups and other civic organizations are still showing kinescopes of the play, which CBS has lent them. This kind of thing is immensely gratifying to a writer, and I remain quite impressed at the effect which a single showing on television can have upon a staggering number of people.

The only thing about The Remarkable Incident at Carson Corners that worries me is this: I sat down to write this script with an intense personal feeling of indignation at mankind's sometimes terrifying irresponsibility and disregard for the basic needs and rights of people. Vaguely I thought of genocide, pogroms, lynchings, wars—the conglomerate tragedies of the ages allowed by human beings to fall upon other human beings through neglect, stupidity, indifference and just sheer laziness. I hoped that I had made clear that the Carson Corners schoolroom was, in effect, our earth, and that the events which transpired in Carson Corners were miniatures of the events which somehow diminish mankind.

But the first letter on the show that I opened, which incidentally was the first letter from a viewer I had ever received, read something like this:

Dear Mr. Rose:

I was thrilled and moved by last night's play on "Studio One" entitled The Remarkable Incident at Carson Corners. My family and I want to thank you most humbly for opening our eyes to a great many things which we had not previously considered. Beginning tomorrow, I have resolved to keep our garden hose in the basement where it belongs, rather than on our lawn where someone may trip over it. Thank you very much.

Sincerely,

Well, you try.

Thunder on Sycamore Street

———— MARCH 15, 1954 ————————

PRODUCER	Felix Jackson
DIRECTOR	Franklin Schaffner
SET DESIGNER	Willard Levitas
ASSISTANT TO PRODUCER	William Markham Altman
STORY EDITOR	Florence Britton
ASSOCIATE DIRECTOR	Joseph Dackow
PROGRAM ASSISTANT	Bette Stein

CAST

FRANK MORRISON
  Whitfield Connor
CLARICE MORRISON
  Nell O'Day
ROGER MORRISON
  Robert Bussard
CHRISTOPHER MORRISON
  Dickie Olsen
ARTHUR HAYES
  Lee Bergere
PHYLLIS HAYES
  Anna Cameron

MR. HARKNESS
  Harry Sheppard
JOSEPH BLAKE
  Kenneth Utt
ANNA BLAKE
  Charlotte Pearson
JUDY BLAKE
  Tirrell Barbery
MRS. BLAKE
  Judith Lowry
CHARLIE DENTON
  Charles Penman

MRS. CARSON
  Mabel Cochran

ACT I

Fade in on a long shot of Sycamore Street in the pleasant and tidy village of Eastmont. It is 6:40 P.M. and just getting dark. We see three houses, modest but attractive, side by side, each an exact replica of the other. Each has a tiny front lawn and a tree or two in front of it. Each has been lived in and cared for by people who take pride in their own hard-won respectability. The street is quiet. Walking toward the houses now we see Arthur Hayes, a quiet, bespectacled man between thirty-five and thirty-eight years of age. He lives in the second of the three houses. He walks slowly, carrying a newspaper under his arm and smoking a pipe. He stops in front of his house and, almost in a daze, knocks the dottle out of his pipe against his heel. As he is doing this, we see Frank Morrison enter, also carrying a newspaper. He is a heavy man, forceful and aggressive, with a loud voice and a hearty laugh. He is about forty years of age. Frank Morrison lives right next door to Arthur in the first of the three houses. He sees Arthur and waves.

FRANK (*Jovially*): Hey, Artie. How ya doin'?

Arthur is preoccupied. He doesn't register at first. He looks blankly at Frank.

FRANK (*Laughing*): Hey . . . wake up, boy. It's almost time for supper.

Arthur snaps out of it and forces a smile.

ARTHUR (*Quietly*): Oh . . . hello, Frank. Sorry. I didn't see you.

FRANK: Didn't see me? Hey, wait till I tell Clarice. That diet she's got me on must be working. You have to look twice to see me! (*Laughing hard, Frank reaches for his keys*) That's a hot one!

Arthur smiles weakly.

FRANK: Say . . . isn't this late for you to be getting home?

ARTHUR: No, I don't think so. (*He looks at his watch*) It's twenty to seven. I always get home about this time.

FRANK: Yeah. Well, I wouldn't want you to be late tonight. You know what tonight is, don't you?

ARTHUR (*Slowly*): Yes, I know what tonight is.

FRANK (*A little hard*): Good.

We hear footsteps and see a man walk by them. He is Joseph Blake, a man in his late thirties, a big, powerful, but quiet man. Joseph Blake lives in the third house on the street. As he walks by them, they both look at him silently. Arthur turns away then, but Frank continues to stare at him. Camera moves in on Frank as he stares coldly at Joseph Blake. His face is hard, full of hatred. The footsteps recede.

FRANK (*Low*): See you later, Artie.

Frank turns and fits the key into the lock. There is

utter silence. He fumbles with the lock, then silently
swings the door open. He walks into the small foyer.
The living room ahead is brightly lighted, but we see
no one. Frank walks slowly, silently into the living
room. As he enters it, we hear a dozen pistol shots.
Frank stiffens, clutches himself and falls to the floor
as if dead. Then we hear a chorus of shrill screams and
two small boys wearing cowboy hats and carrying pistols fling themselves upon Frank's body. Frank doesn't
move as they clamber over him. One is Roger, age ten;
the other is Christopher, age six. Christopher wears
"Dr. Dentons."

CHRISTOPHER (*Screaming*): I got him! I got him first.

ROGER: You did not!

CHRISTOPHER: I did so! Get offa him. I got him first. (*Calling*)
Hey, Mom . . .

ROGER (*Superior*): Boy, are you stupid! I got him three times
before you even pulled the trigger.

CHRISTOPHER (*Squeaking*): What d'ya mean? I got him before you even—(*Roger tries to push Christopher off Frank's
still motionless body*) Before you even—(*Christopher grunts
and fights back*) Cut it out! Hey, Mom . . .
     *Clarice, Frank's wife, a pleasant-looking woman in her
     early thirties, comes to living-room door from kitchen.
     She wears an apron. She calls out before she sees them.*

CLARICE: Now you boys stop that noise. (*She sees Roger pushing Christopher*) Roger!

CHRISTOPHER: Cut it out, willya. I got him—

CLARICE: Roger! Stop that pushing. . . .

CHRISTOPHER: I'm gonna sock you. . . .

CLARICE (*Angrily*): Christopher, don't you dare! Frank! Will
you do something . . . please!

ROGER: Go ahead. Sock me. You couldn't hurt a flea!

CHRISTOPHER (*Winding up*): Who says so?

ROGER: Boy, you must be deaf. I said so!

CLARICE: Frank!

> As Christopher swings at Roger, Frank suddenly comes to life with a tremendous roar. He rolls over, toppling both boys to the floor and with lightning swiftness he grabs both of their cap pistols. He stands up grinning. They both look at him, startled.

FRANK (*Barking*): Get up! (*They both do, slowly*) Get your hands up! (*They look at each other*) Make it snappy if you don't want to draw lead. (*Christopher shrugs and raises his hands.*) (*To Roger*) You too, hombre!

ROGER: Aaaah, Dad . . .

FRANK: Last warning.

ROGER (*Disgusted*): Come on . . . (*Frank shoots him with the cap pistol*) What are you so serious about?

> He walks away. Frank watches him, still not giving up the cowboy pose.

CLARICE: All right. Now that's enough gunplay. All three of you can just settle down. (*To Frank*) Hand 'em over.

> He grins and gives her the guns. Then he bends over and kisses her.

FRANK: Hello, honey.

> She kisses him dutifully, then speaks to Roger, handing him the guns.

CLARICE: Put these in your room and come back with your hands washed. We're sitting down to supper right now.

ROGER (*Desperately*): Right now? I gotta watch "Range-busters."

CLARICE: Not tonight. I told you we were eating early.

ROGER: Ah, Mom . . . please . . .

CLARICE: Absolutely not. Come on, now. Inside . . .

> Roger slumps off. Clarice turns to Christopher as Frank begins to take off his coat.

CLARICE: And you're going to bed, mister.

CHRISTOPHER: No! I can't go to bed!

CLARICE: Christopher!

CHRISTOPHER (*Backing away*): I'm not tired yet. Honest!

> Frank is hanging his coat up in the foyer. Clarice advances towards Chris, who looks for means of escape.

CLARICE: I'm not going to argue with you.

CHRISTOPHER: Mom, fifteen minutes. Come on. Please . . .

CLARICE: I'm going to start counting. One, two—

CHRISTOPHER (*Fast*): Three four five six seven eight nine ten.

> He runs away from her, but right into the arms of Frank, who picks him up.

FRANK: Trapped! Let's go, pal.

CHRISTOPHER: Aaah . . .

> Frank carries him past Clarice, who kisses him on the way by. As they reach the door which leads into bedroom, Roger comes out. Christopher, in his father's arms, raps Roger on the head with his knuckle.

ROGER: Hey!

CHRISTOPHER (*Grinning*): Good night, Rog.

ROGER: Stupid!

FRANK: All right, now. That's enough out of both of you. I don't want to hear another peep.

> Frank takes Christopher into bedroom. Camera follows Roger over to a dining table set at one end of living room near a picture window. This would probably be an L-shaped living room–dining room set-up and would be exactly the same in all three houses. The only difference in the three interior sets will be the way in which they are decorated. There are dishes on the table, glassware, etc. Roger slumps into his chair and takes a piece of bread. He munches on it as Clarice comes in from kitchen carrying a steaming bowl of stew. She sets it down and sits down.

CLARICE (*Calling*): Frank!

FRANK (*Off*): Okay. I'll be right there.

ROGER: Hey, Mom, what are we eating so early for?

CLARICE (*Serving*): Don't say "Hey, Mom."

ROGER: Well, what are we eating so early for?

CLARICE: Because we feel like eating early. (*Calling*) Frank!

Frank walks in, loosening his tie.

FRANK: What's for supper?

CLARICE: Beef stew.

ROGER: Look, if I could see the first five minutes of "Range-busters"—

Clarice ladles out the stew as Frank sits at the table.

CLARICE: Roger, I'm not going to tell you again.

ROGER (*Anguished*): But, Mom, you don't know what's happening. There's this sneaky guy—

FRANK: Come on boy, dig into your dinner.

Roger makes a face and gives up the battle.

FRANK (*To Clarice*): What time is the sitter coming?

CLARICE: Ten after seven. Do you know that's the third time today you've asked me.

FRANK: Just want to be sure.

CLARICE: I don't see why they have to make it so early anyway.

Frank has a mouthful of food, so he shrugs.

ROGER: Make what so early, Dad?

CLARICE: Nothing. Eat your dinner.

FRANK: Good stew.

CLARICE: There's plenty more.

FRANK (*Chewing*): Mmmm. Hmmmm. Do anything special today, Rog?

ROGER: Nope. Just kinda hung around.

FRANK: Well, I don't know why you don't get out and do something. A boy your age . . .

ROGER: Some of the kids dumped garbage on the Blakes' lawn again.

FRANK (*Casually*): That so? What about you?

ROGER: Ah, what fun is that after you do it a couple of times?

FRANK (*Chewing*): Mmmm. Hey, how about eating your stew.

ROGER: I'm not hungry.

CLARICE: Frank, I wish you'd do something about that boy's eating. He's beginning to look like a scarecrow.

FRANK: He'll be all right. What time is it?

CLARICE (*Looking at watch*): Five of seven.

FRANK: We'd better snap it up.

CLARICE: Plenty of time. I'm leaving the dishes till later.

FRANK: Y'know, Clarry, this really ought to be something tonight.

Roger starts to get up, but stops.

ROGER: What ought to be something?

CLARICE: You just sit down and pay attention to your dinner. There's a glass of milk to be finished before you get up.

ROGER (*Grudgingly*): Okay. (*He sips the milk for a moment*) Where you going tonight, Dad?

FRANK: We're going for a little walk.

ROGER: Well, what d'ya have to go out so early for?

FRANK: Just like that.

ROGER (*Aggressively*): Well, what the heck is the big secret, that's what I'd like to know. Everybody's acting so mysterious.

FRANK (*Sharply*): That's enough. Now I don't want to hear any more questions out of you. Your mother and I have some business to attend to, and that's it. You mind yours.

Roger, stunned, looks at his father, then down at his plate. There is an awkward silence. Frank eats stolidly. They watch him.

FRANK (*To Clarice*): Where's that sitter?

CLARICE: It's not time yet. Take it easy, Frank.

Frank gets up from the table, goes over to a box of

cigars on top of the TV set and lights one. Clarice and Roger watch him silently.*

CLARICE: Aren't you going to have some dessert, Frank? There's some cherry pie left.

FRANK: I'll have it later.

He puffs on the cigar.

ROGER (*Low*): I'm sorry, Dad.

FRANK (*Turning*): Well, it's about time you learned some respect, d'you hear me? If I want you to know something I'll tell it to you.

ROGER (*Softly*): Okay . . .

CLARICE (*Quickly*): Have some pie, honey. I heated it special. *Frank goes to the table and sits down. He puts the cigar down and Clarice begins to cut him some pie.*

CLARICE: How late do you think we'll be, Frank?

FRANK: I don't know.

CLARICE: Do you think I ought to pack a thermos of hot coffee? It's going to be chilly.

FRANK: Might not be a bad idea.

Frank now begins to show the first signs of being excited about the evening. He speaks, almost to himself.

FRANK: Boy, I can't wait till I see his face. The nerve of him. The absolute nerve. (*Grinning*) What d'you think he'll do when we all—

CLARICE (*Looking at Roger*): Frank . . .

FRANK (*As Roger stares*): Oh. Yeah. Okay, go ahead, Rog. You can turn on your program.

ROGER: Gee thanks, Dad.

He jumps up, goes to the TV set and turns it on. Frank and Clarice watch him get settled in front of TV set. We hear dialogue from set faintly. Roger watches in background, enraptured.

FRANK (*Quietly*): What are they saying on the block?

CLARICE: I didn't speak to anyone. I was ironing all day.

FRANK: Charlie Denton called me at the office. I was right in the middle of taking an order from Martin Brothers for three A-81 tractors.

CLARICE: Three! Frank, that's wonderful!

FRANK: Not bad. Anyway, I made Mr. Martin wait while I spoke to Charlie. Charlie says its gonna be one hundred per cent. Every family on the block. He just called to tell me that.

CLARICE: Well, that's good. Everyone should be in on this.

FRANK (*Eating*): Clarry, I'm telling you this is going to be a job well done. It's how you have to do these things. Everybody getting together fast . . . and boom, it's over. I can't wait till it's started. It's been long enough.

CLARICE: I saw her out the window today, hanging clothes in her yard like nothing was wrong. She didn't even look this way.

FRANK: What time is it?

CLARICE: Now you just asked me two minutes ago. Its about three minutes to seven. What's the matter with you? You'll be getting yourself an ulcer over this thing. Relax, Frank. Here, have some more pie.

FRANK: No. No more.

> He gets up and walks around nervously, slapping his fist into his palm. Roger is looking at him now. He is tense, excited, completely caught up in the impending event.

FRANK: This is something big, you know that, Clarry? We're getting action without pussyfooting for once. That's it. That's the big part. There's too much pussyfooting going on all the time. Can't hurt anyone's feelings. Every time you turn around you're hurting some idiot's feelings. Well that's tough, I say. . . .

CLARICE (*Indicating Roger*): Frank . . .

FRANK: He can hear! He's old enough. You want something bad, you gotta go out and get it! That's how this world is. Boy, I like this, Clarry. You know what it makes me feel like? It makes me feel like a man!

> *He stalks up and down the room for a few moments as they watch him. Then he goes to the window and stands there looking out.*

CLARICE (*Quietly*): I think I'll just stack the dishes.

> *She starts to do it. The doorbell rings. Roger jumps up.*

ROGER: I'll get it.

> *He goes to the door and opens it. Arthur Hayes stands there a bit apologetically. He wears no overcoat, having just come from next door. He looks extremely upset.*

ARTHUR: Rog, is your dad in?

ROGER: Sure. Come on in, Mr. Hayes.

> *Arthur walks in slowly. Frank turns around, still excited. He goes over to Arthur.*

FRANK (*Loud*): Hey, Artie. Come on in.

ARTHUR: Hello, Frank . . .

FRANK (*Laughing*): What can I do for you? (*Arthur looks hesitantly at Roger*) Oh, sure. Rog, go help your mother.

ROGER (*Annoyed*): Okay . . .

> *He walks off to dining table.*

FRANK (*Chuckling*): That's some kid, isn't he, Artie? How old is yours now?

ARTHUR: Twenty-one months.

FRANK: Yeah. Well that's still nothing but a crying machine. Wait a coupla years. He'll kill you.

ARTHUR: I guess so.

FRANK: And how! Sit down for a minute, Artie. What's on your mind?

ARTHUR (*Sitting. Hesitantly*): Well, I don't know . . . I just . . . well . . . I just wanted . . . to talk.

FRANK: No kidding. Say, y'know you look a little green around the gills? What's the matter?

Arthur Hayes takes off his eyeglasses and begins to polish them, a nervous habit in which he indulges when upset.

ARTHUR: Nothing. I've had an upset stomach for a couple of days. Maybe that's it.

FRANK (*Nodding*): Yeah, that'll get you down all right. Probably a virus.

Arthur nods and they look at each other awkwardly for a moment.

FRANK: Well, what did you want to talk to me about?

Arthur looks at the floor, trying to frame his answer carefully, afraid to offend. Finally he blurts it out.

ARTHUR: What do you think about this thing tonight?

FRANK (*Surprised*): What do you mean what do I think about it?

ARTHUR: Well, I've been kind of going over it all day, Frank. I talked with Phyllis before.

FRANK (*A little hard*): And . . .

ARTHUR: Well, it was just talk. We were just talking it over to get clear on it, you know.

FRANK: Go ahead.

ARTHUR: And . . . well, look, Frank, it's a pretty hard thing. Supposing it were you?

FRANK: It's not.

ARTHUR: Well, I know that, but supposing it were?

Frank stands up and goes over to Arthur.

FRANK: Your glasses are clean. You wear 'em out, you have to buy a new pair. (*Arthur looks down at his glasses, then puts them on nervously*) Now what about it, Artie? What if I was the guy?

ARTHUR: Well, you know . . . how would you feel?

FRANK: How would I feel, huh? Now that's a good question,

Artie. I'll answer it for you. It doesn't make any difference how I'd feel. Now let me ask you a question. Is he a life-long buddy of yours?

ARTHUR: Well, now, you know he's not, Frank.

FRANK: Do you know him to say hello to?

ARTHUR: That's not the idea. He's—

FRANK: Artie . . . you don't even know the guy. What are you getting yourself all hot and bothered about? We all agreed, didn't we?

ARTHUR: Yes . . . everybody agreed . . .

FRANK: You. Me. The Dentons. The McAllisters. The Fredericks. The Schofields. Every family on Sycamore Street for that matter. We all agreed. That's how it is. The majority. Right?

ARTHUR: Well . . . I think we all ought to talk it over, maybe. Let it wait a few days.

He takes off his glasses again and begins to wipe them.

FRANK: Artie . . . we talked it over. (*Frank takes the handkerchief out of Arthur's hand and tucks it into his pocket*) In about ten minutes we're starting. We expect to have a solid front, you know what I mean? Everybody. You included. You're my next door neighbor, boy. I don't want to hear people saying Artie Hayes wasn't there.

ARTHUR (*Hesitantly*): Well, I don't know, Frank. I thought—

The phone rings. Frank goes toward it.

FRANK: Go home, Artie. Don't worry about it. I'll see you in a few minutes. (*Frank goes to the phone and picks it up. Arthur stares at him*) Hello . . . (*Arthur turns away and walks slowly to door*) Speaking.

Arthur goes out, dazed and frightened. Clarice comes into living room and stands waiting as Frank listens to phone.

FRANK (*Angry*): What do you mean you can't get here?

(*Pause*) Well, this is a great time to call! (*Pause*) I know. Yeah. (*He slams the phone down. To Clarice*) Our sitter can't get here. How d'you like that?

CLARICE: What's wrong with her?

FRANK: I don't know. She's got a cold, or something. Nice dependable girl you pick.

CLARICE (*Snapping*): Well, I didn't exactly arrange for her to get a cold, you know.

FRANK: Look, Clarry, we're going to this thing no matter what.

CLARICE: Well, I'm not leaving Chris with Roger. They'll claw each other to pieces.

FRANK: Then we'll take 'em with us.

CLARICE: You wouldn't . . .

FRANK: Who wouldn't? We're doing it for them as much as anyone else, aren't we? Well, they might as well see it.

CLARICE: Maybe I'd better stay home with them.

FRANK: No, sir. You've been in on this from the beginning. You're going. Come on, get Chris dressed. We haven't got much time.

CLARICE: Well . . . whatever you think, Frank . . .

FRANK: I'm telling you it's all right. Won't hurt 'em a bit. (*To Roger*) What d'you say, son? Want to come along?

ROGER (*Eagerly*): Oh boy! Really? (*Frank nods and grins. Roger leaps happily*) Gee, Dad, you're the greatest guy in the whole world.

He runs over and hugs Frank.

FRANK (*Grinning*): Go on, Clarry. Make it snappy.

Clarice goes into the bedroom. Doorbell rings.

ROGER: I'll get it, Dad.

He runs to the door and opens it. Charlie Denton, forty years old and eager as a child, stands there. He comes in fast, excited.

CHARLIE: Hiya, Rog. Frank, you all set?

FRANK: Hello, Charlie. Another minute or two. How's it look?

CHARLIE: Great. I'm checking house to house. Everybody's ready.

FRANK: Good. Any changes?

CHARLIE: Nope. It's gonna be fast and quiet. What time you got?

FRANK (*Calling*): Clarry, what time is it?

CLARICE (*Calling*): Twelve after.

CHARLIE (*Looking at watch*): Make it thirteen. At fifteen we go.

FRANK: Right. Hey listen, you better look in on Artie Hayes next door. He's been acting a little peculiar.

CHARLIE: I spoke to him a little while ago on the street. I think he was coming over to see you. Don't worry about a thing. I'll be watching him. See you, Frank. Let's make this good.

FRANK: You bet we will. It looks like a beaut. Take off. (*Charlie goes out fast*) Get on your coat, Rog. (*Calling*) Clarry!

> Roger goes to closet and begins to get his coat. Frank stalks nervously up and down.

CLARICE (*Calling*): In a minute . . .

> Frank goes to the window and looks out. He watches and waits. We can see the excitement building within him. Roger, hat and coat on, joins him at window. Frank puts his arm on Roger's shoulder and talks, half to himself.

FRANK (*Low*): How do you like that Artie Hayes? Maybe we ought to think it over! I could've belted him one. How do you like that guy!

ROGER: What do you mean, Dad?

FRANK (*Calling*): Clarry!

CLARICE (*Calling*): Here I am. Come on, Chris.

> Clarice walks into living room followed by a very

> sleepy Christopher. He is in his hat and coat. He
> wanders over to Frank.

FRANK: What time is it?

CLARICE: Almost fourteen after.

FRANK: Almost fifteen. Put on your coat.

> Clarice goes to the closet and does so. Frank follows
> her and gets his. He puts it on. Clarice picks up a large
> thermos from the foyer table.

CLARICE (*Low*): Frank . . . I'm busting with excitement.

FRANK (*Low*): Yeah. So'm I, honey. (*Louder*) Come over
here, boys. (*The two boys walk over to them*) Stand here.

> They wait now behind the closed front door, all four
> of them tense, quiet, hardly able to stand the suspense.
> They wait for several seconds, and then, in the street,
> we begin to hear the heavy tread of marching feet.

CHRISTOPHER: Hey, Daddy . . . where we going?

FRANK: Ssh. Be quiet, son.

> He bends over and picks Christopher up. The sound of
> marching feet grows louder and stronger. They wait till
> it reaches a crescendo. Frank speaks quietly now.

FRANK: Let's go.

> He opens the front door and they walk into a mob of
> grimly advancing men and women. They join the mob
> and walk with them quietly, and the only sound we
> hear is the frightening noise of the tramping feet. Fade
> out.

—— ACT II ——

Fade in on long shot of Sycamore Street. It is once
again 6:40 P.M., the same night. We have gone backward in time and we now duplicate exactly the scene
which opened Act I. Arthur Hayes walks on, stops in

front of his house, knocks his pipe against his heel. Frank Morrison enters. Each of the movements they make, the attitudes they strike and the inflections they use must be exact imitations of the Act I business. The audience must feel that this scene is a clip of film which we are rerunning.

FRANK (*Jovially*): Hey, Artie. How ya doin?

Arthur is preoccupied. He doesn't register at first. He looks blankly at Frank.

FRANK (*Laughing*): Hey . . . wake up, boy. It's almost time for supper.

Arthur snaps out of it and forces a smile.

ARTHUR (*Quietly*): Oh . . . hello, Frank. Sorry. I didn't see you.

FRANK: Didn't see me? Hey, wait till I tell Clarice. That diet she's got me on must be working. You have to look twice to see me! (*Laughing hard, Frank reaches for his keys*) That's a hot one! (*Arthur smiles weakly*) Say . . . isn't this late for you to be getting home?

ARTHUR: No, I don't think so. (*He looks at his watch*) It's twenty to seven. I always get home about this time.

FRANK: Yeah. Well, I wouldn't want you to be late tonight. You know what tonight is, don't you?

ARTHUR (*Slowly*): Yes, I know what tonight is.

FRANK (*A little hard*): Good.

We hear footsteps and see a man walk by them. He is Joseph Blake, a man in his late thirties, a big, powerful, but quiet man. Joseph Blake lives in the third house on the street. As he walks by them they both look at him silently. And now, for the first time, this scene moves in a different direction than did the scene at the beginning of Act I. Instead of coming in close on Frank, the camera comes in close on Arthur Hayes as he stands nervously in front of his door, afraid to look at either

*Joseph Blake or Frank Morrison. We hear Joseph's
footsteps fade out. Arthur reaches for his keys.*

FRANK (*Low, off*): See you later, Artie.

*Arthur winces at this. We hear Frank's door opening
and closing softly. Arthur turns now and looks off at
Joseph Blake's house for a moment. Then he turns and
opens his door. As he enters his foyer we hear dance
music playing softly. The living room is lighted, and
looking in from the foyer, we can see Mr. Harkness,
Arthur's father-in-law, seated in an armchair, reading
the newspaper. He is perhaps sixty-five years old, and
usually does nothing much more than sit reading the
newspapers. He looks up as Arthur comes in.*

MR. HARKNESS: Hello, Arthur. (*Calling off*) Here he is, Phyllis.
(*To Arthur*) Little bit late, aren't you?

*Arthur is hanging up his coat. He is obviously worried.
His face shows concern. His entire manner is subdued.
He speaks quietly, even for Arthur.*

ARTHUR: No. Usual time.

*Mr. Harkness takes out a pocket watch, looks at it,
shakes it.*

MR. HARKNESS: Mmm. Must be fast.

*He goes back to his newspaper. Arthur walks into the
living room tiredly.*

ARTHUR (*Not caring*): How's your cough?

MR. HARKNESS (*Reading*): Still got it. I guess I must've swigged
enough cough syrup to float a rowboat today. Waste of time
and money!

*Phyllis enters from kitchen as Arthur goes over to
phonograph from which the dance music is blasting.
He is just ready to turn it off as she enters.*

MR. HARKNESS: Cough'll go away by itself like it always does.

PHYLLIS (*Brightly*): Hello, darling. Ah . . . don't turn it off.

He turns as she walks over to him. She kisses him pos-

sessively and leads him away from the phonograph.
The music continues.

PHYLLIS: How did it go today, dear?

ARTHUR: All right. Nothing special.

PHYLLIS: What about the Franklin closing?

ARTHUR: It's called off till tomorrow.

PHYLLIS: How come?

ARTHUR: I didn't ask them.

PHYLLIS: Well, you'd think they'd at least give you a reason. You should've asked. I don't like it when people push you around like that.

> *Arthur goes over to a chair without answering. A pipe is on an end table next to the chair. He begins to fill it. Phyllis goes to a small bar on which is a cocktail shaker and one glass. She picks up the shaker.*

ARTHUR: What's that?

PHYLLIS: I made you a drink.

ARTHUR: No. No thanks. I don't want a drink now.

PHYLLIS: Oh, Artie! I made it specially for you. You look tired. Come on, it'll do you good. (*She begins to pour the drink*) Sit down, dear. I'll bring it over to you.

> *Arthur sits down. Phyllis finishes pouring the drink and brings it to him. He takes it. She waits, smiling, for him to drink it.*

ARTHUR: How come you made me a drink tonight?

PHYLLIS: Just for luck. Taste it. (*She sits on the arm of the chair. He tastes it slowly. She puts her arm around him*) Good?

ARTHUR (*Slowly*): It's good.

PHYLLIS: I thought you'd like it.

ARTHUR: Where's Billy?

PHYLLIS: Asleep.

ARTHUR: Isn't it kind of early?

PHYLLIS: He didn't get much of a nap today. The poor baby

couldn't keep his eyes open. Artie, he's getting to be such a devil. You should've seen him this afternoon. He got into my bag and took my lipstick. If I only could've taken a picture of his face. He walked into the kitchen and I swear I almost screamed. You never saw anything so red in your life. Drink your drink, darling. It took me ten minutes to scrub it off.

    Obediently, Arthur sips his drink.

ARTHUR (*Mildly*): I'd like to have seen him before he went to bed.

PHYLLIS: Now you know I had to get finished early tonight, Artie. (*She gets up and goes toward the kitchen*) We're eating in a few minutes. I'm just making melted cheese sandwiches. We can have a snack later if you're hungry.

ARTHUR: Later?

PHYLLIS (*Looking at him oddly*): Yes, later. When we get back.

    Arthur puts his drink down. All of his movements are slow, almost mechanical, as if he has that day aged twenty years. Phyllis goes into kitchen. He takes off his glasses and begins polishing them.

MR. HARKNESS: Melted cheese sandwiches.

ARTHUR (*Not hearing*): What?

MR. HARKNESS: I said melted cheese sandwiches. That gluey cheese. Do you like it?

ARTHUR: No.

MR. HARKNESS: Me neither. Never did.

    He goes back to his paper. Arthur gets up and goes to phonograph. He stands over it, listening. Phyllis comes in carrying a tray on which are three glasses of tomato juice. She gives it to Arthur.

PHYLLIS: Put these on the table like a good boy. (*He takes it and looks at her strangely*) What's the matter with you, Artie? You've hardly said a word since you got home . . .

and you keep looking at me. Are you sick, or something?

ARTHUR: No. I'm not sick.

PHYLLIS: Here, let me feel your head. (*She does so*) No, you feel all right. What is it?

ARTHUR: Nothing. I'm just tired, I guess.

PHYLLIS: Well, I hope you perk up a little.

She goes off into kitchen. Arthur goes slowly to dining table which is set in the same spot as the Morrison dining table. He puts the glasses on it, and sets the tray on the end table. He takes a sip of his drink. Phyllis comes in from the kitchen carrying a platter of melted cheese sandwiches. She goes to the table, puts it down.

PHYLLIS: Dinner. Come on, Dad, while they're hot. Artie . . .

ARTHUR: You go ahead. I'm not hungry.

PHYLLIS: Oh, now, let's not start that. You have to eat. Try one. They're nice and runny.

ARTHUR: Really, I'm not hungry.

PHYLLIS: Well, you can at least sit with us. I haven't seen you since half-past eight this morning.

Arthur goes slowly over to the table and sits down. Mr. Harkness ambles over.

MR. HARKNESS: Well, I'm good and hungry. Tell you that. Got any pickles?

PHYLLIS: No pickles. You know they give you heartburn.

MR. HARKNESS: Haven't had heartburn in a long time. Wouldn't mind a slight case if it came from pickles.

They are all seated now, Phyllis facing the window. Arthur sits quietly. Mr. Harkness busies himself drinking water while Phyllis serves the sandwiches, potato salad, etc.

PHYLLIS: Artie . . . potato salad?

ARTHUR: No. Look, Phyllis . . .

PHYLLIS: Just a little.

She puts a spoonful on a heavily loaded plate and passes it to him. He takes it. Now she serves her father.

PHYLLIS: Potato salad, Dad?

MR. HARKNESS: I'll help myself.

She puts the bowl down and helps herself as does Mr. Harkness.

PHYLLIS (*Brightly*): What happened at the office, dear? Anything new?

ARTHUR: No. It was quiet.

PHYLLIS: Did you hear about the Walkers wanting to sell their house?

ARTHUR: No.

PHYLLIS: You know, for a real-estate man you hear less about real estate than anyone I ever saw. I spoke to Margie Walker this morning. I just got to her in time. You're going to handle the sale. She told me she hadn't even thought of you till I called. Why is that, dear?

ARTHUR: I don't know why it is.

PHYLLIS: Well, anyway, she's expecting you to call her to-morrow. It ought to be a very nice sale for you, dear.

Arthur nods and looks down at his plate. There is silence for a moment.

MR. HARKNESS (*Chewing*): This stuff gets under my teeth.

PHYLLIS: Dad!

MR. HARKNESS: Well, I can't help it, can I?

They eat for a moment and then Phyllis, looking out the window, sees movement in the house next door, the Blake house. She can no longer hold back the topic she's been trying not to discuss in front of Arthur.

PHYLLIS: Look at them. Every shade in the house is down. (*She looks at her watch*) There isn't much more time. I wonder if they know. Do you think they do, Artie?

ARTHUR (*Tired*): I don't know.

PHYLLIS: They must. You can't keep a thing like this secret.

I wonder how they feel. (*She looks at Arthur*) Artie, aren't you going to eat your dinner?

ARTHUR (*Slowly*): How can you talk about them and my dinner in the same breath?

PHYLLIS: For Heaven's sakes . . . I don't know what's the matter with you tonight.

ARTHUR (*Quietly*): You don't, do you?

> *He gets up from the table and walks over to the phonograph. He stands there holding it with both hands, listening to the slick dance music. Then abruptly, he turns it off. Phyllis looks as if she is about to protest, but then decides not to.*

MR. HARKNESS: What d'you suppose is gonna happen over there? Boy, wouldn't I like to go along tonight.

PHYLLIS (*Looking at Arthur*): Dad, will you please stop.

MR. HARKNESS: Well, I would! How do you think it feels to be sixty-two years old and baby-sitting when there's real action going on right under your nose? Something a man wants to get into.

ARTHUR (*Turning*): Be quiet!

MR. HARKNESS: Now listen here—

ARTHUR: I said be quiet!

> *He takes off his glasses and walks over to the table.*

PHYLLIS: Artie, stop it! There's no need for you to raise your voice like that.

> *Arthur speaks more quietly now, feeling perhaps that he has gone too far.*

ARTHUR: Then tell your father to keep his ideas to himself!

MR. HARKNESS (*Angrily*): Wait a minute!

> *Phyllis, in the ensuing argument, is quiet, calm, convincing, never losing her temper, always trying to soothe Arthur, to sweeten the ugly things she says by saying them gently.*

PHYLLIS: Dad, be quiet. Listen, Artie, I know you're tired,

darling, but there's something we might as well face. In about fifteen or twenty minutes you and I and a group of our friends and neighbors are going to be marching on that house next door. Maybe it's not such a pleasant thing to look forward to, but something has to be done. You know that, Artie. You agreed to it with all the others.

ARTHUR: I didn't agree to anything. You agreed for the Hayes household. Remember?

PHYLLIS: All right, I agreed. I didn't hear you disagreeing. Oh, what's the difference, darling? You've been acting like there's a ten-ton weight on your back ever since you heard about it. And there's no point to it. It's all decided.

ARTHUR: All decided. What right have we got to decide?

PHYLLIS: It's not a question of right, Artie. Don't you see? It's something we have to do, right or wrong. Do you want them to live next door to you? Do you really want them?

ARTHUR: I always thought a man was supposed to be able to live anywhere he chooses no matter what anyone else wants.

PHYLLIS: But, dear, this isn't anywhere. This is Sycamore Street. It's not some back alley in a slum! This is a respectable neighborhood. Artie, let's be realistic. That's one of the few things we can really say we have. We're respectable. Do you remember how hard we worked to get that way?

ARTHUR: Respectable! Phyllis, for Heaven's sakes. We're talking about throwing a man out of his own home. What is the man? He's not a monster. He's a quiet guy who minds his own business. How does that destroy our respectability?

PHYLLIS (*Hard*): He got out of prison two months ago. He's a common hoodlum.

ARTHUR: We don't know for sure.

PHYLLIS: We know. Charlie Denton doesn't lie. He saw the man's picture in the Rockville papers just fifty miles from here the day he got out. Tell me, what does he do for a living? Where did he get the money to buy that house?

ARTHUR: I don't think that's any of your business.

PHYLLIS: But, Artie, the man was in jail for four years. That's our business! How do you know what he did? How do you know he won't do it again?

ARTHUR: We have police.

PHYLLIS: Police! Will the police stop his child from playing with Billy? What kind of a child must that be? Think about it. Her father is an ex-convict. That's a lovely thing to tell our friends. Why, yes . . . you know Billy's little friend Judy. Of course you do. Her father spent a great deal of time in prison. Charming people. It's beautiful for the neighborhood, isn't it, Artie? It makes real-estate prices just skyrocket up. Tell me, who do you think'll be moving in next . . . and where'll we go?

> Arthur doesn't answer. He sits down in a chair, troubled, trying to find an argument. Phyllis watches him closely.

MR. HARKNESS: Listen, Artie—

> But Phyllis puts her hand on his arm to shut him up. Arthur is thinking and she wants to see if her argument has worked.

ARTHUR: Look, Phyllis, this is a mob we're getting together. We're going to order this man out of his house . . . or we're going to throw him out. What right have we got to do it? Maybe most of us'd rather not have him as a neighbor, but, Phyllis, the man is a human being, not an old dog. This is an ugly thing we're doing. . . .

PHYLLIS: We've got to do something to keep our homes decent. There's no other way. Somebody's always got to lose, Artie. Why should it be all of us when there's only one of him?

ARTHUR: I . . . I don't know.

> Arthur suddenly gets up and goes toward the front

door as if going out. He buttons his jacket. Phyllis gets up, concerned.

PHYLLIS: Where are you going?

ARTHUR: I'm going to talk to Frank Morrison.

PHYLLIS: All right. Maybe Frank'll make sense to you. (*Calling*) Wear your coat.

> *But Arthur has opened the door and intends to go out without it. Phyllis looks at her watch.*

PHYLLIS: Arthur, it's freezing out! (*He is outside the door now*) You'll catch cold. (*The door closes. She stands watching after him, obviously upset. Her father resumes his eating. She looks at the door for a long time. Then, without looking around*) Dad . . .

MR. HARKNESS: Mmmm?

PHYLLIS: What do you think he'll do?

MR. HARKNESS: Well . . . I don't know. You got any more of these melted cheese businesses? I'm hungry.

PHYLLIS: No.

> *She goes to the window and looks out.*

MR. HARKNESS: Why don't you sit down, Phyl? He'll be all right.

PHYLLIS: What do you mean all right? Look at him. He's standing in front of Frank's house afraid to ring the bell.

MR. HARKNESS: He'll calm down. Come away from that window and sit down. Have some coffee.

> *She moves away from window and sits at table.*

PHYLLIS: I've never seen him like this before.

MR. HARKNESS: Well, what are you worried about? Tell you what. I'll go along with you. Boy, wouldn't I like to be in on a thing like this once. Let Artie stay home and mind the baby if that's how he feels.

> *Phyllis turns on her father violently and for the first time we see how much Arthur's decision means to her.*

PHYLLIS (*Fiercely*): He's got to go! Don't you understand?

MR. HARKNESS: What the dickens is eating you? No, I don't understand. (*Phyllis gets up and goes to the window. She looks out tensely*) Would you mind telling me what you're talking about?

PHYLLIS (*Startled*): Oh no!

> *She turns and runs to the front door. She starts to open it and run out. As she gets it half open we hear a low voice calling, Charlie Denton's voice.*

CHARLIE (*Low*): Artie! Hey, Artie!

> *She closes the door silently and stands against it, frightened. Cut to street in front of Frank's house. Arthur stands there, having just been hailed by Charlie. He turns, and then we see Charlie hurrying down the street toward him. Charlie gets to him, takes him by the arm.*

CHARLIE (*Low*): What are you doing out here now?

ARTHUR (*Guiltily*): Nothing. I was . . . well, I was getting some air, that's all.

CHARLIE: Look, boy, this thing has got to be timed on the button. Everybody's supposed to be in his house right now. Nobody's supposed to be wandering around the streets. What time've you got?

ARTHUR (*With an effort*): Listen, Charlie, I want to talk to you about tonight.

CHARLIE: I haven't got time to talk.

ARTHUR: Please. It's important.

CHARLIE (*Tough*): What the heck's the matter with you?

ARTHUR: Nothing. Nothing, Charlie . . .

CHARLIE: What time've you got? (*He grabs Arthur's wrist and holds it up in the light. He holds his own wrist next to it and compares the watches*) You're three minutes slow.

ARTHUR: I know. This watch . . . it runs slow. Charlie . . .

CHARLIE: Well, fix it, will ya? The timing's the most important part.

ARTHUR: I will. Look, about this thing tonight . . .

CHARLIE: Listen, if you're gonna start in with me about the plan, take it up with the committee, will ya, please? All of a sudden everybody's an expert on how to run the show. If you want the organizing job I'll be glad to give it to you.

ARTHUR: No, it's not that. It's organized very well. There's something else.

CHARLIE: Are you gonna fix that watch?

ARTHUR: I will. I've been meaning to set it all day. Listen . . . these people . . . the Blakes. They've got a kid . . .

CHARLIE: So has my mother. Here, gimme this. (*He grabs Arthur's wrist and sets his watch*) There. At seven-fifteen on the nose we go. Now get back into your house.

He walks off fast.

ARTHUR: Charlie . . .

But Charlie keeps going. Arthur watches him. Then he goes up to Frank Morrison's front door and rings the bell. From inside we hear Roger calling.

ROGER (Off): I'll get it.

Roger opens the front door, and now again, Roger's and Arthur's movements must be exactly as they were in the first act, except that now the camera catches them from outside the house.

ARTHUR: Rog, is your Dad in?

ROGER: Sure. Come on in, Mr. Hayes.

Arthur walks in slowly. The door closes.

Fade out.

Fade in on the living room of Arthur's house. Phyllis sits tensely waiting for him. The dining table is cleared. Mr. Harkness is back in his easy chair reading the papers. We hear a key in the lock, the door opens and Arthur enters. He walks slowly, despising himself for not

*having been stronger with Frank or Charlie. Phyllis
gets up as he comes in. He doesn't look at her but
walks over to the window and stands there. She comes
up behind him. He doesn't turn around.*

PHYLLIS: Artie . . . Artie, are you all right?

He turns around slowly, speaks heavily.

ARTHUR: Yeah. I'm fine.

PHYLLIS: What happened? What'd you say to them?

ARTHUR: I said nothing.

PHYLLIS (*Hopefully*): Well, what do you mean you said
nothing. Didn't you talk about it?

ARTHUR: No, I didn't talk about it. I didn't talk about anything. Will you leave me alone?

She backs away, alarmed. Then she looks at her watch.

PHYLLIS (*Softly*): We only have a couple of minutes, dear.

ARTHUR: I'm not going out there.

PHYLLIS: I'd better get our coats.

ARTHUR: Did you hear what I just said?

PHYLLIS: We'll have to bundle up. It's only about twenty
degrees out. Did you know that?

ARTHUR: I said I'm not going.

*Phyllis backs away from him. He turns to the window.
We can see that she is hugely upset, almost desperate.
She looks at him fiercely. Mr. Harkness gets up quietly
with his paper and goes into the next room. We hear
the door close. Arthur doesn't move.*

PHYLLIS (*Strongly*): I want to tell you something. I'm going
to get our coats now, and we're going to put them on, and
we're going to stand in the doorway of our house until it's
seven-fifteen.

ARTHUR (*Turning*): Stop it.

PHYLLIS: And then we're going to walk out into the gutter,
you and me, the Hayes family, and we're going to be just
like everybody else on Sycamore Street!

ARTHUR (*Shouting*): Phyllis! I've told you . . . I'm not going
to be a part of this thing!

> *Phyllis studies him for a long moment.*

PHYLLIS: Listen to me, Artie. Listen to me good. I didn't
think you needed to hear this before. But you're going to
hear it now. We're going out there. Do you want to know
why? Because we're not going to be next!

ARTHUR: You're out of your mind!

PHYLLIS (*Roaring*): Sure I am! I'm out of my mind all right.
I'm crazy with fear because I don't want to be different.
I don't want my neighbors looking at us and wondering
why we're not like them.

ARTHUR (*Amazed*): Phyllis . . . you're making this up! They
won't think that.

PHYLLIS: They will think that! We'll be the only ones, the
odd ones who wanted to let an ex-convict live with us.
They'll look the other way when we walk the streets. They'll
become cold and nasty . . . and all of a sudden we won't
have any neighbors. (*Pointing at the Blake house*) We'll
be like them!

> *Arthur stands looking at her and it begins to sink in.*
> *She knows it and goes after him.*

PHYLLIS: We can't be different! We can't afford it! We live
on the good will of these people. Your business is in this
town. Your neighbors buy us the bread we eat! Do you want
them to stop?

ARTHUR: I don't know . . . Phyllis . . . I don't know what
to think . . . I . . . can't . . . throw a stone at this man.

PHYLLIS (*Strong*): You can! You've got to, or we're finished
here.

> *He stares at her, not knowing what to say next. She has*
> *almost won and knows it. She looks at her watch.*

PHYLLIS: Now just . . . wait . . . just stand there. . . .

> *She runs to the closet and takes out their overcoats.*

She throws hers on and brings his to him, holds it for him.

PHYLLIS: Put it on!

ARTHUR: I . . . can't. They're people. It's their home.

PHYLLIS (*Shouting*): We're people too! I don't care what happens to them. I care what happens to us. We belong here. We've got to live here. Artie, for the love of God, we don't even know them. What's the difference what happens to them? What about us?

He has no answer. She begins to put his coat on. He stands there, beaten, wrecked, moving his arms automatically, no longer knowing the woman who is putting on his coat. She talks as she helps him.

PHYLLIS: There. It won't be long. I promise you. It won't be long. That's my Artie. That's my darling. Let's button up, dear. It's cold. We'll be back in an hour, and it'll be over. There. Now put on your gloves, darling.

She takes him by the arm and he stands there letting her do as she will. He puts on his gloves without knowing he is doing it, and they wait together, there in the doorway. She looks at him, trying to read him, as we begin to hear the cold and chilling sound of the tramping feet. Mr. Harkness comes out of the bedroom and stands there looking at them. Phyllis looks at her watch. The tramping grows louder. They wait in silence. Then she opens the door. We see the crowd, grimly marching, and the Morrisons are at the head of it. No one looks at the Hayes. The dull thud of the tramping feet is sickening to hear. Arthur closes his eyes. Slowly now Phyllis pushes him forward. He steps out of the house and moves ahead to join the others, as if in a dream. Phyllis follows, catches up and takes his arm as they join the marching mob. Fade out.

─── **ACT III** ──────────────────

Fade in on a long shot of Sycamore Street. It is once again 6:40 P.M., same night. We have gone backward in time, and again we duplicate the scene which opened Acts I and II. Arthur Hayes walks on, stops in front of his house, knocks his pipe against his heel. Frank Morrison enters. Again, each of the movements must be exact imitations of the movements in Acts I and II. It is as if we are starting the play again.

FRANK (*Jovially*): Hey, Artie. How ya doin'?
Arthur is preoccupied. He doesn't register at first. He looks blankly at Frank.

FRANK (*Laughing*): Hey . . . wake up, boy. It's almost time for supper.
Arthur snaps out of it and forces a smile.

ARTHUR (*Quietly*): Oh . . . hello, Frank. Sorry. I didn't see you.

FRANK: Didn't see me? Hey, wait till I tell Clarice. That diet she's got me on must be working. You have to look twice to see me! (*Laughing hard, Frank reaches for his keys*) That's a hot one! (*Arthur smiles weakly*) Say . . . isn't this late for you to be getting home?

ARTHUR: No, I don't think so. (*He looks at his watch*) It's twenty to seven. I always get home about this time.

FRANK: Yeah. Well, I wouldn't want you to be late tonight. You know what tonight is, don't you?

ARTHUR (*Slowly*): Yes, I know what tonight is.

FRANK (*A little hard*): Good.
We hear footsteps and see a man walk by them. He is Joseph Blake. They both look at him silently. Camera now follows him as he walks silently toward his house, the third of the three houses we see. As he walks, we hear faintly in background.

FRANK (Off): See you later, Artie.

> We hear Frank's door open and close. Then we hear Arthur's door open, and for an instant, we hear the same dance music coming from Arthur's house that we heard in Act II. Then Arthur's door closes. By this time Joseph Blake is in front of his door. He looks off silently at the other two houses. Then he opens his front door and enters his house. As he closes the door we hear running feet, and then we see Judy, Joe's six-year-old daughter, in a bathrobe and slippers, running at him.

JUDY (Calling): Daddy Daddy Daddy Daddy.

> She runs into his arms. He lifts her up and hugs her.

JOE: Mmm. You smell sweet.

JUDY (Excited): I had a hairwash with Mommy's special shampoo. It smells like gar . . . gar . . .

JOE: Gardenias. Did anyone ever tell you you smelled like gardenias even without Mommy's shampoo?

JUDY (Grinning): You're silly.

> He tickles her and she giggles.

ANNA (Calling): Judy!

JUDY (Importantly): We've got company.

JOE: Oh? Who is it, darling?

JUDY: A lady.

ANNA (Calling): Judy!

> Joe puts her down. She runs inside. Joe takes off his coat, puts it into the closet and walks into the living room. Joe's wife, Anna, stands near a chair. Anna, in her early thirties, is a quiet, small woman who has obviously been through a great deal of suffering in the past five years. She looks extremely nervous and upset now. Seated at the far end of the room in a rocking chair is Joe's mother, Mrs. Blake. She is quite old, quite spry for her years and inclined to be snappish. Also

seated in the room is a middle-aged woman, a neighbor-hood busybody named Mrs. Carson. She wears an odd, old-fashioned hat and sits stiffly, not at home, quite uncomfortable, but determined to do what she has come to do. The living room again is an exact duplicate of the Morrison and Hayes living rooms. It is furnished sparsely and not well. It is obvious that the Blakes have not been living there long. As Joe gets into the room, Anna comes toward him.

ANNA: Joe, this is Mrs. Carson.

JOE (*Politely*): Mrs. Carson.

He turns to her for a moment. She nods curtly. Then he turns back to Anna and kisses her gently.

JOE: Hello, darling.

ANNA: Joe . . .

But he walks away from her and goes to his mother. He bends over and kisses her on the forehead.

MRS. BLAKE: Your face is cold.

JOE (*Smiling*): It's freezing out. How do you feel?

MRS. BLAKE: Just fine, Joe.

He pats her cheek and turns to find Judy behind him, holding a piece of drawing paper and a crayon. On the paper is a childish scribble that looks vaguely like a boat. Anna, a tortured expression on her face, wants to say something, but Joe looks at the drawing, grinning.

JUDY: Daddy . . .

JOE: The Queen Mary! Now that is what I call beautiful.

JUDY: It is not! It's just s'posed to be a sailboat. How do you draw a sail?

ANNA (*Shakily*): Joe . . . Mrs. Carson . . .

JOE: Well, let's see. . . . (*He takes the crayon and paper and studies it*) I suppose you think it's easy to draw a sail.

JUDY (*Serious*): No. I don't.

ANNA (*Sharply*): Joe. (*She comes over and snatches the paper away from him. He looks at her*) Judy, go into your room.

JOE: Wait a minute, Anna. Take it easy.

ANNA (*Near tears*): Judy, did you hear me?

JOE: Darling, what's the matter with you?

ANNA: Joe . . .

JUDY: Mommy, do I have to?

JOE (*Gently*): Maybe you'd better go inside for a few minutes, baby.

> *Judy unhappily goes into her room. Anna waits till we hear the door close. Joe puts his arms around her.*

JOE: Tell me. What's wrong, Anna?

ANNA (*Almost sobbing*): Joe! I don't understand it! Mrs. Carson says . . . She . . .

JOE (*Gently*): Mrs. Carson says what?

ANNA (*Breaking down*): She says . . . Joe . . . they're going to throw us out of our house. Tonight! Right now! What are we going to do?

JOE (*Softly*): Well, I don't know. Who's going to throw us out of our house?

> *But Anna can't answer. Joe grips her tightly, then releases her and walks to Mrs. Carson who sits stolidly, waiting.*

JOE: Who's going to throw us out, Mrs. Carson? Do you know?

MRS. CARSON: Well, like I told Mrs. Blake there, I suppose it's none of my business, but I'm just not the kind that thinks a thing like this ought to happen to people without them getting at least a . . . well, a warning. Know what I mean?

JOE: No, I don't know what you mean, Mrs. Carson. Did someone send you here?

MRS. CARSON (*Indignantly*): Well, I should say not! If my husband knew I was here he'd drag me out by the hair. No,

I sneaked in here, if you please, Mr. Blake. I felt it was my Christian duty. A man ought to have the right to run away, I say.

JOE: What do you mean run away, Mrs. Carson?

MRS. CARSON: Well, you know what I mean.

JOE: Who's going to throw us out?

MRS. CARSON: Well, everybody. The people on Sycamore Street. You know. They don't feel you ought to live here, because . . . Now I don't suppose I have to go into that.

JOE (*understanding*): I see.

ANNA (*Breaking in*): Joe, I've been waiting and waiting for you to come home. I've been sitting here . . . and waiting. Listen . . .

JOE (*Quietly*): Hold it, Anna. (*To Mrs. Carson*) What time are they coming, Mrs. Carson?

MRS. CARSON: Quarter after seven. That's the plan. (*She looks at her watch and gets up*) It's near seven now. They're very angry people, Mr. Blake. I don't think it'd be right for anyone to get hurt. That's why I'm here. If you take my advice, you'll just put some stuff together in a hurry and get out. I don't think there's any point in your calling the police either. There's only two of 'em in Eastmont and I don't think they'd do much good against a crowd like this.

JOE: Thank you, Mrs. Carson.

MRS. CARSON: Oh, don't thank me. It's like I said. I don't know you people, but there's no need for anyone getting hurt long as you move out like everybody wants. No sir. I don't want no part nor parcel to any violence where it's not necessary. Know what I mean?

JOE: Yes, I know what you mean.

MRS. CARSON: I don't know why a thing like this has to start up anyway. It's none of my business, but a man like you ought to know better than to come pushing in here . . . a fine old neighborhood like this! After all, right is right.

JOE (*Controlled*): Get out, Mrs. Carson.

MRS. CARSON: What? Well I never! You don't seem to know what I've done for you, Mr. Blake.

ANNA: Joe . . .

JOE: Get out of this house.

> *He goes to a chair in which lies Mrs. Carson's coat. He picks it up and thrusts it at her. She takes it, indignant and a bit frightened. Joe turns from her. She begins to put her coat on.*

MRS. CARSON: Well, I should think you'd at least have the decency to thank me. I might've expected this though. People like you!

ANNA: Mrs. Carson, please . . .

JOE: Anna, stop it!

> *He strides to the door and holds it open. Mrs. Carson walks out.*

MRS. CARSON: I think maybe you'll be getting what you deserve, Mr. Blake. Good night.

> *She goes out. Joe slams the door.*

ANNA: It's true. I can't believe it! Joe! Did you hear what she said? (*She goes to Joe, who still stands at the door, shocked*) Well, what are you standing there for?

JOE (*Amazed*): I don't know.

ANNA: Joe, I'm scared. I'm so scared, I'm sick to my stomach. What are we going to do?

> *Joe puts his arms around her as she begins to sob. He holds her close till she quiets down. Then he walks her slowly over to his mother.*

JOE (*To his mother*): Will you read to Judy for a few minutes, Mother? It's time for her story. (*Mrs. Blake starts to get up*) Winnie the Pooh. She'll tell you what page.

> *Mrs. Blake nods and gets up and goes into Judy's room.*

ANNA: What are you doing, Joe? We've only got fifteen minutes. . . . Don't you understand?

JOE (*Quietly*): What do you want me to do? I can't stop them from coming here.

> *She goes to him and looks up at him, pleading now.*

ANNA (*Whispering*): Joe. Let's get out. We've got time. We can throw some things into the car. . . .

JOE: Isn't it a remarkable thing? A quiet street like this and people with thunder in their hearts.

ANNA: Listen to me, Joe—please. We can get most of our clothes in the car. We can stop at a motel. I don't care where we go. Anywhere. Joe, you're not listening. (*Loud*) What's the matter with you?

JOE: We're staying.

ANNA (*Frightened*): No!

JOE: Anna, this is our home and we're staying in it. No one can make us get out of our home. No one. That's a guarantee I happen to have since I'm born.

ANNA (*Sobbing*): Joe, you can't! Do you know what a mob is like? Do you know what they're capable of doing?

JOE: It's something I've never thought of before . . . a mob. I guess they're capable of doing ugly things.

ANNA: Joe, you're talking and talking and the clock is ticking so fast. Please . . . please . . . Joe. We can run. We can go somewhere else to live. It's not so hard.

JOE: It's very hard, Anna, when it's not your own choice.

ANNA (*Sobbing*): What are you talking about? What else've we got to do? Stand here and fight them? We're not an army. We're one man and one woman and an old lady and a baby.

JOE: And the floor we stand on belongs to us. Not to anyone else.

ANNA: They don't care about things like that. Joe, listen to me, please. You're not making sense. Listen . . . Judy's inside. She's six years old now and she's only really known you for a few weeks. We waited four years for you, and she didn't remember you when you picked her up and kissed her hello, but, Joe, she was so happy. What are you gonna tell her when they set fire to her new house?

JOE: I'm gonna tell her that her father fought like a tiger to stop them.

ANNA (*Crying*): Oh, no! No! No! What good will that do? Joe . . . please . . . please . . .

JOE (*Thundering*): Stop it! (*Anna turns away from him and covers her face. After a long pause, quietly*) It's this way, Anna. We have a few things we own. We have this house we've just bought with money left from before . . . money you could have used many times. We have a mortgage and a very old car and a few pieces of furniture. We have my job.

ANNA (*Bitterly*): Selling pots and pans at kitchen doors.

JOE (*Patiently*): We have my job. And we have each other and that's what we have. Except there's one more thing. We have the right to live where we please and how we please. We're keeping all of those things, Anna. They belong to us.

> He comes up behind her and puts his hands on her shoulders. She sinks down in a chair, turned away from him, and sobs. He stands over her. She continues to sob. He holds her and tries to quiet her. The bedroom door opens and Judy bounces into the room. Joe gets up and goes to her as Anna tries to dry her tears.

JUDY: Grandma says I'm supposed to go to bed now. Do I have to, Daddy?

JOE (*Smiling*): It's time, honey.

JUDY (*Disappointed*): Gee whiz. Some night, I'm gonna stay up until four o'clock in the morning!

JOE: Some night you can. *He kisses her.*

Good night, baby. Give Mommy a kiss.

> Judy goes to Anna and speaks as she is kissing her.

JUDY: Really? I really can stay up till four o'clock?

JOE: Really.

JUDY: Night, Mommy.

ANNA: Good night, darling.

> *Judy runs off gleefully to the bedroom.*

JUDY: Oh boy! (*Calling*) Grandma . . .

> *The door closes. Anna gets up and goes to window. She is still terrified, but a bit calmer now. She looks out and then turns to Joe. He watches her.*

ANNA: What've we done to hurt them? What've we done? I don't understand.

JOE (*Softly*): Well, I guess maybe they think we've destroyed the dignity of their neighborhood, darling. That's why they've thrown garbage on our lawn.

ANNA: Dignity! Throwing garbage. Getting together a mob. Those are dignified things to do. Joe, how can you want to stay? How can you want to live on the same street with them? Don't you see what they are?

JOE: They're people, Anna. And I guess they're afraid, just like we are. That's why they've become a mob. It's why people always do.

> *The bedroom door opens and Joe's mother enters. She goes to her rocker and sits in it and begins to rock.*

ANNA: What are they afraid of?

JOE: Living next door to someone they think is beneath them, An ex-convict. Me.

> *Anna runs to Joe and grips him excitedly.*

ANNA: What do you think you did? They must think you're a thief or a murderer.

JOE: Maybe they do.

ANNA: Well, they can't. You'll tell them. You'll tell them. Joe.

JOE: Anna, listen . . .

ANNA: It could've happened to any one of them. Tell them

you're not a common criminal. You were in an accident, and that's all it was. An accident. Joe, they'll listen. I know they will.

JOE: No, Anna . . .

ANNA (*Eagerly*): All you have to do is tell them and they'll go away. It's not like you committed a crime or anything. You were speeding. Everybody speeds. You hit an old man, and he died. He walked right in front—

JOE: They're not asking what I did, Anna.

ANNA (*Pleading*): Joe, please. Look at me. I'm so frightened. . . . You have to tell them.

JOE: Anna, we have our freedom. If we beg for it, then it's gone. Don't you see that?

ANNA (*Shouting*): No!

> *He comes to her and grips her, and speaks to her with his face inches from hers.*

JOE: How can I tell it to you? Listen, Anna, we're only little people, but we have certain rights. Judy's gonna learn about them in school in a couple of years . . . and they'll tell her that no one can take them away from her. She's got to be able to believe that. They include the right to be different. Well, a group of our neighbors have decided that we have to get out of here because they think we're different. They think we're not nice. (*Strongly*) Do we have to smile in their faces and tell them we are nice? We don't have to win the right to be free! It's the same as running away, Anna. It's staying on their terms, and if we can't stay here on our terms, then there are no more places to stay anywhere. For you—for me—for Judy—for anyone, Anna.

> *She sees it now and she almost smiles, but the tears are running down her cheeks and it's difficult to smile. Joe kisses her forehead.*

JOE (*Quietly*): Now we'll wait for them.

> *Anna goes slowly to a chair and sits in it. Mrs. Blake*

rocks rhythmically on her rocking chair. *Joe stands firm at one side of the room and they wait in silence. Suddenly the ticking of the clock on the mantelpiece thunders in our ears and the monotonous beat of it is all we hear. They wait. Anna looks at Joe and then speaks softly.*

ANNA: Joe. My hands are shaking. I don't want them to shake. *Joe walks over to her, stands over her strongly and clasps both her hands together. Then he holds them in his till they are still. The clock ticks on, and now we cut to it. It reads ten after seven. Dissolve to a duplicate of the clock which now reads quarter after seven. Cut to long shot of room as we begin to hear the tramping of the feet down the street. They wait. The rocker rocks. The clock ticks. The tramping grows louder. Joe stands in the center of the room, hard and firm. Then he turns to his mother and speaks gently and softly.*

JOE: Go inside, Mother.

MRS. BLAKE (*Slowly*): No, Joe. I'm staying here. I want to watch you. I want to hear you. I want to be proud.

She continues to rock and now the tramping noise reaches a crescendo and then stops. For a moment there is silence, absolute silence, and then we hear a single angry voice.

CHARLIE DENTON (*Shouting*): Joseph Blake! (*There is a chorus of shouts and a swelling of noise*) Joseph Blake . . . come out here!

The noise from outside grows in volume. Inside only the rocking chair moves.

FIRST MAN (*Shouting*): Come out of that house!

The noise, the yelling of the crowd, continues to grow. Inside the room no one gives a signal that they have heard.

SECOND MAN (*Shouting*): We want you, Joseph Blake!

FRANK MORRISON (Shouting): Come out—or we'll drag you out!

> The yelling continues, grows louder. Still the Blakes do not move. Then suddenly a rock smashes through the window. Glass sprays to the floor. The pitch of the noise outside rises even more. Joe begins to walk firmly to the door.

ANNA (Softly): Joe . . .

> But he doesn't hear her. He gets to the door and flings it open violently and steps outside. As he does, the shouting, which has reached its highest pitch, stops instantly and from deafening noise we plunge into absolute silence, broken only by the steady creaking of the rocking chair inside. Joe stands there in front of his house like a rock. Now for the first time we see the crowd. The camera plays over the silent faces watching him—the faces of the men and women and children. The Morrisons are directly in front, Charlie Denton is further back. Mrs. Carson is there. And far to the rear we see Arthur Hayes and Phyllis. Still the silence holds. Then, little by little, the people begin to speak. At first we only hear single voices from different parts of the crowd.

FIRST MAN (Shouting): Look at him, standing there like he owns the block!

> There is a chorus of ad-lib approvals.

SECOND MAN (Shouting): Who do you think you are busting in where decent people live?

> Another chorus of approvals. Joe stands like a fierce and powerful statue.

FIRST WOMAN (Shouting): Why don't you go live with your own kind . . . in a gutter somewhere?

> Another chorus of approvals. The camera moves about

catching the eagerness, the mounting temper of the
crowd, then the shame and anguish of Arthur Hayes,
then the giant strength of Joe.

FIRST MAN (*Shouting*): Your limousine is waiting, Mr. Blake.
You're taking a one-way trip!

There are a few laughs at this, and now the crowd, although not moving forward, is a shouting mass again.
Still Joe waits quietly.

CHARLIE DENTON (*Shouting*): Well, what are we waiting for?
Let's get him!

The intensity of the noise grows and the mob begins to
move forward. Then, with a tremendous roar, Frank
Morrison stops them.

FRANK (*Roaring*): Quiet! Everybody shut up.

The noise dies down gradually.

FRANK (*To crowd*): Now listen to me! This whole thing is
gonna be handled the way we planned at the meeting.

Roger, standing next to Frank, looks at him adoringly.
Chris holds Clarice's hand and looks around calmly.

CLARICE (*Loud*): That's right! It's what we agreed on.

FRANK (*Shouting*): This man here is gonna be asked politely
and quietly to pack his things and get his family out of
here. We don't have to tell him why. He knows that. He's
gonna be given a chance to leave right now. If he's got any
brains in his head he'll be out in one hour—and nobody'll
touch him or his house. If he hasn't—

There is a low-throated, ominous murmur from the
crowd.

FRANK: Right! This thing is gonna be done fair and square.
(*Turning to Joe*) What d'ya say, Mr. Blake?

Joe looks at him for a long time. The crowd waits
silently. Arthur Hayes lowers his head and clenches his
fists, and looks as if he wants to be sick. The crowd

waits. When Joe speaks, it is with a controlled fury that these people have never heard before. He speaks directly to Frank.

JOE: I spit on your fairness! (*The crowd gasps. Joe waits, then he thunders out*) I own this house and God gave me the right to live in it. The man who tries to take it away from me is going to have to climb over a pile of my bones to do it. You good people of Sycamore Street are going to have to kill me tonight! Are you ready, Mr. Morrison? Don't bother to be fair. You're the head man here. Be first!

The crowd, rocked back on its heels, doesn't know what to do. Behind Joe, in the house, we see framed in the doorway the rocking chair moving steadily, and Anna standing next to it. Frank is stunned by this outburst. He calls for action. But not with the force he displayed earlier.

FRANK: You heard him, everybody. . . . Let's get him.

JOE: I asked for you first, Mr. Morrison!

FRANK (*Shouting*): Listen to me! Let's go, men!

But the crowd is no longer moving as a whole. Some of them are still strongly with Frank, including Charlie, the first man, the second man, and several of the others. But others are not so sure of themselves now.

CHARLIE (*Roaring*): Don't let him throw you, Frank! He asked for it. Let's give it to him!

Joe looks only at Frank. Waits calmly for him.

FRANK (*Roaring*): Come on!

He takes a step forward, but the people behind him don't follow. He turns to them.

FRANK: What's the matter with you people?

JOE: They're waiting for you, Mr. Morrison.

Frank whirls and faces him and they look long and hard at each other. Cut to Charlie Denton at rear of crowd. He has a stone in his hand.

CHARLIE (*Shouting*): Let's start it off, Frankie boy.

He flings the stone. We hear it hit and drop to the ground. The crowd gasps. Cut to Joe. There is blood running down the side of his head. He stands there firmly. Cut to Arthur Hayes. He looks up in horror, and then a transformation comes over him. He seems to grow taller and broader. His face sets strongly and he begins to stride forward, elbowing people aside. Phyllis knows. She clings to him, trying to pull him back.

PHYLLIS (*Screaming*): Artie . . . Artie . . . don't . . .

But he breaks loose from her and pushes forward. Whoever is in his way is knocked aside, and finally he reaches Joe. He looks up at Joe. Then he turns and stands next to him. He takes off his eyeglasses and flings them into the crowd.

ARTHUR (*Strong*): Throw the next stone at me, neighbors. I live here too!

Now the crowd is uncertain as the two men stand together and the blood runs down Joe's face. Frank tries to rally them. During his next lines we shoot through the open door into the living room. Mrs. Blake gets up from her rocking chair and takes Anna's hand. Together they walk to the front door, come outside and stand proudly behind Joe and Arthur.

FRANK: Listen to me! Pay attention, you people. Let's remember what we came here to do . . . and why! This man is garbage! He's cluttering up our street. He's wrecking our neighborhood. We don't want him here. We agreed, every last man and woman of us . . . we agreed to throw him out! Are we gonna let him stop us? If we do—you know what'll happen.

Mrs. Blake and Anna are out of the house now. They wait, along with Joe and Arthur. The crowd listens. Frank shouts on, running from person to person as the crowd begins ashamedly to drift away. Christopher clings to Frank's jacket, and begins to sob.

FRANK: You know what Sycamore Street'll be like. I don't have to tell you. How do we know who we'll be rubbing elbows with next? Listen, where are you going? We're all together in this! What about our kids? Listen to me, people. Our kids'll be playing and going to school with his. How do you like that, neighbors? Makes you a little sick, doesn't it? Come back here! I'm telling you we've got to do this! Come back here!

But the crowd continues to drift away. Finally only the Morrisons and Phyllis Hayes are left in the street. Joe and his family, and Arthur, watch them proudly. Roger looks at his bewildered father and then he turns away takes Clarice's hand, and his father is no longer the greatest guy in the world. Frank looks down at the sobbing Christopher, and picks him up and walks slowly off. Clarice and Roger follow. The Blakes turn and go into their house, leaving Arthur on the porch. And standing alone, starkly in the middle of the street, is Phyllis. Arthur looks at her as she stands, heartbreakingly alone, for a long time.

ARTHUR (Sadly): Well, what are you standing there for? My neighbor's head is bleeding!

And then, slowly, knowing that Arthur is no longer a grown-up child, Phyllis moves forward into Joseph Blake's house.

Fade out.

There are elements in Thunder on Sycamore Street which, two years after the writing of it, I would like to be able to duplicate in a new play, and there are other elements which nettle me each time I reread the play. Actually, I believe that this play should have been prepared for Broadway rather than for television. The reasons for this feeling may not be immediately evident, but since perhaps they may have some interest to those of you who want to write for television, I'll try to explain them here.

First, the elements of the play which have always intrigued me, and which are so ideally suited to the peculiar demands of television, are the simplicity of the plot and the suspense-generating construction of the play itself. Second, this play had something quite intangible yet tremendously important in its favor. It was prompted by a series of events which infuriated me, and written with a passion I have not felt since while working on a script. In late 1953 I had read about the incredible reactions of tenants in a housing development in Cicero, a suburb of Chicago, to the news that some of their neighbors would be Negroes. The inhuman, medieval attitudes of these free, white Americans had so disturbed me that I had decided to do a play about them in an attempt to explore the causes behind their mass sickness. For various reasons it was necessary, however, to put this project aside. But finally, in February 1954, I saw newsreel films and photographs of these people stoning Negroes in front of their apartments and rioting on the lawns of the housing development in which they themselves lived, and I saw the fearsome, hate-twisted faces of women in the mob, some of them actually holding small children by the hand as they hurled rocks at their neighbors. I sat down then and within a very few minutes had worked out the basic story of Thunder on Sycamore Street.

I felt, as I nearly always feel about television plays, that the tighter I was able to compress the span of time in which the action took place, the more suspenseful and effective would be the play. This one, I reasoned, required as much suspense as could be generated, since I wanted to be sure to lose the least possible audience to rival shows. This, of course, is always a consideration in television, but I felt it to be more important for this show than any I had yet written. At any rate, I set the problem of reducing the time span of the play to twenty minutes. To accomplish this it was necessary to have each act take place during the same time span, and then to . move backward in time at the end of each act so that the following act would begin at precisely the time the previous act had begun.

To further the suspense I felt it necessary to withhold from the audience the actual details of what was happening until the middle of the second act. Basically, the framework was set now. Each act would take place in one of three houses on a quiet street in a small town, and each would explore the problems and motivations of the inhabitants of these houses as they concerned the single act of violence in question. Acts I and II would end as the inhabitants of houses 1 and 2 join the mob marching on house 3. I felt that, for this particular story, this rather involved construction could not be improved upon, and I still feel this way. Further, I had something to say in this play about which I felt as strongly as I've ever felt about anything in my life.

What actually happened, however, when I sat down to write Thunder on Sycamore Street is this: Eliminating the time taken by the three identical act openings (about four minutes) and the mob scene (about four minutes) the actual playing time after commercials, credits, etc., was approximately thirty-eight minutes. In this amount of time the problems, the motivations and the basic character delineations of the members of three families had to be presented. At thirteen minutes per family the type of probing this play required is impossible. Therefore, Thunder on Sycamore Street became a play revolving around the action itself rather than the people who created the action. Their problems were real enough, but what motivated the problems was left for an audience to guess at if it so desired.

The three families in this play are composed of people who, in the context of the immediate problem in which they are involved, would have made fascinating and exciting studies were there the time in which to present them properly. This is why I feel that Thunder on Sycamore Street should actually have been written for the theater, where it could have been nearly three times as long and much more complete.

One interesting point to note is this: Originally, Thunder on Sycamore Street was conceived as the story of a Negro who moves into a white community. This was unpalatable to the networks since many of their stations are situated in Southern states and it was felt that viewers might be appalled at the sight of a Negro as the beleaguered hero of a television drama. I felt that a compromise would weaken the play but I decided to make one anyway, hoping that the principle under observation was strong enough to arouse an audience, no matter what strata of society the mob's intended victim represented. The selection of an ex-convict as the protagonist was the obvious choice since this could offend no known organized pressure groups. (I might note here that in Act II of Thunder on Sycamore Street there is a derogatory reference to melted cheese sandwiches, which I sincerely hope did not offend lovers of same.)

It seems, however, that no matter how the protagonist of

the play was disguised, viewers recognized him either for what he was meant to be or for a representative of a minority group in their particular area. It was variously felt by viewers with whom I discussed the show that Joseph Blake was meant to symbolize a Negro, a Jew, a Catholic, a Puerto Rican, an ex-Communist or fellow traveler, a Japanese or Chinese, a Russian, an anarchist or an avowed atheist. Not one single person I spoke to felt that he was actually meant to be an ex-convict. This was extremely gratifying to me and made me feel that perhaps Thunder on Sycamore Street had more value in its various interpretations than it would have had had it simply presented the Negro problem.

It is interesting to note that a week or so after the show I received a letter which contained a bitter, shocking point of view. It was signed by ten married couples living in a Far Western city, and stated in effect that the events depicted in this show could never happen in America and that the author was obviously trying to foment some kind of mysterious anti-American trouble. This after the events in Cicero!

The actual production of Thunder on Sycamore Street was superbly handled by director Franklin Schaffner and producer Felix Jackson. The set itself, designed by Willard Levitas, brilliantly captured the drab middle-class respectability of a right-side-of-the-tracks small-town street, and was somehow crammed into what is actually an inadequate studio. As for casting, it was felt that to maintain the illusion of a living small town this play required faces which were relatively unfamiliar to television audiences. The men of the three families, played by Whitfield Connor, Lee Bergere and Kenneth Utt, gave distinguished performances. Especially exciting was Mr. Utt's portrayal of Joseph Blake, the man of giant strength and quiet dignity, and it was quite a surprise to most viewers to discover, in subsequent magazine and newspaper stories, that Kenny Utt is actually the floor manager for "Studio One" thirty-nine weeks of the year, and was plucked out from behind his microphone for this role by Felix Jackson.

I have not seen Thunder on Sycamore Street since the night it was performed, March 15, 1954, but I don't think I'll ever forget hearing and seeing Kenny Utt thunder out the lines "I own this house and God gave me the right to live in it. The man who tries to take it away from me is going to have to climb over a pile of my bones to do it," and then watching him walk off the studio floor minutes later as the play ended, tears flowing down his cheeks, trying to work his way out of a role which he had really lived as he played it.

Somehow this still remains one of the most moving experiences of my life.

Twelve Angry Men

SEPTEMBER 20, 1954

PRODUCER	Felix Jackson
DIRECTOR	Franklin Schaffner
SET DESIGNER	Willard Levitas
ASSISTANT TO PRODUCER	William M. Altman
STORY EDITOR	Florence Britton
ASSOCIATE DIRECTOR	Joseph Dackow
PROGRAM ASSISTANT	Bette Stein

CAST

FOREMAN	JUROR No. 8
Norman Feld	Robert Cummings
JUROR No. 2	JUROR No. 9
John Beal	Joseph Sweeney
JUROR No. 3	JUROR No. 10
Franchot Tone	Edward Arnold
JUROR No. 4	JUROR No. 11
Walter Abel	George Voskovec
JUROR No. 5	JUROR No. 12
Lee Phillips	Will West
JUROR No. 6	JUDGE
Bart Burns	Joseph Foley
JUROR No. 7	GUARD
Paul Hartman	Vincent Gardenia

DESCRIPTIONS OF JURORS

FOREMAN: A small, petty man who is impressed with the authority he has and handles himself quite formally. Not overly bright, but dogged.

JUROR NO. 2: A meek, hesitant man who finds it difficult to maintain any opinions of his own. Easily swayed and usually adopts the opinion of the last person to whom he has spoken.

JUROR NO. 3: A very strong, very forceful, extremely opinionated man within whom can be detected a streak of sadism. A humorless man who is intolerant of opinions other than his own and accustomed to forcing his wishes and views upon others.

JUROR NO. 4: Seems to be a man of wealth and position. A practiced speaker who presents himself well at all times. Seems to feel a little bit above the rest of the jurors. His only concern is with the facts in this case, and he is appalled at the behavior of the others.

JUROR NO. 5: A naive, very frightened young man who takes his obligations in this case very seriously, but who finds it difficult to speak up when his elders have the floor.

JUROR NO. 6: An honest but dull-witted man who comes upon his decisions slowly and carefully. A man who finds it difficult to create positive opinions, but who must listen to and digest and accept those opinions offered by others which appeal to him most.

JUROR NO. 7: A loud, flashy, gladhanded salesman type who has more important things to do than to sit on a jury. He is quick to show temper, quick to form opinions on things about which he knows nothing. Is a bully and, of course, a coward.

JUROR NO. 8: A quiet, thoughtful, gentle man. A man who sees all sides of every question and constantly seeks the truth. A man of strength tempered with compassion. Above all, a man who wants justice to be done and will fight to see that it is.

JUROR NO. 9: A mild, gentle old man, long since defeated by life and now merely waiting to die. A man who recognizes himself for what he is and mourns the days when it would have been possible to be courageous without shielding himself behind his many years.

JUROR NO. 10: An angry, bitter man. A man who antagonizes almost at sight. A bigot who places no values on any human life save his own. A man who has been nowhere and is going nowhere and knows it deep within him.

JUROR NO. 11: A refugee from Europe who has come to this country in 1941. A man who speaks with an accent and who is ashamed, humble, almost subservient to the people around him, but who will honestly seek justice because he has suffered through so much injustice.

JUROR NO. 12: A slick, bright advertising man who thinks of human beings in terms of percentages, graphs and polls and has no real understanding of people. A superficial snob, but trying to be a good fellow.

—— **ACT I** —————————————————

Fade in on a jury box. Twelve men are seated in it, listening intently to the voice of the judge as he charges them. We do not see the judge. He speaks in slow, measured tones and his voice is grave. The camera drifts over the faces of the jurymen as the judge speaks and we see that most of their heads are turned to camera's left. No. 7 looks down at his hands. No. 3 looks off in another direction, the direction in which the defendant would be sitting. No. 10 keeps moving his head back and forth nervously. The judge drones on.

JUDGE: Murder in the first degree—premeditated homicide— is the most serious charge tried in our criminal courts. You've heard a long and complex case, gentlemen, and it is now your duty to sit down to try and separate the facts from the fancy. One man is dead. The life of another is at stake. If there is a reasonable doubt in your minds as to the guilt of the accused . . . then you must declare him not guilty. If, however, there is no reasonable doubt, then he must be found guilty. Whichever way you decide, the verdict must be unanimous. I urge you to deliberate honestly and thoughtfully. You are faced with a grave responsibility. Thank you, gentlemen.

There is a long pause.

CLERK (Droning): The jury will retire.

And now, slowly, almost hesitantly, the members of the jury begin to rise. Awkwardly, they file out of the jury box and off camera to the left. Camera holds on jury box, then fades out.

Fade in on a large, bare, unpleasant-looking room. This is the jury room in the county criminal court of a large Eastern city. It is about 4:00 P.M. The room is furnished with a long conference table and a dozen chairs. The walls are bare, drab and badly in need of a fresh coat of paint. Along one wall is a row of windows which look out on the skyline of the city's financial district. High on another wall is an electric clock. A washroom opens off the jury room. In one corner of the room is a water fountain. On the table are pads, pencils, ashtrays. One of the windows is open. Papers blow across the table and onto the floor as the door opens. Lettered on the outside of the door are the words "Jury Room." A uniformed guard holds the door open. Slowly, almost self-consciously, the twelve jurors file in. The guard counts them as they enter the door, his lips moving, but no sound coming forth. Four or five of the jurors light cigarettes as they enter the room. Juror No. 5 lights his pipe, which he smokes constantly throughout the play. Jurors No. 2 and 12 go to the water fountain. No. 9 goes into the washroom, the door of which is lettered "Men." Several of the jurors take seats at the table. Others stand awkwardly around the room. Several look out the windows. These are men who are ill at ease, who do not really know each other to talk to and who wish they were anywhere but here. No. 7, standing at window, takes out a pack of gum, takes a piece and offers it around. There are no takers. He mops his brow.

NO. 7 (To No. 6): Y'know something? It's hot. (No. 6 nods) You'd think they'd at least air-condition the place. I almost dropped dead in court.

No. 7 opens the window a bit wider. The guard looks

*them over and checks his count. Then, satisfied, he
makes ready to leave.*

GUARD: Okay, gentlemen. Everybody's here. If there's anything you want, I'm right outside. Just knock.

*He exits, closing the door. Silently they all look at the
door. We hear the lock clicking.*

NO. 5: I never knew they locked the door.

NO. 10 (*Blowing nose*): Sure, they lock the door. What did
you think?

NO. 5: I don't know. It just never occurred to me.

*Some of the jurors are taking off their jackets. Others
are sitting down at the table. They still are reluctant to
talk to each other. Foreman is at head of table, tearing
slips of paper for ballots. Now we get a close shot of
No. 8. He looks out the window. We hear No. 3 talking to No. 2.*

NO. 3: Six days. They should have finished it in two. Talk, talk,
talk. Did you ever hear so much talk about nothing?

NO. 2 (*Nervously laughing*): Well . . . I guess . . . they're
entitled.

NO. 3: Everybody gets a fair trial. (*He shakes his head.*) That's
the system. Well, I suppose you can't say anything against
it.

*No. 2 looks at him nervously, nods and goes over to
water cooler. Cut to shot of No. 8 staring out window.
Cut to table. No. 7 stands at the table, putting out a
cigarette.*

NO. 7 (*To No. 10*): How did you like that business about the
knife? Did you ever hear a phonier story?

NO. 10 (*Wisely*): Well, look, you've gotta expect that. You
know what you're dealing with.

NO. 7: Yeah, I suppose. What's the matter, you got a cold?

NO. 10 (*Blowing*): A lulu. These hot-weather colds can kill
you.

No. 7 nods sympathetically.

FOREMAN (*Briskly*): All right, gentlemen. Let's take seats.

NO. 7: Right. This better be fast. I've got tickets to *The Seven Year Itch* tonight. I must be the only guy in the whole world who hasn't seen it yet. (*He laughs and sits down*) Okay, your honor, start the show.

> *They all begin to sit down. The foreman is seated at the head of the table. No. 8 continues to look out the window.*

FOREMAN (*To No. 8*): How about sitting down? (*No. 8 doesn't hear him*) The gentleman at the window.

> *No. 8 turns, startled.*

FOREMAN: How about sitting down?

NO. 8: Oh. I'm sorry.

> *He heads for a seat.*

NO. 10 (*To No. 6*): It's tough to figure, isn't it? A kid kills his father. Bing! Just like that. Well, it's the element. They let the kids run wild. Maybe it serves 'em right.

FOREMAN: Is everybody here?

NO. 12: The old man's inside.

> *The foreman turns to the washroom just as the door opens. No. 9 comes out, embarrassed.*

FOREMAN: We'd like to get started.

NO. 9: Forgive me, gentlemen. I didn't mean to keep you waiting.

FOREMAN: It's all right. Find a seat.

> *No. 9 heads for a seat and sits down. They look at the foreman expectantly.*

FOREMAN: All right. Now, you gentlemen can handle this any way you want to. I mean, I'm not going to make any rules. If we want to discuss it first and then vote, that's one way. Or we can vote right now to see how we stand.

NO. 7: Let's vote now. Who knows, maybe we can all go home.

NO. 10: Yeah. Let's see who's where.

NO. 3: Right. Let's vote now.

FOREMAN: Anybody doesn't want to vote? (*He looks around the table. There is no answer*) Okay, all those voting guilty raise your hands.

> *Seven or eight hands go up immediately. Several others go up more slowly. Everyone looks around the table. There are two hands not raised, No. 9's and No. 8's. No. 9's hand goes up slowly now as the foreman counts.*

FOREMAN: . . . Nine . . . ten . . . eleven . . . That's eleven for guilty. Okay. Not guilty? (*No. 8's hand is raised*) One. Right. Okay. Eleven to one, guilty. Now we know where we are.

NO. 3: Somebody's in left field. (*To No. 8*) You think he's not guilty?

NO. 8 (*Quietly*): I don't know.

NO. 3: I never saw a guiltier man in my life. You sat right in court and heard the same thing I did. The man's a dangerous killer. You could see it.

NO. 8: He's nineteen years old.

NO. 3: That's old enough. He knifed his own father. Four inches into the chest. An innocent little nineteen-year-old kid. They proved it a dozen different ways. Do you want me to list them?

NO. 8: No.

NO. 10 (*To No. 8*): Well, do you believe his story?

NO. 8: I don't know whether I believe it or not. Maybe I don't.

NO. 7: So what'd you vote not guilty for?

NO. 8: There were eleven votes for guilty. It's not so easy for me to raise my hand and send a boy off to die without talking about it first.

NO. 7: Who says it's easy for me?

NO. 8: No one.

NO. 7: What, just because I voted fast? I think the guy's guilty. You couldn't change my mind if you talked for a hundred years.

NO. 8: I don't want to change your mind. I just want to talk for a while. Look, this boy's been kicked around all his life. You know, living in a slum, his mother dead since he was nine. That's not a very good head start. He's a tough, angry kid. You know why slum kids get that way? Because we knock 'em on the head once a day, every day. I think maybe we owe him a few words. That's all.

> *He looks around the table. Some of them look back coldly. Some cannot look at him. Only No. 9 nods slowly. No. 12 doodles steadily. No. 4 begins to comb his hair.*

NO. 10: I don't mind telling you this, mister. We don't owe him a thing. He got a fair trial, didn't he? You know what that trial cost? He's lucky he got it. Look, we're all grown-ups here. You're not going to tell us that we're supposed to believe him, knowing what he is. I've lived among 'em all my life. You can't believe a word they say. You know that.

NO. 9 (*To No. 10 very slowly*): I don't know that. What a terrible thing for a man to believe! Since when is dishonesty a group characteristic? You have no monopoly on the truth——

NO. 3 (*Interrupting*): All right. It's not Sunday. We don't need a sermon.

NO. 9: What this man says is very dangerous. . . .

> *No. 8 puts his hand on No. 9's arm and stops him. Somehow his touch and his gentle expression calm the old man. He draws a deep breath and relaxes.*

NO. 4: I don't see any need for arguing like this. I think we ought to be able to behave like gentlemen.

NO. 7: Right!

NO. 4: If we're going to discuss this case, let's discuss the facts.

FOREMAN: I think that's a good point. We have a job to do. Let's do it.

NO. 11 (*With accent*): If you gentlemen don't mind, I'm going to close the window. (*He gets up and does so*) (*Apologetically*): It was blowing on my neck.

> No. 10 blows his nose fiercely.

NO. 12: I may have an idea here. I'm just thinking out loud now, but it seems to me that it's up to us to convince this gentleman (*Indicating No. 8*) that we're right and he's wrong. Maybe if we each took a minute or two, you know, if we sort of try it on for size . . .

FOREMAN: That sounds fair enough. Supposing we go once around the table.

NO. 7: Okay, let's start it off.

FOREMAN: Right. (*To No. 2*) I guess you're first.

NO. 2 (*Timidly*): Oh. Well . . . (*Long pause*) I just think he's guilty. I thought it was obvious. I mean nobody proved otherwise.

NO. 8 (*Quietly*): Nobody has to prove otherwise. The burden of proof is on the prosecution. The defendant doesn't have to open his mouth. That's in the Constitution. The Fifth Amendment. You've heard of it.

NO. 2 (*Flustered*): Well, sure, I've heard of it. I know what it is. I . . . what I meant . . . well, anyway, I think he was guilty.

NO. 3: Okay, let's get to the facts. Number one, let's take the old man who lived on the second floor right underneath the room where the murder took place. At ten minutes after twelve on the night of the killing he heard loud noises in the upstairs apartment. He said it sounded like a fight. Then he heard the kid say to his father, "I'm gonna kill you." A second later he heard a body falling, and he ran to the door of his apartment, looked out, and saw the kid running down the stairs and out of the house. Then he called the police. They found the father with a knife in his chest.

FOREMAN: And the coroner fixed the time of death at around midnight.

NO. 3: Right. Now what else do you want?

NO. 4: The boy's entire story is flimsy. He claimed he was at the movies. That's a little ridiculous, isn't it? He couldn't even remember what pictures he saw.

NO. 3: That's right. Did you hear that? (*To No. 4*) You're absolutely right.

NO. 10: Look, what about the woman across the street? If her testimony don't prove it, then nothing does.

NO. 12: That's right. She saw the killing, didn't she?

FOREMAN: Let's go in order.

NO. 10 (*Loud*): Just a minute. Here's a woman who's lying in bed and can't sleep. It's hot, you know. (*He gets up and begins to walk around, blowing his nose and talking*) Anyway, she looks out the window, and right across the street she sees the kid stick the knife into his father. She's known the kid all his life. His window is right opposite hers, across the el tracks, and she swore she saw him do it.

NO. 8: Through the windows of a passing elevated train.

NO. 10: Okay. And they proved in court that you can look through the windows of a passing el train at night and see what's happening on the other side. They proved it.

NO. 8: I'd like to ask you something. How come you believed her? She's one of "them" too, isn't she?

No. 10 walks over to No. 8.

NO. 10: You're a pretty smart fellow, aren't you?

FOREMAN (*Rising*): Now take it easy.

No. 3 gets up and goes to No. 10.

NO. 3: Come on. Sit down. (*He leads No. 10 back to his seat*) What're you letting him get you all upset for? Relax.

No. 10 and No. 3 sit down.

FOREMAN: Let's calm down now. (*To No. 5*) It's your turn.

NO. 5: I'll pass it.

FOREMAN: That's your privilege. (*To No. 6*) How about you?

NO. 6 (*Slowly*): I don't know. I started to be convinced, you know, with the testimony from those people across the hall. Didn't they say something about an argument between the father and the boy around seven o'clock that night? I mean, I can be wrong.

NO. 11: I think it was eight o'clock. Not seven.

NO. 8: That's right. Eight o'clock. They heard the father hit the boy twice and then saw the boy walk angrily out of the house. What does that prove?

NO. 6: Well, it doesn't exactly prove anything. It's just part of the picture. I didn't say it proved anything.

FOREMAN: Anything else?

NO. 6: No.

> No. 6 goes to the water fountain.

FOREMAN (*To No. 7*): All right. How about you?

NO. 7: I don't know, most of it's been said already. We can talk all day about this thing, but I think we're wasting our time. Look at the kid's record. At fifteen he was in reform school. He stole a car. He's been arrested for mugging. He was picked up for knife-fighting. I think they said he stabbed somebody in the arm. This is a very fine boy.

NO. 8: Ever since he was five years old his father beat him up regularly. He used his fists.

NO. 7: So would I! A kid like that.

NO. 3: You're right. It's the kids. The way they are—you know? They don't listen. (*Bitter*) I've got a kid. When he was eight years old he ran away from a fight. I saw him. I was so ashamed, I told him right out, "I'm gonna make a man out of you or I'm gonna bust you up into little pieces trying." When he was fifteen he hit me in the face. He's big, you know. I haven't seen him in three years. Rotten kid! You work your heart out. . . . (*Pause*) All right. Let's get on with it.

Looks away embarrassed.

NO. 4: We're missing the point here. This boy—let's say he's a product of a filthy neighborhood and a broken home. We can't help that. We're not here to go into the reasons why slums are breeding grounds for criminals. They are. I know it. So do you. The children who come out of slum backgrounds are potential menaces to society.

NO. 10: You said it there. I don't want any part of them, believe me.

There is a dead silence for a moment, and then No. 5 speaks haltingly.

NO. 5: I've lived in a slum all my life—

NO. 10: Oh, now wait a second!

NO. 5: I used to play in a back yard that was filled with garbage. Maybe it still smells on me.

FOREMAN: Now let's be reasonable. There's nothing personal—

No. 5 stands up.

NO. 5: There is something personal!

Then he catches himself and, seeing everyone looking at him, sits down, fists clenched.

NO. 3 (*Persuasively*): Come on, now. He didn't mean you, feller. Let's not be so sensitive. . . .

There is a long pause.

NO. 11: I can understand this sensitivity.

FOREMAN: Now let's stop the bickering. We're wasting time. (*To No. 8*) It's your turn.

NO. 8: All right. I had a peculiar feeling about this trial. Somehow I felt that the defense counsel never really conducted a thorough cross-examination. I mean, he was appointed by the court to defend the boy. He hardly seemed interested. Too many questions were left unasked.

NO. 3 (*Annoyed*): What about the ones that were asked? For instance, let's talk about that cute little switch-knife. You know, the one that fine, upright kid admitted buying.

NO. 8: All right. Let's talk about it. Let's get it in here and look at it. I'd like to see it again, Mr. Foreman.

The foreman looks at him questioningly and then gets up and goes to the door. During the following dialogue the foreman knocks, the guard comes in, the foreman whispers to him, the guard nods and leaves, locking the door.

NO. 3: We all know what it looks like. I don't see why we have to look at it again. (*To No. 4*) What do you think?

NO. 4: The gentleman has a right to see exhibits in evidence.

NO. 3 (*Shrugging*): Okay with me.

NO. 4 (*To No. 8*): This knife is a pretty strong piece of evidence, don't you agree?

NO. 8: I do.

NO. 4: The boy admits going out of his house at eight o'clock after being slapped by his father.

NO. 8: Or punched.

NO. 4: Or punched. He went to a neighborhood store and bought a switch-knife. The storekeeper was arrested the following day when he admitted selling it to the boy. It's a very unusual knife. The storekeeper identified it and said it was the only one of its kind he had in stock. Why did the boy get it? (*Sarcastically*) As a present for a friend of his, he says. Am I right so far?

NO. 8: Right.

NO. 3: You bet he's right. (*To all*) Now listen to this man. He knows what he's talking about.

NO. 4: Next, the boy claims that on the way home the knife must have fallen through a hole in his coat pocket, that he never saw it again. Now there's a story, gentlemen. You know what actually happened. The boy took the knife home and a few hours later stabbed his father with it and even remembered to wipe off the fingerprints.

The door opens and the guard walks in with an oddly

> designed knife with a tag on it. No. 4 gets up and takes
> it from him. The guard exits.

NO. 4: Everyone connected with the case identified this knife.
Now are you trying to tell me that someone picked it up
off the street and went up to the boy's house and stabbed
his father with it just to be amusing?

NO. 8: No, I'm saying that it's possible that the boy lost the
knife and that someone else stabbed his father with a similar
knife. It's possible.

> No. 4 flips open the knife and jams it into the table.

NO. 4: Take a look at that knife. It's a very strange knife. I've
never seen one like it before in my life. Neither had the
storekeeper who sold it to him.

> No. 8 reaches casually into his pocket and withdraws
> an object. No one notices this. He stands up quietly.

NO. 4: Aren't you trying to make us accept a pretty incredible
coincidence?

NO. 8: I'm not trying to make anyone accept it. I'm just saying
it's possible.

NO. 3 (Shouting): And I'm saying it's not possible.

> NO. 8 swiftly flicks open the blade of a switch-knife and
> jams it into the table next to the first one. They are
> exactly alike. There are several gasps and everyone stares
> at the knife. There is a long silence.

NO. 3 (Slowly amazed): What are you trying to do?

NO. 10 (Loud): Yeah, what is this? Who do you think you
are?

NO. 5: Look at it! It's the same knife!

FOREMAN: Quiet! Let's be quiet.

> They quiet down.

NO. 4: Where did you get it?

NO. 8: I got it last night in a little junk shop around the corner
from the boy's house. It cost two dollars.

NO. 3: Now listen to me! You pulled a real smart trick here, but you proved absolutely zero. Maybe there are ten knives like that, so what?

NO. 8: Maybe there are.

NO. 3: The boy lied and you know it.

NO. 8: He may have lied. (*To No. 10*) Do you think he lied?

NO. 10 (*Violently*): Now that's a stupid question. Sure he lied!

NO. 8 (*To No. 4*): Do you?

NO. 4: You don't have to ask me that. You know my answer. He lied.

NO. 8 (*To No. 5*): Do you think he lied?

> *No. 5 can't answer immediately. He looks around nervously.*

NO. 5: I . . . I don't know.

NO. 7: Now wait a second. What are you, the guy's lawyer? Listen, there are still eleven of us who think he's guilty. You're alone. What do you think you're gonna accomplish? If you want to be stubborn and hang this jury, he'll be tried again and found guilty, sure as he's born.

NO. 8: You're probably right.

NO. 7: So what are you gonna do about it? We can be here all night.

NO. 9: It's only one night. A man may die.

> *No. 7 glares at No. 9 for a long while, but has no answer. No. 8 looks closely at No. 9 and we can begin to sense a rapport between them. There is a long silence. Then suddenly everyone begins to talk at once.*

NO. 3: Well, whose fault is that?

NO. 6: Do you think maybe if we went over it again? What I mean is . . .

NO. 10: Did anyone force him to kill his father? (*To No. 3*) How do you like him? Like someone forced him!

NO. 11: Perhaps this is not the point.

NO. 5: No one forced anyone. But listen . . .

NO. 12: Look, gentlemen, we can spitball all night here.

NO. 2: Well, I was going to say—

NO. 7: Just a minute. Some of us've got better things to do than sit around a jury room.

NO. 4: I can't understand a word in here. Why do we all have to talk at once?

FOREMAN: He's right. I think we ought to get on with it.

> *No. 8 has been listening to this exchange closely.*

NO. 3 (To No. 8): Well, what do you say? You're the one holding up the show.

NO. 8 (Standing): I've got a proposition to make.

> *We catch a close shot of No. 5 looking steadily at him as he talks. No. 5, seemingly puzzled, listens closely.*

NO. 8: I want to call for a vote. I want you eleven men to vote by secret ballot. I'll abstain. If there are still eleven votes for guilty, I won't stand alone. We'll take in a guilty verdict right now.

NO. 7: Okay. Let's do it.

FOREMAN: That sounds fair. Is everyone agreed?

> *They all nod their heads. No. 8 walks over to the window, looks out for a moment and then faces them.*

FOREMAN: Pass these along.

> *The foreman passes ballot slips to all of them, and now No. 8 watches them tensely as they begin to write. Fade out.*

——— ACT II ———

> *Fade in on same scene, no time lapse. No. 8 stands tensely watching as the jurors write on their ballots. He stays perfectly still as one by one they fold the ballots and pass them along to the foreman. The foreman takes them, riffles through the folded ballots, counts*

eleven *and now begins to open them. He reads each one out loud and lays it aside. They watch him quietly, and all we hear is his voice and the sound of No.* 2 *sucking on a cough drop.*

FOREMAN: Guilty. Guilty. Guilty. Guilty. Guilty. Guilty. Guilty. Guilty. Guilty. (*He pauses at the tenth ballot and then reads it*) Not Guilty. (*No.* 3 *slams down hard on the table. The foreman opens the last ballot*) Guilty.

NO. 10 (*Angry*): How do you like that!

NO. 7: Who was it? I think we have a right to know.

NO. 11: Excuse me. This was a secret ballot. We agreed on this point, no? If the gentleman wants it to remain secret—

NO. 3 (*Standing up angrily*): What do you mean? There are no secrets in here! I know who it was. (*He turns to No.* 5) What's the matter with you? You come in here and you vote guilty and then this slick preacher starts to tear your heart out with stories about a poor little kid who just couldn't help becoming a murderer. So you change your vote. If that isn't the most sickening—

No. 5 *stares at No.* 3, *frightened at this outburst.*

FOREMAN: Now hold it.

NO. 3: Hold it? We're trying to put a guilty man into the chair where he belongs—and all of a sudden we're paying attention to fairy tales.

NO. 5: Now just a minute . . .

NO. 11: Please. I would like to say something here. I have always thought that a man was entitled to have unpopular opinions in this country. This is the reason I came here. I wanted to have the right to disagree. In my own country, I am ashamed to say—

NO. 10: What do we have to listen to now—the whole history of your country?

NO. 7: Yeah, let's stick to the subject. (*To No.* 5) I want to ask you what made you change your vote.

There is a long pause as No. 7 and No. 5 eye each other angrily.

NO. 9 (*Quietly*): There's nothing for him to tell you. He didn't change his vote. I did. (*There is a pause*) Maybe you'd like to know why.

NO. 3: No, we wouldn't like to know why.

FOREMAN: The man wants to talk.

NO. 9: Thank you. (*Pointing at No. 8*) This gentleman chose to stand alone against us. That's his right. It takes a great deal of courage to stand alone even if you believe in something very strongly. He left the verdict up to us. He gambled for support and I gave it to him. I want to hear more. The vote is ten to two.

NO. 10: That's fine. If the speech is over, let's go on.

Foreman gets up, goes to door, knocks, hands guard the tagged switch-knife and sits down again.

NO. 3 (*To No. 5*): Look, buddy, I was a little excited. Well, you know how it is. I . . . I didn't mean to get nasty. Nothing personal.

No. 5 looks at him.

NO. 7 (*To No. 8*): Look, supposing you answer me this. If the kid didn't kill him, who did?

NO. 8: As far as I know, we're supposed to decide whether or not the boy on trial is guilty. We're not concerned with anyone else's motives here.

NO. 9: Guilty beyond a reasonable doubt. This is an important thing to remember.

NO. 3 (*To No. 10*): Everyone's a lawyer. (*To No. 9*) Supposing you explain what your reasonable doubts are.

NO. 9: This is not easy. So far, it's only a feeling I have. A feeling. Perhaps you don't understand.

NO. 10: A feeling! What are we gonna do, spend the night talking about your feelings? What about the facts?

NO. 3: You said a mouthful. (*To No. 9*) Look, the old man

heard the kid yell, "I'm gonna kill you." A second later he heard the father's body falling, and he saw the boy running out of the house fifteen seconds after that.

NO. 12: That's right. And let's not forget the woman across the street. She looked into the open window and saw the boy stab his father. She saw it. Now if that's not enough for you . . .

NO. 8: It's not enough for me.

NO. 7: How do you like him? It's like talking into a dead phone.

NO. 4: The woman saw the killing through the windows of a moving elevated train. The train had five cars, and she saw it through the windows of the last two. She remembers the most insignificant details.

> *Cut to close shot of No. 12 who doodles a picture of an el train on a scrap of paper.*

NO. 3: Well, what have you got to say about that?

NO. 8: I don't know. It doesn't sound right to me.

NO. 3: Well, supposing you think about it. (*To No. 12*) Lend me your pencil.

> *No. 12 gives it to him. He draws a tic-tac-toe square on the same sheet of paper on which No. 12 has drawn the train. He fills in an X, hands the pencil to No. 12.*

NO. 3: Your turn. We might as well pass the time.

> *No. 12 takes the pencil. No. 8 stands up and snatches the paper away. No. 3 leaps up.*

NO. 3: Wait a minute!

NO. 8 (*Hard*): This isn't a game.

NO. 3 (*Angry*): Who do you think you are?

NO. 7 (*Rising*): All right, let's take it easy.

NO. 3: I've got a good mind to walk around this table and belt him one!

FOREMAN: Now, please. I don't want any fights in here.

NO. 3: Did ya see him? The nerve! The absolute nerve!

NO. 10: All right. Forget it. It don't mean anything.

NO. 6: How about sitting down.

NO. 3: This isn't a game. Who does he think he is?

He lets them sit him down. No. 8 remains standing, holding the scrap of paper. He looks at it closely now and seems to be suddenly interested in it. Then he throws it back toward No. 3. It lands in center of table. No. 3 is angered again at this, but No. 4 puts his hand on his arm. No. 8 speaks now and his voice is more intense.

NO. 8 (To No. 4): Take a look at that sketch. How long does it take an elevated train going at top speed to pass a given point?

NO. 4: What has that got to do with anything?

NO. 8: How long? Guess.

NO. 4: I wouldn't have the slightest idea.

NO. 8 (To No. 5): What do you think?

NO. 5: About ten or twelve seconds, maybe.

NO. 8: I'd say that was a fair guess. Anyone else?

NO. 11: I would think about ten seconds, perhaps.

NO. 2: About ten seconds.

NO. 4: All right. Say ten seconds. What are you getting at?

NO. 8: This. An el train passes a given point in ten seconds. That given point is the window of the room in which the killing took place. You can almost reach out of the window of that room and touch the el. Right? (*Several of them nod*) All right. Now let me ask you this. Did anyone here ever live right next to the el tracks? I have. When your window is open and the train goes by, the noise is almost unbearable. You can't hear yourself think.

NO. 10: Okay. You can't hear yourself think. Will you get to the point?

NO. 8: The old man heard the boy say, "I'm going to kill you," and one second later he heard a body fall. One second. That's the testimony, right?

NO. 2: Right.

NO. 8: The woman across the street looked through the windows of the last two cars of the el and saw the body fall. Right? The *last two* cars.

NO. 10: What are you giving us here?

NO. 8: An el takes ten seconds to pass a given point or two seconds per car. That el had been going by the old man's window for at least six seconds, and maybe more, *before the body fell*, according to the woman. The old man would have had to hear the boy say, "I'm going to kill you," while the front of the el was roaring past his nose. It's not possible that he could have heard it.

NO. 3: What d'ya mean! Sure he could have heard it.

NO. 8: Could he?

NO. 3: He said the boy yelled it out. That's enough for me.

NO. 9: I don't think he could have heard it.

NO. 2: Maybe he didn't hear it. I mean with the el noise . . .

NO. 3: What are you people talking about? Are you calling the old man a liar?

NO. 5: Well, it stands to reason.

NO. 3: You're crazy. Why would he lie? What's he got to gain?

NO. 9: Attention, maybe.

NO. 3: You keep coming up with these bright sayings. Why don't you send one in to a newspaper? They pay two dollars.

No. 8 looks hard at No. 3 and then turns to No. 9.

NO. 8 (*Softly*): Why might the old man have lied? You have a right to be heard.

NO. 9: It's just that I looked at him for a very long time. The seam of his jacket was split under the arm. Did you notice that? He was a very old man with a torn jacket, and he carried two canes. I think I know him better than anyone here. This is a quiet, frightened, insignificant man who has been nothing all his life, who has never had recognition— his name in the newspapers. Nobody knows him after seventy-five years. That's a very sad thing. A man like this needs to be recognized. To be questioned, and listened to and quoted just once. This is very important.

NO. 12: And you're trying to tell us he lied about a thing like this just so that he could be important?

NO. 9: No. He wouldn't really lie. But perhaps he'd make himself believe that he heard those words and recognized the boy's face.

NO. 3 (Loud): Well, that's the most fantastic story I've ever heard. How can you make up a thing like that? What do you know about it?

NO. 9 (Low): I speak from experience.

There is a long pause. Then the foreman clears his throat.

FOREMAN (*To No. 8*): All right. Is there anything else?

No. 8 is looking at No. 9. No. 2 offers the foreman a box of cough drops. The foreman pushes it away.

NO. 2 (Hesitantly): Anybody . . . want a cough . . . drop?

FOREMAN (Sharply): Come on. Let's get on with it.

NO. 8: I'll take one. (*No. 2 almost gratefully slides him one along the table*) Thanks.

No. 2 nods and No. 8 puts the cough drop into his mouth.

NO. 8: Now. There's something else I'd like to point out here. I think we proved that the old man couldn't have heard the boy say, "I'm going to kill you," but supposing he really did hear it? This phrase: how many times has each of you used it? Probably hundreds. "If you do that once more, Junior, I'm going to murder you." "Come on, Rocky, kill him!" We say it every day. This doesn't mean that we're going to kill someone.

NO. 3: Wait a minute. The phrase was "I'm going to kill you," and the kid screamed it out at the top of his lungs. Don't try and tell me he didn't mean it. Anybody says a thing like that the way he said it—they mean it.

NO. 10: And how they mean it!

NO. 8: Well, let me ask you this. Do you really think the boy would shout out a thing like that so the whole neighborhood would hear it? I don't think so. He's much too bright for that.

NO. 10 (*Exploding*): Bright! He's a common, ignorant slob. He don't even speak good English!

NO. 11 (*Slowly*): He *doesn't* even speak good English.

> *No. 10 stares angrily at No. 11, and there is silence for a moment. Then No. 5 looks around the table nervously.*

NO. 5: I'd like to change my vote to not guilty.

> *No. 3 gets up and walks to the window, furious, but trying to control himself.*

FOREMAN: Are you sure?

NO. 5: Yes. I'm sure.

FOREMAN: The vote is nine to three in favor of guilty.

NO. 7: Well, if that isn't the end. (*To No. 5*) What are you basing it on? Stories this guy (*Indicating No. 8*) made up! He oughta write for *Amazing Detective Monthly.* He'd make a fortune. Listen, the kid had a lawyer, didn't he? Why didn't his lawyer bring up all these points?

NO. 5: Lawyers can't think of everything.

NO. 7: Oh, brother! (*To No. 8*) You sit in here and pull stories out of thin air. Now we're supposed to believe that the old man didn't get up out of bed, run to the door and see the kid beat it downstairs fifteen seconds after the killing. He's only saying he did to be important.

NO. 5: Did the old man say he *ran* to the door?

NO. 7: Ran. Walked. What's the difference? He got there.

NO. 5: I don't remember what he said. But I don't see how he could run.

NO. 4: He said he *went* from his bedroom to the front door. That's enough, isn't it?

NO. 8: Where was his bedroom again?

NO. 10: Down the hall somewhere. I thought you remembered everything. Don't you remember that?

NO. 8: No. Mr. Foreman, I'd like to take a look at the diagram of the apartment.

NO. 7: Why don't we have them run the trial over just so you can get everything straight?

NO. 8: Mr. Foreman . . .

FOREMAN (*Rising*): I heard you.

> The foreman gets up, goes to door during following dialogue. He knocks on door, guard opens it, he whispers to guard, guard nods and closes door.

NO. 3: (*To No. 8*): All right. What's this for? How come you're the only one in the room who wants to see exhibits all the time.

NO. 5: I want to see this one, too.

NO. 3: And I want to stop wasting time.

NO. 4: If we're going to start wading through all that nonsense about where the body was found . . .

NO. 8: We're not. We're going to find out how a man who's had two strokes in the past three years, and who walks with a pair of canes, could get to his front door in fifteen seconds.

NO. 3: He said twenty seconds.

NO. 2: He said fifteen.

NO. 3: How does he know how long fifteen seconds is? You can't judge that kind of a thing.

NO. 9: He said fifteen. He was very positive about it.

NO. 3 (*Angry*): He's an old man. You saw him. Half the time he was confused. How could he be positive about . . . anything?

No. 3 *looks around sheepishly, unable to cover up his blunder. The door opens and the guard walks in, carrying a large pen-and-ink diagram of the apartment. It is a railroad flat. A bedroom faces the el tracks. Behind it is a series of rooms off a long hall. In the front bedroom is a diagram of the spot where the body was found. At the back of the apartment we see the entrance into the apartment hall from the building hall. We see a flight of stairs in the building hall. The diagram is clearly labeled and included in the information on it are the dimensions of the various rooms. The guard gives the diagram to the foreman.*

GUARD: This what you wanted?

FOREMAN: That's right. Thank you.

The guard nods and exits. No. 8 goes to foreman and reaches for it.

NO. 8: May I?

The foreman nods. No. 8 takes the diagram and sets it up on a chair so that all can see it. No. 8 looks it over. Several of the jurors get up to see it better. No. 3, No. 10 and No. 7, however, barely bother to look at it.

NO. 7 (*To No. 10*): Do me a favor. Wake me up when this is over.

NO. 8 (*Ignoring him*): All right. This is the apartment in which the killing took place. The old man's apartment is directly beneath it and exactly the same. (*Pointing*) Here are the el tracks. The bedroom. Another bedroom. Living room. Bathroom. Kitchen. And this is the hall. Here's the front door to the apartment. And here are the steps. (*Pointing to front bedroom and then front door*) Now, the old man was in bed in this room. He says he got up, went out into the hall, down the hall to the front door, opened it and looked out just in time to see the boy racing down the stairs. Am I right?

NO. 3: That's the story.

NO. 8: Fifteen seconds after he heard the body fall.

NO. 11: Correct.

NO. 8: His bed was at the window. It's (*Looking closer*) twelve feet from his bed to the bedroom door. The length of the hall is forty-three feet, six inches. He had to get up out of bed, get his canes, walk twelve feet, open the bedroom door, walk forty-three feet and open the front door— all in fifteen seconds. Do you think this possible?

NO. 10: You know it's possible.

NO. 11: He can only walk very slowly. They had to help him into the witness chair.

NO. 3: You make it sound like a long walk. It's not.

>   *No. 8 gets up, goes to the end of the room and takes two chairs. He puts them together to indicate a bed.*

NO. 9: For an old man who uses canes, it's a long walk.

NO. 3 (*To No. 8*): What are you doing?

NO. 8: I want to try this thing. Let's see how long it took him. I'm going to pace off twelve feet—the length of the bedroom.

>   *He begins to do so.*

NO. 3: You're crazy. You can't recreate a thing like that.

NO. 11: Perhaps if we could see it . . . this is an important point.

NO. 3 (*Mad*): It's a ridiculous waste of time.

NO. 6: Let him do it.

NO. 8: Hand me a chair. (*Someone pushes a chair to him*) All right. This is the bedroom door. Now how far would you say it is from here to the door of this room?

NO. 6: I'd say it was twenty feet.

NO. 2: Just about.

NO. 8: Twenty feet is close enough. All right, from here to the door and back is about forty feet. It's shorter than the length of the hall, wouldn't you say that?

NO. 9: A few feet, maybe.

NO. 10: Look, this is absolutely insane. What makes you think you can—

NO. 8: Do you mind if I try it? According to you, it'll only take fifteen seconds. We can spare that. (*He walks over to the two chairs now and lies down on them*) Who's got a watch with a second hand?

NO. 2: I have.

NO. 8: When you want me to start, stamp your foot. That'll be the body falling. Time me from there. (*He lies down on the chairs*) Let's say he keeps his canes right at his bedside. Right?

NO. 2: Right!

NO. 8: Okay. I'm ready.

> *They all watch carefully. No. 2 stares at his watch, waiting for the second hand to reach 60. Then, as it does, he stamps his foot loudly. No. 8 begins to get up. Slowly he swings his legs over the edges of the chairs, reaches for imaginary canes and struggles to his feet. No. 2 stares at the watch. No. 8 walks as a crippled old man would walk, toward the chair which is serving as the bedroom door. He gets to it and pretends to open it.*

NO. 10 (*Shouting*): Speed it up. He walked twice as fast as that.

> *No. 8, not having stopped for this outburst, begins to walk the simulated forty-foot hallway.*

NO. 11: This is, I think, even more quickly than the old man walked in the courtroom.

NO. 8: If you think I should go faster, I will.

> *He speeds up his pace slightly. He reaches the door and turns now, heading back, hobbling as an old man would hobble, bent over his imaginary canes. They watch him tensely. He hobbles back to the chair, which also serves*

> as the front door. *He stops there and pretends to un-lock the door. Then he pretends to push it open.*

NO. 8 (*Loud*): Stop.

NO. 2: Right.

NO. 8: What's the time?

NO. 2: Fifteen . . . twenty . . . thirty . . . thirty-one seconds exactly.

NO. 11: Thirty-one seconds.

> *Some of the jurors ad-lib their surprise to each other.*

NO. 8: It's my guess that the old man was trying to get to the door, heard someone racing down the stairs and assumed that it was the boy.

NO. 6: I think that's possible.

NO. 3 (*Infuriated*): Assumed? Now, listen to me, you people. I've seen all kinds of dishonesty in my day . . . but this little display takes the cake. (*To No. 4*) Tell him, will you?

> *No. 4 sits silently. No. 3 looks at him and then he strides over to No. 8.*

NO. 3: You come in here with your heart bleeding all over the floor about slum kids and injustice and you make up these wild stories, and you've got some softhearted old ladies listening to you. Well I'm not. I'm getting real sick of it. (*To all*) What's the matter with you people? This kid is guilty! He's got to burn! We're letting him slip through our fingers here.

NO. 8 (*Calmly*): Our fingers. Are you his executioner?

NO. 3 (*Raging*): I'm one of 'em.

NO. 8: Perhaps you'd like to pull the switch.

NO. 3 (*Shouting*): For this kid? You bet I'd like to pull the switch!

NO. 8: I'm sorry for you.

NO. 3 (*Shouting*): Don't start with me.

NO. 8: What it must feel like to want to pull the switch!

NO. 3: Shut up!

NO. 8: You're a sadist.

NO. 3 (*Louder*): Shut up!

NO. 8 (*Strong*): You want to see this boy die because you personally want it—not because of the facts.

NO. 3 (*Shouting*): Shut up!

> He lunges at No. 8, but is caught by two of the jurors and held. He struggles as No. 8 watches calmly.

NO. 3 (*Screaming*): Let me go! I'll kill him. I'll kill him!

NO. 8 (*Softly*): You don't really mean you'll kill me, do you?

> No. 3 stops struggling now and stares at No. 8. All the jurors watch in silence as we fade out.

―――― **ACT III** ――――――――――――――――――――   *Le*

> Fade in on same scene. No time lapse. No. 3 glares angrily at No. 8. He is still held by two jurors. After a long pause, he shakes himself loose and turns away. He walks to the windows. The other jurors stand around the room now, shocked by this display of anger. There is silence. Then the door opens and the guard enters. He looks around the room.

GUARD: Is there anything wrong, gentlemen? I heard some noise.

FOREMAN: No. There's nothing wrong. (*He points to the large diagram of the apartment*) You can take that back. We're finished with it.

> The guard nods and takes the diagram. He looks curiously at some of the jurors and exits. The jurors still are silent. Some of them slowly begin to sit down. No. 3 still stands at the window. He turns around now. The jurors look at him.

NO. 3 (*Loud*): Well, what are you looking at?

> They turn away. He goes back to his seat now. Silently

the rest of the jurors take their seats. No. 12 begins to doodle. No. 10 blows his nose, but no one speaks. Then, finally—

NO. 4: I don't see why we have to behave like children here.

NO. 11: Nor do I. We have a responsibility. This is a remarkable thing about democracy. That we are . . . what is the word? . . . Ah, notified! That we are notified by mail to come down to this place and decide on the guilt or innocence of a man we have not known before. We have nothing to gain or lose by our verdict. This is one of the reasons why we are strong. We should not make it a personal thing.

There is a long, awkward pause.

NO. 12: Well—we're still nowhere. Who's got an idea?

NO. 6: I think maybe we should try another vote. Mr. Foreman?

FOREMAN: It's all right with me. Anybody doesn't want to vote?

He looks around the table.

NO. 7: All right, let's do it.

NO. 3: I want an open ballot. Let's call out our votes. I want to know who stands where.

FOREMAN: That sounds fair. Anyone object? (*No one does*) All right. I'll call off your jury numbers.

He takes a pencil and paper and makes marks now in one of two columns after each vote.

FOREMAN: I vote guilty. No. 2?

NO. 2: Not guilty.

FOREMAN: No. 3?

NO. 3: Guilty.

FOREMAN: No. 4?

NO. 4: Guilty.

FOREMAN: No. 5?

NO. 5: Not guilty.

FOREMAN: No. 6?

NO. 6: Not guilty.

FOREMAN: No. 7?

NO. 7: Guilty.

FOREMAN: No. 8?

NO. 8: Not guilty.

FOREMAN: No. 9?

NO. 9: Not guilty.

FOREMAN: No. 10?

NO. 10: Guilty.

FOREMAN: No. 11?

NO. 11: Not guilty.

FOREMAN: No. 12?

NO. 12: Guilty.

NO. 4: Six to six.

NO. 10 (*Mad*): I'll tell you something. The crime is being committed right in this room.

FOREMAN: The vote is six to six.

NO. 3: I'm ready to walk into court right now and declare a hung jury. There's no point in this going on any more.

NO. 7: I go for that, too. Let's take it in to the judge and let the kid take his chances with twelve other guys.

NO. 5 (*To No. 7*): You mean you still don't think there's room for reasonable doubt?

NO. 7: No, I don't.

NO. 11: I beg your pardon. Maybe you don't understand the term "reasonable doubt."

NO. 7 (*Angry*): What do you mean I don't understand it? Who do you think you are to talk to me like that? (*To all*) How do you like this guy? He comes over here running for his life, and before he can even take a big breath he's telling us how to run the show. The arrogance of him!

NO. 5 (*To No. 7*): Wait a second. Nobody around here's asking where you came from.

NO. 7: I was born right here.

NO. 5: Or where your father came from. . . . (*He looks at No. 7, who doesn't answer but looks away*) Maybe it wouldn't hurt us to take a few tips from people who come running here! Maybe they learned something we don't know. We're not so perfect!

NO. 11: Please—I am used to this. It's all right. Thank you.

NO. 5: It's not all right!

NO. 7: Okay, okay, I apologize. Is that what you want?

NO. 5: That's what I want.

FOREMAN: All right. Let's stop the arguing. Who's got something constructive to say?

NO. 2 (*Hesitantly*): Well, something's been bothering me a little . . . this whole business about the stab wound and how it was made, the downward angle of it, you know?

NO. 3: Don't tell me we're gonna start that. They went over it and over it in court.

NO. 2: I know they did—but I don't go along with it. The boy is five feet eight inches tall. His father was six two. That's a difference of six inches. It's a very awkward thing to stab *down* into the chest of someone who's half a foot taller than you are.

> *No. 3 jumps up, holding the knife.*

NO. 3: Look, you're not going to be satisfied till you see it again. I'm going to give you a demonstration. Somebody get up.

> *He looks around the table. No. 8 stands up and walks toward him. No. 3 closes the knife and puts it in his pocket. They stand face to face and look at each other for a moment.*

NO. 3: Okay. (*To No. 2*) Now watch this. I don't want to have to do it again. (*He crouches down now until he is quite a bit shorter than No. 8*) Is that six inches?

NO. 12: That's more than six inches.

NO. 3: Okay, let it be more.

He reaches into his pocket and takes out the knife. He flicks it open, changes its position in his hand and holds the knife aloft, ready to stab. He and No. 8 look steadily into each other's eyes. Then he stabs downward, hard.

NO. 2 (*Shouting*): Look out!

He stops short just as the blade reaches No. 8's chest. No. 3 laughs.

NO. 6: That's not funny.

NO. 5: What's the matter with you?

NO. 3: Now just calm down. Nobody's hurt, are they?

NO. 8 (*Low*): No. Nobody's hurt.

NO. 3: All right. There's your angle. Take a look at it. Down and in. That's how I'd stab a taller man in the chest, and that's how it was done. Take a look at it and tell me I'm wrong.

No. 2 doesn't answer. No 3 looks at him for a moment, then jams the knife into the table and sits down. They all look at the knife.

NO. 6: Down and in. I guess there's no argument.

No. 8 picks the knife out of the table and closes it. He flicks it open and, changing its position in his hand, stabs downward with it.

NO. 8 (*To No. 6*): Did you ever stab a man?

NO. 6: Of course not.

NO. 8 (*To No. 3*): Did you?

NO. 3: All right, let's not be silly.

NO. 8: Did you?

NO. 3 (*Loud*): No, I didn't!

NO. 8: Where do you get all your information about how it's done?

NO. 3: What do you mean? It's just common sense.

NO. 8: Have you ever seen a man stabbed?

NO. 3 (*Pauses and looks around the room nervously*): No.

NO. 8: All right. I want to ask you something. The boy was an experienced knife fighter. He was even sent to reform school for knifing someone, isn't that so?

NO. 12: That's right.

NO. 8: Look at this. (*No. 8 closes the knife, flicks it open and changes the position of the knife so that he can stab overhanded*) Doesn't it seem like an awkward way to handle a knife?

NO. 3: What are you asking me for?

> *No. 8 closes the blade and flicks it open, holds it ready to slash underhanded.*

NO. 5: Wait a minute! What's the matter with me? Give me that.

> *He reaches out for the knife.*

NO. 8: Have you ever seen a knife fight?

NO. 5: Yes, I have.

NO. 8: In the movies?

NO. 5: In my back yard. On my stoop. In the vacant lot across the street. Too many of them. Switch-knives came with the neighborhood where I lived. Funny I didn't think of it before. I guess you try to forget those things. (*Flicking the knife open*) Anyone who's ever used a switch-knife would never have stabbed downward. You don't handle a switch-knife that way. You use it underhanded.

NO. 8: Then he couldn't have made the kind of wound which killed his father.

NO. 5: No. He couldn't have. Not if he'd ever had any experience with switch-knives.

NO. 3: I don't believe it.

NO. 10: Neither do I. You're giving us a lot of mumbo jumbo.

NO. 8 (*To No. 12*): What do you think?

NO. 12 (*Hesitantly*): Well . . . I don't know.

NO. 8 (*To No. 7*): What about you?

NO. 7: Listen, I'll tell you something. I'm a little sick of this whole thing already. We're getting nowhere fast. Let's break it up and go home. I'm changing my vote to not guilty.

NO. 3: You're what?

NO. 7: You heard me. I've had enough.

NO. 3: What do you mean, you've had enough? That's no answer.

NO. 11 (*Angry*): I think perhaps you're right. This is not an answer. (*To No. 7*) What kind of a man are you? You have sat here and voted guilty with everyone else because there are some theater tickets burning a hole in your pocket. Now you have changed your vote for the same reason. I do not think you have the right to play like this with a man's life. This is an ugly and terrible thing to do.

NO. 7: Now wait a minute . . . you can't talk like that to me.

NO. 11 (*Strong*): I can talk like that to you! If you want to vote not guilty, then do it because you are convinced the man is not guilty. If you believe he is guilty, then vote that way. Or don't you have the . . . the . . . guts—the guts to do what you think is right?

NO. 7: Now listen . . .

NO. 11: Is it guilty or not guilty?

NO. 7 (*Hesitantly*): I told you. Not . . . guilty.

NO. 11 (*Hard*): Why?

NO. 7: I don't have to—

NO. 11: You have to! Say it! Why?

They stare at each other for a long while.

NO. 7 (*Low*): I . . . don't think . . . he's guilty.

NO. 8 (*Fast*): I want another vote.

FOREMAN: Okay, there's another vote called for. I guess the quickest way is a show of hands. Anybody object? (*No one does*) All right. All those voting not guilty, raise your hands.

Numbers 2, 5, 6, 7, 8, 9 and 11 raise their hands imme-

diately. *Then, slowly, No. 12 raises his hand. The foreman looks around the table carefully and then he too
raises his hand. He looks around the table, counting
silently.*

FOREMAN: Nine. (*The hands go down*) All those voting
guilty.

Numbers 3, 4 and 10 raise their hands.

FOREMAN: Three. (*They lower their hands*) The vote is nine
to three in favor of acquittal.

NO. 10: I don't understand you people. How can you believe
this kid is innocent? Look, you know how those people lie.
I don't have to tell you. They don't know what the truth
is. And lemme tell you, they—(*No. 5 gets up from table,
turns his back to it and goes to window*)—don't need any
real big reason to kill someone either. You know, they get
drunk, and bang, someone's lying in the gutter. Nobody's
blaming them. That's how they are. You know what I
mean? Violent!

*No. 9 gets up and does the same. He is followed by
No. 11.*

NO. 10: Human life don't mean as much to them as it does
to us. Hey, where are you going? Look, these people are
drinking and fighting all the time, and if somebody gets
killed, so somebody gets killed. They don't care. Oh, sure,
there are some good things about them, too. Look, I'm the
first to say that.

*No. 8 gets up, and then No. 2 and No. 6 follow him
to the window.*

NO. 10: I've known a few who were pretty decent, but that's
the exception. Most of them, it's like they have no feelings.
They can do anything. What's going on here?

*The foreman gets up and goes to the windows, fol-
lowed by No. 7 and No. 12.*

NO. 10: I'm speaking my piece, and you—Listen to me! They're

no good. There's not a one of 'em who's any good. We better watch out. Take it from me. This kid on trial . . .

*No. 3 sits at table toying with the knife and No. 4 gets
up and starts for the window. All have their backs to
No. 10.*

NO. 10: Well, don't you know about them? Listen to me!
What are you doing? I'm trying to tell you something. . . .

*No. 4 stands over him as he trails off. There is a dead
silence. Then No. 4 speaks softly.*

NO. 4: I've had enough. If you open your mouth again, I'm
going to split your skull.

*No. 4 stands there and looks at him. No one moves or
speaks. No. 10 looks at him, then looks down at the
table.*

NO. 10 (*Softly*): I'm only trying to tell you . . .

There is a long pause as No. 4 stares down at No. 10.

NO. 4 (*To all*): All right. Sit down everybody.

*They all move back to their seats. When they are all
seated, No. 4 then sits down.*

NO. 4 (*Quietly*): I still believe the boy is guilty of murder.
I'll tell you why. To me, the most damning evidence was
given by the woman across the street who claimed she actually saw the murder committed.

NO. 3: That's right. As far as I'm concerned, that's the most
important testimony.

NO. 8: All right. Let's go over her testimony. What exactly
did she say?

NO. 4: I believe I can recount it accurately. She said that she
went to bed at about eleven o'clock that night. Her bed
was next to the open window, and she could look out of
the window while lying down and see directly into the window across the street. She tossed and turned for over an
hour, unable to fall asleep. Finally she turned toward the
window at about twelve-ten and, as she looked out, she

saw the boy stab his father. As far as I can see, this is un-shakable testimony.

NO. 3: That's what I mean. That's the whole case.

No. 4 takes off his eyeglasses and begins to polish them, as they all sit silently watching him.

NO. 4 (*To the jury*): Frankly, I don't see how you can vote for acquittal. (*To No. 12*) What do you think about it?

NO. 12: Well . . . maybe . . . there's so much evidence to sift.

NO. 3: What do you mean, maybe? He's absolutely right. You can throw out all the other evidence.

NO. 4: That was my feeling.

No. 2, polishing his glasses, squints at clock, can't see it. No. 6 watches him closely.

NO. 2: What time is it?

NO. 11: Ten minutes of six.

NO. 2: It's late. You don't suppose they'd let us go home and finish it in the morning. I've got a kid with mumps.

NO. 5: Not a chance.

NO. 6 (*To No. 2*): Pardon me. Can't you see the clock with-out your glasses?

NO. 2: Not clearly. Why?

NO. 6: Oh, I don't know. Look, this may be a dumb thought, but what do you do when you wake up at night and want to know what time it is?

NO. 2: What do you mean? I put on my glasses and look at the clock.

NO. 6: You don't wear them to bed.

NO. 2: Of course not. No one wears eyeglasses to bed.

NO. 12: What's all this for?

NO. 6: Well, I was thinking. You know the woman who testi-fied that she saw the killing wears glasses.

NO. 3: So does my grandmother. So what?

NO. 8: Your grandmother isn't a murder witness.

NO. 6: Look, stop me if I'm wrong. This woman wouldn't wear her eyeglasses to bed, would she?

FOREMAN: Wait a minute! Did she wear glasses at all? I don't remember.

NO. 11 (*Excited*): Of course she did! The woman wore bifocals. I remember this very clearly. They looked quite strong.

NO. 9: That's right. Bifocals. She never took them off.

NO. 4: She did wear glasses. Funny. I never thought of it.

NO. 8: Listen, she wasn't wearing them in bed. That's for sure. She testified that in the midst of her tossing and turning she rolled over and looked casually out the window. The murder was taking place as she looked out, and the lights went out a split second later. She couldn't have had time to put on her glasses. Now maybe she honestly thought she saw the boy kill his father. I say that she saw only a blur.

NO. 3: How do you know what she saw? Maybe she's far-sighted.

He looks around. No one answers.

NO. 3 (*Loud*): How does he know all these things?
There is silence.

NO. 8: Does anyone think there still is not a reasonable doubt?
He looks around the room, then squarely at No. 10. No. 10 looks down and shakes his head no.

NO. 3 (*Loud*): I think he's guilty!

NO. 8 (*Calmly*): Does anyone else?

NO. 4 (*Quietly*): No. I'm convinced.

NO. 8 (*To No. 3*): You're alone.

NO. 3: I don't care whether I'm alone or not! I have a right.

NO. 8: You have a right.

There is a pause. They all look at No. 3.

NO. 3: Well, I told you I think the kid's guilty. What else do you want?

NO. 8: Your arguments.

They all look at No. 3.

NO. 3: I gave you my arguments.

NO. 8: We're not convinced. We're waiting to hear them again. We have time.

No. 3 runs to No. 4 and grabs his arm.

NO. 3 (Pleading): Listen. What's the matter with you? You're the guy. You made all the arguments. You can't turn now. A guilty man's gonna be walking the streets. A murderer. He's got to die! Stay with me.

NO. 4: I'm sorry. There's a reasonable doubt in my mind.

NO. 8: We're waiting.

No. 3 turns violently on him.

NO. 3 (Shouting): Well, you're not going to intimidate me! (*They all look at No. 3*) I'm entitled to my opinion! (*No one answers him*) It's gonna be a hung jury! That's it!

NO. 8: There's nothing we can do about that, except hope that some night, maybe in a few months, you'll get some sleep.

NO. 5: You're all alone.

NO. 9: It takes a great deal of courage to stand alone.

No. 3 looks around at all of them for a long time. They sit silently, waiting for him to speak, and all of them despise him for his stubbornness. Then, suddenly, his face contorts as if he is about to cry, and he slams his fist down on the table.

NO. 3 (Thundering): All right!

No. 3 turns his back on them. There is silence for a moment and then the foreman goes to the door and knocks on it. It opens. The guard looks in and sees them all standing. The guard holds the door for them as they begin slowly to file out. No. 8 waits at the door as the others file past him. Finally he and No. 3 are the only ones left. No. 3 turns around and sees that they are alone. Slowly he moves toward the door. Then he

stops at the table. He pulls the switch-knife out of the table and walks over to No. 8 with it. He holds it in the approved knife-fighter fashion and looks long and hard at No. 8, pointing the knife at his belly. No. 8 stares back. Then No. 3 turns the knife around. No. 8 takes it by the handle. No. 3 exits. No. 8 closes the knife, puts it away and, taking a last look around the room, exits, closing the door. The camera moves in close on the littered table in the empty room, and we clearly see a slip of crumpled paper on which are scribbled the words "Not guilty."
Fade out.

AUTHOR'S COMMENTARY ON

Twelve Angry Men

Of all the plays in this volume, Twelve Angry Men is certainly the most difficult to read. In reading plays, most of which generally are devoid of any descriptive matter whatsoever (outside of brief outlines of the sets), the first task a reader has is that of separating the characters from each other. In most cases, after several pages have been read, the names of the characters in the play have been memorized by the reader, mental images of these characters have been formed, and it is a relatively simple thing to distinguish between the characters and to know, almost automatically, who is speaking each line. In reading Twelve Angry Men, however, I realize that it is almost impossible to form immediate and distinct pictures of each of the twelve men, designated as they are only by number. This play was constructed to fall into shape upon being seen, and since I felt that a dozen names would be quite meaningless to a viewing audience (members of a jury rarely address each other by name), I omitted the sometimes annoying chore of selecting names for my characters. It is for this reason that thumbnail descriptions of characteristics which pertain to the action in this play have been included for purposes of reference.

Twelve Angry Men is the only play I've written which has any relation at all to actual personal experience. A month or so before I began the play I sat on the jury of a manslaughter case in New York's General Sessions Court. This was my first experience on a jury, and it left quite an impression on me. The receipt of my jury notice activated many grumblings and mutterings, most of which began with lines like "My God, eight million people in New York and they have to call me!"

All the prospective jurors I met in the waiting room the first day I appeared had the same grim, horribly persecuted attitude. But, strangely, the moment I walked into the courtroom to be empaneled and found myself facing a strange man whose fate was suddenly more or less in my hands, my entire attitude changed. I was hugely impressed with the almost frightening stillness of the courtroom, the impassive, masklike face of the judge, the brisk, purposeful scurrying of the various officials in the room, and the absolute finality of the decision I and my fellow jurors would have to make at the end of the trial. I doubt whether I have ever been so impressed in my life with a role I had to play, and I suddenly became so earnest that, in thinking about it later, I probably was unbearable to the eleven other jurors.

It occurred to me during the trial that no one anywhere ever knows what goes on inside a jury room but the jurors, and I thought then that a play taking place entirely within a jury room might be an exciting and possibly moving experience for an audience.

Actually, the outline of Twelve Angry Men, which I began shortly after the trial ended, took longer to write than the script itself. The movements in the play were so intricate that I wanted to have them down on paper to the last detail before I began the construction of the dialogue. I worked on the idea and outline for a week and was stunned by the time I was finished to discover that the outline was twenty-seven typewritten pages long. The average outline is perhaps five pages long, and many are as short as one or two pages. This detailed setting down of the moves of the play paid off, however. The script was written in five days and could have been done in four had I not written it approximately fifteen pages too long.

In writing Twelve Angry Men I attempted to blend four elements which I had seen at work in the jury room during my jury service. These elements are: a) the evidence as remembered and interpreted by each individual juror (the disparities here were incredible); b) the relationship of juror to juror in a life-and-death situation; c) the emotional pattern of each individual juror; and d) physical problems such as the weather, the time, the uncomfortable room, etc. All of these elements are of vital importance in any jury room, and all of them presented excellent dramatic possibilities.

Before I began to plot the play, I felt that the basic problem was going to consist of a constant search for drama and movement in order to prevent a normally static situation from becoming too static. Actually, as it turned out, the writing of Twelve Angry Men became a struggle to cram all of the detail, action and character I had devised into the less than fifty minutes of air time available.

Before the play went into rehearsal I had to cut large chunks of dialogue, and, since I was dealing with quite an involved plot, all the cuts were made on passages that had been written to give some depth to the characters. This left the bare frame of the plot and the skeletons of the people. To this day I have not been able to decide whether the cuts made Twelve Angry Men more effective or not. The men of the play were easily recognizable as types, but I believe that whatever dimension they had as real people was achieved as much by the excellence of the performance as it was by the personal insights revealed in dialogue. What Twelve Angry Men has to say about democracy, justice, social responsibilities and the pressure of the times upon the people who live them has some importance, I believe, and perhaps helps to overshadow the meager development of some of the characters.

As a motion picture, soon to be released, I think that Twelve Angry Men has grown in stature. It is nearly twice as long as the television play, and much of the extra time has been spent in exploring the characters and their motivations for behaving as they do toward the defendant and each other.

The time limitations of television tend to restrict the complete development of a play so that it is necessary to show only brief fragments of people if the plot is fairly involved, or the barest sketch of a plot if the characters are to be fully developed. The only way out of this stifling trap is longer, more expensive shows, of which I, for one, am heartily in favor.

The production problems of Twelve Angry Men were, for what seemed like a reasonably simple show, incredibly involved. The set, to be realistic, had to be small and cramped. This, of course, inhibited the movement of cameras and presented director Frank Schaffner with an endless traffic jam which would have had Robert Moses spinning like a ball-bearing top. Somehow, however, Mr. Schaffner managed to capture the speaker of each line on camera at precisely the right moment and composed starkly realistic, tension-filled pictures of the reactions to these lines. This was perhaps the best-directed show I've ever seen on television and Mr. Schaffner won a mantelpieceful of awards for it, including the Christopher Award, the Sylvania Award and the Academy of Television Arts and Sciences Emmy Award.

Twelve Angry Men, incidentally, was the first of my shows to be seen by my two youngsters—Jonathan, then five and a half, and Richard, three. (Since then, two more small twin boys have joined our family!) I hadn't intended to have them see it at all, but one Sunday afternoon they discovered that I had made arrangements to run off a kinescope of the show for some people who had missed it and they begged to be allowed to see it. Never one to resist the accomplished wheedling of small, determined boys, I agreed, provided that they swore up and down to sit like lumps and not utter a sound. They said they would and they kept their word. From time to time I looked at them, two little figures squatting on hassocks, wide-eyed, unmoving, terribly impressed with the entire situation, and I felt, I must admit, a tinge of pride that they were obviously so fascinated with something I had created. At the end of the show, after much small talk, I went over to the hassock where Jonathan still sat, silent and obviously impressed. With what must have been some smugness I asked, "Well, how'd you like it, Jon?"

He looked at me gravely. Then he whispered, "Boy, were they angry!"

He has never mentioned it again, and if he thinks I'm going to ask him . . .

An Almanac of Liberty

(*Suggested by the book* An Almanac of Liberty *by William O. Douglas, published by Doubleday & Company, Inc.*)

——— NOVEMBER 8, 1954 ———

PRODUCER	Felix Jackson
DIRECTOR	Paul Nickell
SET DESIGNER	Kim Swados
STORY EDITOR	Florence Britton
ASSOCIATE PRODUCER	William Markham Altman
ASSOCIATE DIRECTOR	Paul Stanley
PROGRAM ASSISTANT	Joan Pilkington

CAST

HARMON JONES
Archie Smith
HANK LE SEUER
Karl Lukas
MAC HUNT
Jock MacGregor
GEORGE WILKINSON
Lawrence Fletcher
JOHN CARTER
Sandy Kenyon
MR. NEARY
P. J. Kelly
WOMAN ON PHONE
Mary Lou Taylor
MRS. CHURCH
Ethel Everett
MICHAEL LESTER
Bruce Marshall
SUSIE LESTER
Ginger MacManus
HORACE SWEETSER
Brandon Peters

MATTY WILKINSON
Dorothy Patten
SYBIL HUNT
Clarice Blackburn
TED FRANKLIN
Fred Herrick
BILLY SWEETSER
Gene Sultan
DOCTOR SLATTERY
James Winslow
MR. NATHAN
Eli Mintz
MRS. NATHAN
Frieda Altman
BEN PHILLIPS
Lee Richardson
MR. FALION
Martin Rudy
OPERATOR (VOICE)
Allyn Rice
NARRATOR
Charles Collingwood

OTTILIE SWEETSER
Florence Sundstrom

ACT I

Fade in on a street corner. All we see is a stretch of pavement, a lamppost, a small piece of store front. It is morning. We are tight on a group of struggling men. Among the group we see Harmon Jones, Hank Le Seuer, Mac Hunt, George Wilkinson and three or four extras. They are all attacking one man. We do not see him. Silently, ferociously, they beat at him with their fists. Their faces are enraged, yet several of them are grinning. We hear no sound save the sound of fists meeting flesh and the grunting of the men. The man they are beating goes down and they stand over him for a moment. He lies motionless on the pavement. Now, silently, they begin to drift away and finally we see only John Carter, battered, beaten, bloody, lying on the sidewalk. He gets to his hands and knees, looks up, and suddenly we see a flash bulb go off. He blinks groggily and stays there on his hands and knees, unable to get up. Fade out.

Fade in on the narrator.

NARRATOR: Good evening. What you have just seen is the opening few seconds of the "Studio One" presentation, An Almanac of Liberty. For just a moment or two, I'd like to tell you something of the background of this play. An Almanac of Liberty is the title of a remarkable book written by Supreme Court Justice William O. Douglas, and published this week. It is a book about the countless episodes, the gradual accretion of precedents, the slow growth of habits and attitudes which have made us free men. It was written by one of the truly great men of our time. It would be as impossible to dramatize this book as it would be to dramatize the Constitution of the United States. But Reginald Rose has distilled from An Almanac of Liberty the moving spirit of freedom in which it was written, and shaped this spirit alone into an original teleplay for "Studio One." It is the spirit of the prayer for liberty by Rabindranath Tagore which closes Mr. Justice Douglas' book.

"Where the mind is without fear and the head is held high;
Where knowledge is free;
Where the world has not been broken up into fragments by narrow domestic walls;

Where words come out from the depth of truth.

Where tireless striving stretches its arms towards perfection;

Where the clear stream of reason has not lost its way into the
dreary desert sand of dead habit;

Where the mind is led forward by Thee into ever-widening
thought and action—

Into that Heaven of freedom, my Father, let my country
awake."

*Dissolve to the interior of the Ridgeville Town Hall.
We see a large, dark, musty room which might once
have been a town-meeting hall many years ago. This
room has rarely been used in recent years, since there is
a brand-new community center in Ridgeville where all
the local raffles, bingo games and dances take place.
The old town hall still functions as headquarters for
civic officials, etc., and is equipped with offices, conference rooms, etc., but this room, with its rows of old-
fashioned wooden benches, its antique lectern, its faded
American flag is now merely a dust collector and a burden to the ancient janitor, Mr. Neary, whom we see
shuffling silently through the room, carrying a thermos
bottle and a feather duster. Mr. Neary's bones ache.
Walking is an effort to him, but somehow, as he makes
his way to the lectern, we see that he goes with the
room. They are both anachronisms, past their prime,
ready to be torn down, and there are merely faint echoes
for both of them of the days when they had their youth
and their own special glories. Mr. Neary raises one of
the torn window shades, spraying dust about the sill,
and the sunlight streams into the darkness. Now he
goes to the lectern and he puts his thermos bottle on
it. He looks up at the ancient clock above the lectern.
He checks his pocket watch. Then he begins to move*

slowly among the benches, flicking softly at them with
the feather duster.

The phone rings. Mr. Neary goes to it and picks it up.
The clock behind him reads exactly 10:23.

MR. NEARY: Hello?

WOMAN (Exasperated): Now let me tell you something, Mr.
whatever-your-name-is. This had just better be the right
extension. They've been switching me all over this building,
but all over it. I mean, how difficult can it be to find out
where to get a dog license? Hello?

MR. NEARY (Puzzled): Hello?

WOMAN: His name is Sweetie, S–w–e–e–t–i–e, and he's a
Pomeranian, and I don't know why I need a license for him
at all. I mean, you can hardly see him.

MR. NEARY: The license bureau is extension twenty-one.

WOMAN (Angry): Oh, for Heaven's sakes!

She hangs up. Mr. Neary shakes his head and hangs up.
He looks at the clock. It is 10:24. Quietly now, as if by
a signal, he closes his thermos. He takes the duster,
walks to the rows of benches and sits down, facing the
lectern, and waits as if expecting someone to speak.
The door opens now and a man enters briskly. The
man is Harmon Jones and he is a soda jerk. He is dressed
in whites.

HARMON: Hiya, Mr. Neary. How's it going?

Mr. Neary doesn't answer him. Harmon sits down as
the door opens and three people enter. They are: a
very old woman, Mrs. Church, and a boy and a girl,
Michael and Susie Lester, each about ten years old.
The girl races past the boy and bumps him into Mrs.
Church, who tut-tuts indignantly.

MIKE (To Susie): Ah, cut it out, Susie! (To Mrs. Church)
I'm sorry, Mrs. Church. She shoved me. (She glares at him)
Well, I couldn't help it. (Calling to Susie) Hey, wait up!

Susie has scooted to a seat. Mike runs after her and sits next to her. They look back at Mrs. Church and giggle.

SUSIE: Shhh.

They stop, face front and sit quietly, waiting. Mrs. Church walks slowly down the aisle as the door opens again. The president of the city council enters. His name is Horace Sweetser. He is fiftyish and a politician of the old school. He is accompanied by his wife, Ottilie, an overdressed woman in her late forties. He is followed by several extras in working clothes, a bus driver, a telephone linesman and several housewives. One of them, Matty Wilkinson, about forty years old, stops next to Horace Sweetser. Ottilie goes down aisle and sits down. During Matty's and Horace's lines, people continue to enter and ad-lib greetings to each other. Once they sit down, however, they become silent and unmoving. They sit stiffly, facing the lectern. Camera must catch this change in mood several times.

MATTY (*Cute*): Well, if it isn't the illustrious president of our city council! (*Grinning*) Hi, Horace.

HORACE (*Beaming*): Well, Matty, my love! (*Looking around*) Where's George?

MATTY: He'll probably come straight over from the store. (*She looks around*) Looks like there'll be a crowd. Even Mrs. Church is here. What time is it?

Horace looks at the clock.

HORACE: Ten twenty-four on the nose.

MATTY (*Casually*): Why do we have to come here, Horace?

HORACE: Excuse me. Ottilie's saving me a seat.

He moves off down the aisle. Matty follows. Four or five others enter, including Hank Le Seuer, a husky young laborer; Mac and Sybil Hunt, a wealthy, middle-aged farm couple; and Ted Franklin, a local policeman of about forty. Billy Sweetser, age seventeen, enters. He is followed by Dr. Slattery, who is in his late thirties, and Mr. Nathan, a mild, perpetually frightened little man of about fifty-five. Mr. Nathan is a tailor. Mrs. Nathan catches up to Mr. Nathan.

MR. NATHAN: Oh, Dr. Slattery. How are you?

DR. SLATTERY (*Smiling*): Tired. How are you, Mr. Nathan?

MR. NATHAN (*Nodding*): Thanks, fine.

Dr. Slattery walks down the aisle with Mr. Falion. They ad-lib greetings.

MRS. NATHAN: Phil, will you look at me. I forgot to take off my apron! (*He smiles as she takes it off*) How come they made it for ten twenty-four? Such a silly time. I mean why not ten-thirty?

He shrugs and they walk down the aisle. George Wilkinson, a prosperous middle-aged man, enters behind Ben Phillips, a youngish, studious-looking man. Ben is the editor of the Ridgeville Echo. Mr. Wilkinson owns the only department store in town. Mr. Wilkinson catches up to Ben.

MR. WILKINSON (*Smiling*): Whatever this is, I don't know why they have to pull it on a Saturday morning. Busiest time of the week at the store. How are you, Ben?

BEN: I'm okay, thanks, Mr. Wilkinson.

Coming in now we see John Carter, the man who was beaten up in the first scene. His face is battered, but it bears an expression of reverent calm. He walks toward Ben and Mr. Wilkinson.

BEN: Say, how'd you like your ad in the paper today?

MR. WILKINSON: It looked okay. I didn't think much of your editorial, though.

John Carter walks between them.

JOHN: Pardon me, please.

They stand aside and look strangely at him as he walks between them. He searches for a seat, finds one in the center of the room and sits down. The people around him look at him curiously for a moment.

MR. WILKINSON (Low): The nerve of him! Did you see him, Ben?

But Ben is gone, walking quietly down the aisle. The door is closed now and the room is absolutely still. Mr. Wilkinson looks around uncertainly and then begins to walk down the aisle, looking for Matty, his wife. He spots Matty and moves into the row in which she sits. He stands over her and bends down to kiss her on the cheek.

MR. WILKINSON: Hello, dear. Sorry I'm late.

She looks up at him and nods silently. Then suddenly he is seized with a thought. Everyone is sitting so silently. He bends down to her and whispers.

MR. WILKINSON: Listen, this isn't a funeral or something, is it? (She pulls at his arm) Well, what the heck is going on? (She motions him to sit down) (Exasperated) Well, okay. I'll sit.

He sits down, and then he becomes silent too. Now the entire room is still and everyone sits, staring at the lectern and waiting. There is no sound and no movement for a long while. Then finally a few heads begin to turn curiously and it begins to be obvious that no one quite knows what to expect. A few more heads begin to turn and, very slowly, a vague restlessness begins to fill the room and here and there, where there has been no movement, we begin to see people turning to each other and whispering a few words softly. Little by little this grows into a steady buzzing, and curiosity begins to get the better of the strange, silent mood which has been so mysteriously created. The buzzing grows louder and people begin to crane their necks and look around the room, but no one seems to be able to *stand up and ask a question, and no one can answer the whispered words of his neighbor with anything more than a shrug. Finally Mr. Wilkinson turns to Matty and speaks so that just those immediately around him can hear.*

MR. WILKINSON: What's supposed to happen?

MATTY: I don't know.

MR. WILKINSON: Look, you're the one who told me to be here at ten twenty-four.

MATTY: I am not. I never told you any such thing.

MR. WILKINSON: You mentioned it to me right after breakfast.

MATTY: You left the house before I woke up.

MR. WILKINSON: Did I?

HARMON: All right. Let's get the show on the road!

He begins to applaud rhythmically.

MR. WILKINSON (*To Matty*): Well, who told you to be here?

MATTY: I'm trying to remember.

Cut to Dr. Slattery, who sits next to Mr. Falion, the school principal.

DR. SLATTERY: What's it all about, Walt? Something with the school?

MR. FALION: Not that I know of. It's probably something Horace Sweetser arranged.

HARMON: Who knows what's going on around here?

MAC HUNT: Well, somebody oughta know. I've got better things to do this morning than sit and gab.

MR. WILKINSON: All right. Let's find out who's in charge. That's number one. (*To Mr. Sweetser*) Horace, what's supposed to be happening here?

HORACE: You've got me, George.

MR. WILKINSON: Well, somebody must have called this meeting for a specific reason. Who was the first one here?

HARMON: I was.

MR. WILKINSON: Who told you to be here?

HARMON: I think it was Mrs. Church.

MRS. CHURCH (*Standing shakily*): It was not. You can't go accusing me of anything of the kind. I never mentioned it to a soul. I was lyin' in my bed—

HARMON: I just thought of something. Mr. Neary was here before me. Sittin' right where he is now.

MR. WILKINSON: Well, how about it, Mr. Neary?

HANK LE SEUER: If he was first he must know something.

MRS. CHURCH: Getting me out of a sickbed. I'd sure like to know who started this.

MAC HUNT (*Loud*): Come on, speak up, Mr. Neary!

    Mr. Neary rises slowly.

MR. NEARY (*Falteringly*): I was just in here to dust. This place gets very dusty. Then, all of a sudden, instead of dusting I sat down, and he walked in here. (*Pointing at Harmon*) That's all I know. I just sat down. I'm supposed to be dusting.

MAC HUNT (*To Sybil*): What do you suppose it is?

SYBIL HUNT: Now how do I know? Maybe it's just a coincidence.

OTTILIE: Well, now, look, we couldn't have all just walked in here by ourselves. Everybody knew what time to be here. I mean somebody must've started it. It stands to reason that—

HORACE: Ottilie!

    He silences her with an exasperated look. She sits down.

HORACE (*To Ben*): Now, what about you, Ben? You run the paper here. You're supposed to know everything that's going on around town. What about this thing?

    As Ben speaks John Carter looks quietly at him. We see John several times during this exchange of questions, and each time he looks directly at the speaker as if hoping the speaker will say something which hasn't yet been said.

BEN: You've got me, Mr. Sweetser. Maybe there was a town meeting scheduled. No, that's ridiculous. I'd know about it if there were.

MR. WILKINSON: We haven't had a meeting in here in over thirty years.

MR. NATHAN: Maybe it's something with the children . . . a practical joke or something.

HORACE: Well, let's find out. Susie, do you know anything about this?

SUSIE (*Scared*): No, Mr. Sweetser. Mikey told me to be here. Least I think he did.

MIKE: I did not, you big liar. You told me.

SUSIE: Don't you call me a liar, Mikey Lester, or I'll smack you one.

MIKE (*Bristling up*): You and what army?

HORACE (*Sharply*): All right, stop it, children. Let's be quiet. Now . . . does anyone here know anything more about this meeting than we've already heard? (*He looks around. No one answers*) Well, do any of you positively remember how you heard about it? No guessing now. Let's get facts. (*No one answers*) Well, now, since no one can enlighten us, I don't see any reason why we have to sit here and squabble over it any longer. Let's just call it a mistake. It's a beautiful day out and I think we've all got other things to do.

MR. WILKINSON: I'm for that.

MATTY (*To Mr. Wilkinson*): It's very strange, George. Why ten twenty-four? How did everyone know?

MR. WILKINSON: Forget it, Matty. It's over. C'mon, let's go.
    He gets up and starts to leave. Some of the others do, too. The group breaks up into little clusters of people moving toward the door and ad-libbing to each other. John Carter stays in his seat, looking directly forward now as the people around him get up. Everyone moves toward the door. We see the sunlight streaming in

through the windows. Now only John Carter is seated and we see him sitting quietly as everyone goes toward the door. Just as George Wilkinson, the first one up the aisle, reaches for the door, we hear:

HORACE (*Loud*): Wait a minute, everyone! (*They all stop and turn to look at him*) As long as we're all here together, friends, I figure this is a good time to remind you about the Patriot's Day Picnic, a week from next Saturday. Now let's everyone get out there a week from Saturday and remind ourselves that we're one hundred per cent good Americans. Let's make it the biggest Patriot's Day ever. Thanks a lot.

There is a scattering of applause and then George Wilkinson opens the door. As he does so we hear the crash of thunder and the rain begins to pour down in torrents. The room darkens perceptibly. George moves back into the room.

MR. WILKINSON: It's pouring. How do you like that? Ten seconds ago the sun was out.

MATTY: Oh, for Heaven's sakes! And I've got on a new dress. I'm not going out in that, George.

BEN (*Grinning*): It can't be raining. My paper says fair.

MR. WILKINSON: Very funny. Look, Matty, I've got to get back to the store. I'll see you later.

HARMON: Holy smokes. Look at it come down.

George Wilkinson steps out of the door for a second. The rain beats on him and then a blinding bolt of lightning flashes.

BEN: Look out!

MATTY: George!

He jumps back inside.

HANK LE SEUER: Hey, that was pretty close.

MR. WILKINSON: And how.

MATTY: Let's wait, George. Please.

She takes his arm and they move away to sit down.

Everyone is crowded about the aisle and the back and the side of the room. Some of them begin moving back to seats and the buzz of ad-lib conversation is quite loud. Then, almost as if at a signal, they all see that in the midst of the empty seats one man sits still as if he has known they would be back. Standing, grouped around the room, they all look at him and the buzzing dies down. They stare for an uncomfortable moment and he quietly sits there.

HANK LE SEUER (Low): What the heck is he doing here anyway?

Then Horace Sweetser clears his throat.

HORACE: Well . . . I suppose we might as well all stay here for a while. It's . . . quite a storm.

He turns and sits down, and many of the others take seats. They are restless now and they talk to each other almost in whispers, some sitting, others standing by the windows. Now we see Ben Phillips standing alone by the window. Slowly he makes his way to the seat next to John Carter and sits down. No one else has sat near Carter. Ben looks at him for a moment.

JOHN (Nodding): Hello.

BEN: How do you feel?

JOHN: Better, thanks.

BEN: That's good. My name is Ben Phillips.

JOHN: John Carter.

BEN: Nice to meet you. I was a little surprised to see you come in here this morning.

JOHN: Why?

BEN: Well . . . these people haven't treated you very well.

John doesn't answer this, but looks steadily at Ben. Ben is a little uncomfortable.

BEN: How long have you been in town?

JOHN: A week.

BEN: What kind of work do you do?

JOHN: Almost anything. I heard there was a housing development going up here. I thought there might be a job.

There is another uncomfortable pause.

BEN: I was the one who ran out and snapped that picture of
you yesterday.

JOHN: I know.

BEN: Why did they do it?

*Ben opens the paper and shows it to John. John looks
at it briefly.*

JOHN: I don't know.

BEN: No idea?

JOHN: None. I wish I did know.

*Ben looks at him for a long time. Then he turns and
stands up.*

BEN (*Calling*): Listen everybody! (*The buzzing dies down and
everyone looks at him*) Being all together like this . . .
This is something that only happens in Ridgeville at Bingo
parties and funerals. (*They laugh appreciatively*) Anyway,
since we're all here, maybe some of you can answer a question for me. A man was beaten up in our town by a mob last
night. He doesn't know why it happened.

HARMON: He knows why.

BEN: He doesn't know why it happened. I saw the tail end of
it. There must have been fifteen or twenty people in on it.
Most of them are right in this room. I'd like to know why
it happened. A mob attacking one man. What was the
reason?

HARMON: He deserved every bit of it and more.

BEN: Why?

HANK LE SEUER: What's the matter, don't you know about
him?

BEN: Know what?

HANK LE SEUER: He's a dangerous guy—right, Mr. Sweetser?

HORACE (*Standing*): I'll buy that. I don't think we need his kind around here.

BEN: What kind is that?

HORACE: Well, if you don't know what I mean, Ben . . .

BEN: I don't. I'd like to know what Ridgeville's coming to— mobbing a stranger just like that.

HORACE: Now, look, Ben, Ridgeville can take care of itself. We've gotten along fine for a lot of years. We're a hundred per cent American here and that's how we're going to stay.

MR. WILKINSON: Right!

HANK LE SEUER: You said it, Mr. Sweetser.

HORACE: So just sit yourself down, Ben, and mind your business. We'll take care of our town.

> *Ben looks around at the hostile crowd and has nothing more to say. Cut fast to Ottilie, who looks at clock.*

OTTILIE: Oh, the clock stopped. What time is it, Horace?

> *Horace looks at his watch.*

HORACE: I've got ten twenty-four. My watch must've stopped, too.

> *He begins to wind it.*

OTTILIE: Ten twenty-four. That's what the clock says. (*Calling*) Who's got the time?

MATTY: I've got twenty-four minutes after ten. That's funny. My watch must've stopped just as I walked in here.

HORACE (*Shaking watch*): This thing won't start.

MR. NATHAN: Neither will mine. It's stopped at ten twenty-four. What is this?

MR. WILKINSON: I can't get mine going either. I've got ten twenty-four on the nose.

HARMON: So have I. That's what time it was when I came in here.

MATTY (*Frightened*): What's happening? George, what is it?

MR. WILKINSON: I don't know. Take it easy. (*Calling*) Who's got the right time? Speak up!

And the room begins to buzz. People turn to each other. Some of them stand up, frightened.

BEN: My watch won't start. It stopped at ten twenty-four.

OTTILIE: Horace! I'm frightened. What's wrong?

HORACE (*Low*): Be quiet! (*Calling*) All right, let's take it easy! Has everyone's watch stopped?

They all nod and more of them get up and start piling toward the aisle. There is a great deal of pushing and a woman screams.

HORACE (*Roaring*): Now stop that! Let's not lose our heads! Calm down! (*They stop momentarily*) All right. I'm going to telephone for the time.

He goes up front to the telephone. Most of them follow him and crowd around him as he picks it up. He dials a number and holds the phone up for all of them to hear. We hear a click.

OTTILIE: I can't hear.

HORACE: Shhh.

OPERATOR: When you hear the tone the time will be . . . ten twenty-four exactly.

We hear the tone, and we fade out on the frightened faces of the crowd.

——— ACT II ———

Fade in on same scene, no time lapse. Everyone is grouped around the phone. Horace slowly hangs it up.

HORACE: Ten twenty-four exactly.

OTTILIE: It can't be!

MATTY (*Frightened*): Listen, I came in here at ten twenty-four. I set my watch with the radio this morning. (*To Mr. Wilkinson*) George! Did you hear me? It's the watch you gave me. I set it with the radio.

MR. WILKINSON: Call again.

MRS. NATHAN (*Softly*): Phil! What is it? The rain. The black-
ness. All morning it's like I'm walking in a dream. You
know what I mean?

MR. NATHAN (*Nodding*): I know.

MR. WILKINSON (*Loud*): Call again!

HORACE: Take it easy, George.

MR. WILKINSON: Give me the phone! You can't just call once!
Give it to me!

> *He rips it from Horace's hands and begins feverishly to
> dial.*

MR. NATHAN: There's no sense in getting overexcited, Mr.
Wilkinson.

> *Mr. Wilkinson stops dialing and looks at him.*

MR. WILKINSON (*Viciously*): Don't you ever tell me what to
do! But I mean ever!

> *Mr. Nathan backs away quickly. Mr. Wilkinson con-
> tinues to dial. Then we hear a click and he holds up
> the phone.*

OPERATOR: When you hear the tone the time will be . . .
ten twenty-four exactly.

> *He lets the phone fall. He grabs Dr. Slattery.*

MR. WILKINSON (*Frightened*): Did you hear it?

DR. SLATTERY: Dial the operator.

MR. WILKINSON: Did you hear it? What kind of craziness is
this?

MATTY: George . . .

DR. SLATTERY: Take it easy, George. That's just a record the
phone company plays. Dial the operator.

MR. WILKINSON: Everything's stopped!

HORACE: Don't be ridiculous.

MR. WILKINSON: No. I'm telling you. Everything's stopped.
I can feel it.

HORACE: Somebody dial the operator.

Dr. Slattery takes the phone and dials once.

MRS. CHURCH: Well, what does she say? I can't hear.

TED FRANKLIN: Be quiet a minute, Mrs. Church.

OPERATOR TWO: Operator.

DR. SLATTERY: Hello, Operator. Would you mind giving me the time? (*He waits. There is a long silence*) Operator. Hello, Operator. Operator!

He jiggles the phone. There is no answer. He looks around at them. Ben Phillips goes forward and takes the phone from his hand. He hangs it up, picks it up again and dials once.

OTTILIE: Hold the phone up.

HORACE: Will you shut up!

OPERATOR TWO: Operator.

BEN: Listen, Operator, something's happened here . . . Hello . . . hello . . . Operator!

He jiggles the phone. There is no answer. He hangs up and turns to face them.

MR. WILKINSON: Y'hear that? It's stopped! I told you. Everything's stopped.

HARMON: I'm getting out of here!

He starts to push wildly through the crowd.

BEN: Cut it out, Harmon! (*He grabs Harmon by the arm and spins him around*) What are you trying to do? We've got kids in here. Now control yourself!

Mrs. Nathan turns to her husband.

MRS. NATHAN: Phil! This is something I don't understand. . . . What did we do? What did we do?

She begins to cry and he puts his arms around her.

MR. NATHAN (*Wonderingly*): I don't know. . . .

MIKEY (*Screeching*): Look at this!

Cut to window. Mikey stares out into the rain.

MIKEY: It's Mr. Busby. He's just standing there like a statue.

There is a rush for the windows. Everyone crowds against them.

MAC HUNT: It's Al Busby, all right.

BILLY SWEETSER: Look at him, half in and half out of the pick-up truck.

HANK LE SEUER: He's not moving!

Horace Sweetser pushes his way through the crowd.

HORACE: Let me in there.

Horace throws open the window. Rain beats in on him.

HORACE (*Shouting*): Al! Al Busby! Listen! Al Busby!

He looks at him for a moment, then closes the window and turns to face them. They stare at him.

HORACE (*Low*): The rain beats into his face, and he doesn't blink. He just stands there, frozen.

There is a long pause. They all stand there, letting it sink in.

MR. WILKINSON (*Quietly*): It's like I said. Everything's stopped. (*Quietly*) Matty, time is standing still. I said it before. Didn't you hear me say it, Matty? . . . Matty? Didn't you hear? . . .

MATTY (*Softly*): I want to go home.

BEN (*Wonderingly*): Time has stopped.

MIKEY: Why?

MR. FALION (*Gently*): Be quiet, Mike.

MIKEY: No. No kidding. Why?

BEN: We don't know.

There is a long pause as they all look at each other silently. Now they walk away from the windows, singly and in groups, together in their fear but separate in the methods they are using to try and adjust to it. Finally they are scattered about the room. Dr. Slattery is near the phone. He picks it up, looks at it, puts it down again. Everyone stands around silently and they look at each other and wonder.

OTTILIE (*Softly*): I wasn't going to come here. I didn't have to. No one answers her. *Finally Hank Le Seuer sits down.*

HANK LE SEUER: Might as well sit down.

Now they all begin to sit down and we cut to Mrs. Nathan as she finds a seat and sits wonderingly in it.

MRS. NATHAN (*Softly*): What are we going to do?

There are no answers. No one knows what to do or say. They look blankly at each other. There is silence for a moment, and then John Carter stands up.

JOHN: I don't think there's anything we can do except talk, maybe. People never seem to get much of a chance to talk to each other any more.

HARMON: Sit down.

JOHN: We're prisoners here. Time has stopped for everyone but us. If we knew why—

HARMON: Look, will you shut your mouth!

JOHN (*To Harmon*): Maybe you can understand a thing like this. Maybe you know what's going to happen to us. If you could explain . . . (*Harmon can't answer this and turns away*) I can't either. I guess none of us can.

We see that Mrs. Church's lips have begun to move silently.

JOHN (*Quietly*): Perhaps I can ask you a question. I don't know any of you here. Why did you want to hurt me? This is a very hard thing for me to understand. (*He looks around the room for a moment. There is no answer. He walks over to Hank Le Seuer*) You hit me in the face. I never saw you before in my life. Why did you do it?

HANK LE SEUER: You know why. The things you said—things no good American ought to say. I ain't ashamed for hitting you. I'd do it again.

JOHN: What things did you hear me say?

HANK LE SEUER: Don't start giving me any of that. Mr. Wilkinson told me plenty. He heard you—

John turns and looks around.

JOHN: Mr. Wilkinson . . .

MR. WILKINSON: What do you want?

JOHN (*Softly*): What was it I said that offended you?

Mr. Wilkinson gets up as John walks over to him.

MR. WILKINSON: You want to know? Everything about you offends me. You're a troublemaker. You talk like a Red! (*To all*) Let me tell you something, folks. This man came busting into Ridgeville from I don't know where and before his shoes stopped flapping his mouth began. He's the man who knows what's wrong with the way we're thinking and behaving here! Listen, I don't like strangers and especially I don't like strangers that criticize and disagree.

JOHN: Is that why I was attacked?

MR. WILKINSON: You bet it is! (*To all*) There's an element moving in here that's no good. They're not satisfied with anything. They've got radical ideas and they infect good innocent people with 'em. We'd better watch our step, that's all I can tell you. (*To John*) Listen, mister, I'm warning you. You've had one lesson already.

Cut to Mr. Nathan as he gets up.

MR. NATHAN (*Meekly*): Excuse me . . .

MR. WILKINSON: Just wait a second. I'm not finished yet.

MR. NATHAN: Maybe you shouldn't finish.

MRS. NATHAN (*Scared*): Phil!

MR. NATHAN: To talk to a man the way you did. Who gave you the right?

MRS. NATHAN: Phil, what's the matter with you? That's Mr. Wilkinson!

MR. NATHAN: Sometimes it doesn't matter who it is.

MR. WILKINSON: See what I mean, folks? Our tailor. See what's happening to our town. We've gotta watch it.

MRS. NATHAN: Phil, I'm begging you. We've got a store here. He comes in, Mr. Wilkinson.

MR. WILKINSON: There's your example. That's the element. Look who he's defending and you know what he is.

MR. NATHAN: What I am. Maybe you've got a definition. I'm a tailor and I'm a man. What else? Tell me, Mr. Wilkinson.

MR. WILKINSON: I'm telling you to shut your mouth.

MRS. NATHAN (*Desperate*): Phil, you've got to be quiet. Look at me. I can't stand it.

MR. NATHAN: There's free speech here. Nobody can stop me from talking. That's a guarantee from way back before Mr. Wilkinson's time.

Mrs. Nathan begins to sob.

MR. NATHAN: Listen, Mr. Wilkinson, let me tell you something. I may not be much, but I got a right to my opinion, thank God, and my opinion is that for talking to this man the way you did someone should kick you ten times around the room. Also this—

MR. WILKINSON: You better listen to me, Nathan . . .

MR. NATHAN: Also this: I don't like anyone to tell me I'm an element. I may press your pants, Mr. Wilkinson, but we're both the same, you and me. We were born the same way and we'll die the same way, and in between we have the right to be respected, me as well as you. (*Indicating John*) Him as well as both of us. And don't you forget it.

Mr. Nathan sits down and there is silence. Mr. Wilkinson is flabbergasted. Mrs. Nathan cries. He puts his arm around her, looks at his trembling fingers and half whispers to himself.

MR. NATHAN: I shouldn't have to tremble.

In the silence now, John Carter gets up and goes to the tailor and puts his hand on the tailor's shoulder.

MR. WILKINSON: Did you hear him? The man is out of his mind!

JOHN (*To Mr. Nathan*): Thank you.

Mr. Nathan can only nod and hold his sobbing wife.

MR. WILKINSON (*Loud*): And look at the other one. He walks right over to his little friend. Listen, did it ever occur to anyone to find out who he is? What his name is? Maybe the police—

MATTY (*Urgently*): George, haven't you said enough?

MR. WILKINSON (*Mad*): I haven't said half enough.

MATTY: You're making a fool of yourself.

MR. WILKINSON: My wife. My lovely wife. Did you hear what the man said to me?

MATTY: I heard. It's still ten twenty-four. When do you think it'll be ten twenty-five? What's going to happen to us? We'll die.

> He looks blankly at her. Then he sits down. John Carter sits next to the tailor.
>
> Cut to Mrs. Church, who has been mumbling to herself for a long while. Suddenly she struggles to her feet and points hysterically at John.

MRS. CHURCH (*Shrilly*): It's him! That man. (*Mr. Falion gets up quickly and goes toward her*) It's him, sure as we're all sittin' here and waitin' to die. He's a peculiar man, do you hear me? A peculiar man. Look into his face. . . .

MR. FALION: Mrs. Church . . . please . . .

MRS. CHURCH: No! No! No! It's his doing. I can feel it. The lightning and the thunder. The midnight when God in Heaven knows it ought to be noon.

> Mr. Neary gets up and goes to Mrs. Church. She speaks and acts hysterically. Mr. Neary pushes Mr. Falion aside.

MRS. CHURCH: I tell you he brought us here, each and every one of us.

MR. NEARY: Mary, behave yourself!

MRS. CHURCH: He snapped his fingers and he rolled his eyes and we trooped in here like a flock of lambs led to the slaughter.

MR. NEARY (*Firm*): Stop it, or I'm gonna have to slap you one!

MRS. CHURCH: The devil sits in this room . . .

MR. NEARY: Mary! You'll be getting yourself a stroke or something. Sit down.

> *He pushes her into a seat and she sobs and rocks. He stands over her, shaken and puzzled.*

MRS. CHURCH (*Softly*): Oh, help us! Help us, dear God, help us!

MR. NEARY (*To himself*): I don't know what's come over this woman. She's most of the time quiet.

HANK LE SEUER (*Loud*): Maybe she's not so wrong. Who is that guy?

HARMON (*Standing up*): That's right. What's his name?

BEN: His name is John Carter. What's on your mind, Harmon?

HARMON: How do we know his name is John Carter?

TED FRANKLIN: He acts strange, like Mrs. Church says.

> *He gets up and Hank Le Seuer follows suit. They stand with Harmon, facing John Carter.*

HANK LE SEUER: I don't like the looks of him. The old woman maybe knows what she's talking about.

MR. NATHAN: What are you saying?

MAC HUNT: He's the only one who sat in his seat when we were all leaving, like he knew we'd never get out.

HARMON: That's right.

BEN: Now wait a minute . . .

> *Hank, Harmon and Ted Franklin move forward, followed by Mac Hunt. Others stand up and begin to adlib comments. The excitement builds.*

TED FRANKLIN: What do you mean, wait a minute? I'll tell you, men. I'm gonna search him and find out who he really is. That name John Carter is a phony if I ever heard one.

> *John Carter stands up calmly and faces them. Ben stands in front of him.*

TED FRANKLIN: Well, what do ya say, Mr. Phillips?

HARMON (Loud): Come on! Let's get him!

> Ted Franklin pushes past Ben and grabs John Carter's arm. John does not resist.

TED FRANKLIN: Come here, you.

> Ben suddenly shouts fiercely.

BEN: Take your hands off him!

> He shoves Ted violently away and now we see that he is suddenly raging mad. They step back, startled, and he stands facing them, ready to fight if need be.

BEN: Now I've seen it working! The idiot mob. You're a disgusting sight.

HARMON: Now listen, Mr. Phillips . . .

BEN: Call me Ben. Maybe you'll understand me better. Look around you, Harmon. Do you see any trees? Brother, this is no jungle. This is your town hall and you're supposed to be a human being in it. What are you afraid of . . . dying? Listen, Harmon, if you die, (*Pointing at John*) he dies too. He's the same as you. And while you're alive you're going to respect his rights. Ever hear that word? Rights! Nobody's going to search this man. He hasn't committed any crime and he's not suspected of any crime, and whatever he has in his pockets and his head is his own. Now sit down, Harmon, and bite your nails and cry if you want to, but don't touch this man. He's afraid too, and so am I.

> Harmon and the others back away and Ben watches them, and there is an angry grumbling from the crowd, directed against Ben.

SYBIL HUNT: But he got us into this thing.

BEN (Raging): Do you accuse him of witchcraft?

> There is silence and then Ben turns away from them. John Carter sits down and, after a moment, we hear the voice of Horace Sweetser.

HORACE: I'll tell you something, Ben Phillips. Maybe you can talk those boys back into their seats, but you're not gonna buffalo me. You've been shooting off your mouth in this town for a long time, and I'm sick of it. (*We hear an answering chorus of grumbling assents from the crowd*) I don't like your point of view, and I never have. Some of the things I read in your newspaper make my blood boil!

MR. WILKINSON: You can say that again!

HORACE: You're standing up there and defending a dangerous man. Well, I say it's just like you to do it. It goes with the rabble-rousing trash you're always printing. You're a radical, Ben Phillips, and you shouldn't be allowed to print some of the stuff you run. Now I'm telling you this. If we ever get out of here, you're not gonna print it. I'll see to it that the good people in this town squelch you proper, Mr. Phillips. (*Billy Sweetser slowly rises, his face white and frightened*) We'll get up a committee and—

BILLY: Listen. I don't think you ought to—

All eyes turn on him and he seems to shrivel.

HORACE: Ought to what?

BILLY: Well, I don't think you're right. What I mean is . . . what's printed in a newspaper . . . is supposed to be—

HORACE (*Interrupting*): Sit back in that seat, mister.

BILLY (*Stiffening*): No!

OTTILIE (*Scared*): Billy, what are you doing?

BILLY: I'm not doing anything. I'm just talking. Maybe I'm mixed up, I don't know, but in school we were taking up the press last week. You know, newspapers and like that, and how it's important that they can print any kind of opinions they want to print. Listen, I only got a C in Civics, but—

HORACE: I'm going to walk over there and smack your behind for you in a minute.

BILLY: Everyone else is talking. Why can't I say something?

BEN: Every man can speak his piece, Billy. Isn't that right, Mr. Sweetser?

Horace glares angrily at Ben, but shuts up.

BILLY: O.K. Y'know wherever they don't allow the news-papers to print the stuff they want to print, well, that country ends up going down the drain. I can prove it to you six different ways. That's why we've got freedom of the press around here, otherwise nobody would know anything 'cept what a few guys want to tell 'em. Listen, I mean if that's just phony stuff from a book, then what am I wast-ing my time studying it for? But if it's real, then maybe we oughta remember it. (*To Horace*) I don't know—you're al-ways talking about freedom and stuff when you have a speech to make. What's the matter, Dad? Don't you believe in what you say?

Horace starts to move toward Billy.

BILLY (*Softly*): Honest. I'm ashamed a little.

Horace stops and Ottilie goes to Billy.

OTTILIE: Billy . . .

She puts her arms around him.

MR. NATHAN: You said something to remember, Billy—some-thing to remember.

Ottilie takes Billy back to where she was sitting.

HORACE: Ottilie . . . (*Ottilie and Billy sit down*) Well, what do you think I believe in? (*They don't look at him*) You think I'm a fake or something? (*Shouting*) Listen to me . . .

But they choose not to listen. He turns away. Hunt gets up and faces Horace.

MAC HUNT: I don't know about you, Sweetser, but if that was any kid of mine, I wouldn't waste my time talking. I'd take a cat-o'-nine-tails to him so fast his head would spin. Speak-ing to his father like that! (*He turns to Mr. Falion*) Is that what you teach him in your school?

SYBIL HUNT (*Hissing*): Mac Hunt, you stay out of this!

MAC HUNT: Be quiet. (*To Mr. Falion*) Well, what about it,

Falion? Is that your idea of what a good education means? Why don't you teach these kids to respect their folks?

MR. FALION (*Rising*): That's something they're supposed to learn at home, Mr. Hunt.

MAC HUNT: Well, that's a smart answer! Listen, Mr. Principal, I've seen these kids of yours around town and I've heard 'em talk. I tell you it's enough to shock a decent citizen sometimes. They're carping and criticizing. They're talking politics, little seventeen-year-old pipsqueaks, and they've got ideas'd make your hair stand on end. Somebody ought to slap 'em down, and while they're doing it they ought to run a thresher through that school of yours.

MR. FALION: Mr. Hunt . . .

MAC HUNT: Don't you interrupt me! Letting kids read stuff like they've got there in these times. Yeah, I've seen some of the books. They oughta be carted out and burned. These kids're being exposed to foreign ideas and nobody tells 'em they're bad ideas. Is that how you teach 'em to be Americans?

MR. FALION: Are you finished?

MAC HUNT: I'm finished. Now let's hear the double-talk.

MR. FALION: No double-talk, Mr. Hunt. Just sympathy. I'm sorry for you and the people like you who speak out in favor of ignorance. I'm sorry for you because you're afraid.

MAC HUNT (*Roaring*): Afraid! I'm not afraid to walk over there and punch your head in for you.

DR. SLATTERY (*Leaping up*): Stop it! You had your say. Now shut up and listen!

Mac Hunt looks at Dr. Slattery and decides to sit down.

MR. FALION: I don't think you're alone, Mr. Hunt. Many people are afraid, and that's a very strange thing because we've never been afraid before. Never—not in a hundred and seventy-five years. But fear is among us now, and it's nagging at us to burn the alien books. I ask you why. What have we got to be afraid of? You call our democracy the greatest system in history. Can books overthrow it? Can knowledge destroy it? Can curiosity wreck it? If they can, then we're a dying race and freedom is an empty word. If democracy is so fragile that it can be smashed by the open minds of children, then I'll get down on my knees and weep for it with you. But if it's strong—and I know it's strong— then I'll let my boys and girls read every book ever written if they want to, and I'll trust them to decide what ideas are the best ideas. This is what freedom is! (*Strong*) You can bring your fire into my school, Mr. Hunt, but you'll never make me tell my kids that there's anything anywhere that they cannot know! (*Quietly*) You see, I believe in what we've got and you don't. That's why your guts wither and tremble at an idea, while I'm not afraid.

Mr. Falion, almost embarrassed now at his oratory, sits down quickly and Mac Hunt, still standing, stares at him, not fully understanding, but somehow feeling that he has been taught a lesson. There is a long pause and then Mr. Nathan clears his throat.

MR. NATHAN (*Softly*): If we had a child . . . I'd be proud to send him to your school, Mr. Falion.

MR. FALION: Thank you.

MRS. NATHAN (*Shyly*): Likewise.

Mr. Falion nods. There is silence and then we cut to Horace.

HORACE: Well, I've heard rabble-rousing speeches in my time . . .

OTTILIE (*To Horace*): Horace, stop it! We've been sitting here and all we do is fight. Why don't you think about getting us back to our homes?

HORACE: You keep talking to me like I'm the only one here. What do you want me to do?

OTTILIE: I don't know. I've got a feeling that maybe there's a reason why we're here like this.

BEN: Maybe she's right. Maybe we've done something . . .

HORACE: All right, what have we done, Mr. Bleeding Heart? I'll confess to it. I'll yell it out as loud as you want.

BEN: We beat up an innocent man.

MR. WILKINSON (*Rising and shouting*): Innocent? Why, that man belongs in jail and you know it!

> *Ben gets up and goes to Mr. Wilkinson.*

BEN: Then why don't you accuse him of a crime and let him face you? Why don't you see that he has counsel? Why doesn't he hear the charges against him? Why don't you give him a trial by jury? What country are you living in, Mr. Wilkinson?

MR. WILKINSON (*Raging*): All right. You go ahead and dispense justice! It's still ten twenty-four, and we're still here—and he got us here. I'll let him face me with that! (*He gets up and goes over to John Carter. Loud*) I said you got us here! What have you got to say to that?

JOHN (*Gently*): No one got you here. You came of your own free will. Don't you remember?

MR. WILKINSON: That's a lie!

JOHN: Why are you so afraid?

MR. WILKINSON (*Raging*): I'm not afraid!

> *And he reaches out and slaps John Carter viciously across the face. The people in the room gasp and Mr. Wilkinson stands still, shocked at what he has done. John Carter looks at him quietly, and then we hear the sharp ringing of the telephone, sudden and insistent. Terrified, they all stare at it as we fade out.*

——— ACT III ———

Fade in on same scene, no time lapse. Everyone stares at the ringing phone and no one has the courage to move. Finally Mr. Neary gets up and shuffles slowly to the phone. He picks it up.

MR. NEARY: Hello?

WOMAN (*Exasperated*): Now let me tell you something, Mr. Whatever-your-name-is. This had just better be the right extension. They've been switching me all over this building, but all over it. You'd think it was the U.N. or something. I mean how difficult can it be to find out where to get a dog license? Hello?

Mr. Neary stares at the phone, horrified, and hangs up. He turns to face them.

MATTY: Who was it?

MR. NEARY (*Dazed*): It was a woman. I don't understand . . .

HORACE: What did she say?

MR. NEARY: She called before—a minute before everyone started to come in here. This was the same call.

MR. WILKINSON: What are you talking about?

MR. NEARY: The same call. Exactly the same. It was like she was making it for the first time.

SYBIL HUNT (*Screaming*): Look at the clock!

We cut to the clock. It reads ten twenty-three. There is a moment of silence. Cut back to them, staring at clock.

MR. NATHAN (*Slowly*): Ten twenty-three!

MR. WILKINSON: That's impossible.

MR. FALION: My watch has ten twenty-three.

HARMON: So has mine! What is this?

Hank Le Seuer grabs Harmon.

HANK LE SEUER (*Desperately*): Start your watch!

HARMON (*Trying*): I can't.

HANK LE SEUER: Start it! Start it! Do ya hear me?

HARMON: I'm trying!

> Hank grabs the watch and tries for a moment. Then he flings it to the floor and stands facing them.

HANK LE SEUER: Well, what are we gonna do? Where do we go? Don't you hear me?

BEN: We hear you, Hank. Take it easy.

HANK LE SEUER: Take it easy!

> He sits down suddenly, his head in his hands. Cut to Mr. Neary.

MR. NEARY (*Wonderingly*): Originally, I picked up the phone at ten twenty-three.

MR. WILKINSON (*Shouting*): Look! This can't be! We're all going out of our minds.

> There is a babble of excitement and people begin to rise. Dr. Slattery runs and picks up the phone, and some of them see him and crowd around him. The room quiets down as he dials. We hear a click and he holds the phone up for all to hear.

OPERATOR ONE: When you hear the tone, the time will be . . . ten twenty-three exactly.

> Dr. Slattery hangs up the phone.

MRS. CHURCH: I didn't hear. What was it? I didn't hear . . .

DR. SLATTERY: It's gone back a minute. It's ten twenty-three.

MATTY: It can't—

HANK LE SEUER: I wasn't even here at ten twenty-three. I was down the street.

MIKEY (*At window*): Look. Mr. Busby is gone!

> They rush to the window. The rain still pours down. We see a flash of lightning. Ted Franklin gets there first and presses his nose against the window.

MAC HUNT: Where is he? What's happening?

TED FRANKLIN: I see him. He's up near Elm. The truck is stopped in the middle of the block. He's frozen at the wheel.

MR. NEARY: He was here before—right in front of the window.

TED FRANKLIN: He hasn't gotten here yet.

OTTILIE (*Frightened*): What's happened? For the love of God, what is it?

DR. SLATTERY: Well, I guess time has moved backward a minute and stopped again, for everyone but us. We're here, talking. For everyone else . . . there's nothing.

OTTILIE (*Intensely*): But why? Why should it happen?

DR. SLATTERY: I don't know.

MR. FALION (*Pointing to John*): It happened just as we struck this man.

OTTILIE: We didn't. George hit him.

MR. FALION: George is the same as all of us. We hit a man for no reason. That's a step backward, isn't it?

MAC HUNT (*Angry*): What are you talking about?

MR. FALION: I don't know. I think maybe I can see it now. Look, a man loses a fraction of his freedom when he's attacked like that, and so do we! If it can happen to him—well, then, it can happen to all of us, can't it? And when we try to destroy freedoms that've taken centuries to establish—well, it's like time is moving backward instead of forward. Maybe what's happening here is—

OTTILIE: Stop it! That's insanity! You keep making up these fantastic things. It's not our fault! It's not! (*She grabs Horace*) Horace—I'm begging you—do something. Look at me. I can't stand this any more.

BILLY SWEETSER: Mom—take it easy.

    Horace looks at her and around the room at all of them, knowing that he should be the leader, ashamed that he is not.

MR. FALION: If someone has a better understanding, let him speak up.

HORACE: All right! We've had enough talk. Let's have some

action. Listen, you people. I don't pretend to understand this and I'm not going to try.

John Carter stands alone at one side of the room, watching them quietly. Horace points at him.

HORACE: I don't know what he has to do with it, but it's something. I'm telling you that.

BEN: Don't be a fool, Mr. Sweetser!

HORACE: Now hear me. We're going to take him and throw him out of here if we have to break his neck to do it!

MR. WILKINSON: That's the way! We're all with you, Horace. Let's go!

DR. SLATTERY: Now wait a minute. You can't do that!

HORACE: Who can't?

DR. SLATTERY: Don't you see? This is our problem, not his. We can't get rid of it by punishing someone else. No one ever has. Not in all of history! Bigger men than you have tried.

HORACE: Don't tell me that. I'm not listening to you any more. (*To all*) Now let's do it, men. Come on. (*He strides a few steps toward John Carter, then stops*) All right! What are you waiting for? Hank Le Seuer! Let's go! Come on, Ted!

They stand still, looking at him. He walks over to Hank Le Seuer, who is sitting down, not looking at him.

HORACE: Okay, on your feet, boy. We're all together in this. (*Hank doesn't move. Horace shakes him*) Hank! Look, I'm telling you to follow me now.

HANK LE SEUER (*Low*): Go away, Mr. Sweetser.

Horace looks at him, shocked, then turns to Harmon.

HORACE (*Loud*): Harmon! Come on. This is the answer. We'll nail him to the wall, boy. And this thing'll be over! (*Harmon doesn't move. Horace grabs him*) Well, what's the matter with you? You don't have to think. Just do what I tell you! Now come on! (*Harmon turns away. Horace goes to Ted Franklin*) Listen, Ted. You're with me, aren't you?

TED (*Slowly*): Well, Mr. Sweetser, I don't know . . .

HORACE: Are you or aren't you? Answer me! (*Shaking Ted*) Answer me!

TED: No, Mr. Sweetser. I'm not!

HORACE: All right. I don't need you! Do you hear that? (*He runs to Mac Hunt*) Mac! Listen . . . we can stop this thing now. . . .

> *Mac turns away from him. Horace looks at him for a moment, then turns to the others.*

HORACE: Who's with me here? This has got to be done. Look at the clock on the wall and you'll know it. We've got to get this man. Now there's me and there's George Wilkinson. Who else?

OTTILIE: Horace . . .

HORACE: I said who else?

> *No one answers. Enraged, he glares at them, then looks at Mr. Wilkinson.*

HORACE: All right, George! Let's go!

MATTY (*Loud*): No!

HORACE: George!

MATTY: You leave him alone.

HORACE: George, do ya hear me?

MR. WILKINSON (*Slowly*): I hear you.

HORACE: Then come on.

WILKINSON: Listen, Horace, I . . . kind of think . . .

HORACE: You think what? Come on, George. Don't mumble! Talk to me! Do you want to help me or don't you?

> *They look at each other for a moment. Then Mr. Wilkinson looks at John Carter.*

MR. WILKINSON (*Low*): I guess I don't.

HORACE (*Exploding*): Okay!

> *He turns to John Carter and slowly begins to walk over to him as everyone watches. It takes him a long while*

to reach John. *Finally he comes face to face with him. John looks at him calmly as Horace, angry and trembling, raises both of his hands as if to take John by the throat. John waits quietly, not preparing to resist. They look into each other's eyes. Then suddenly Horace drops his hands. He sags, turns and walks away to the window and looks out into the storm. Everyone stands silently for a moment. And then Mrs. Nathan looks at her husband wonderingly.*

MRS. NATHAN (*Softly*): He didn't do anything.

MR. NATHAN: He was alone.

MRS. NATHAN: It's a very strange thing.

MR. NATHAN: Very.

MRS. NATHAN: Why are we here, Phil?

MR. NATHAN: I don't know.

MATTY: There must be a reason for it. Things like this can't happen without a reason. Is it a dream, George?

MR. WILKINSON: It's no dream.

OTTILIE: No. It's no dream.

MRS. NATHAN: It must be something. It has to be something.

MRS. CHURCH: I say God help us.

SYBIL HUNT: If we all tried to think . . .

DR. SLATTERY: What is it, Ben? All of us here together . . .

BEN: Maybe it's the day.

MR. FALION: I don't understand you.

BEN: Why today? What day is it?

MR. NEARY: It's Saturday.

MRS. NATHAN: That's right. It's Saturday.

BEN: A Saturday in December.

DR. SLATTERY: And what's the date?

MR. NEARY: I don't know.

MIKEY: December fifteenth. Tomorrow I'm going to be nine. That's how I know.

BEN: December fifteenth. Is that a special date?

MR. NATHAN: Who knows?

HARMON: What do you mean by special?

BEN: Did something happen on December fifteenth?

DR. SLATTERY: Maybe that's it. Maybe something happened on this day.

MR. FALION: Maybe something did.

OTTILIE: At ten twenty-four . . .

DR. SLATTERY: At ten twenty-four A.M.

HANK LE SEUER: Is it a holiday?

TED FRANKLIN: No. It's not a holiday.

MR. NATHAN: It's just a day. That's all I know. December fifteenth.

MR. FALION: Maybe we did something wrong on this day.

MAC HUNT: What could we have done wrong?

SYBIL HUNT: We could have done something. Last year we could have done something.

OTTILIE: Or the year before.

MRS. NATHAN: Or many years before.

BEN: December fifteenth. Maybe it's a day on which we did something right. Something good.

MR. NATHAN: Maybe.

BILLY SWEETSER (*Standing slowly*): December 15, 1789.

OTTILIE: What's that?

BILLY SWEETSER: December 15, 1789. The Bill of Rights approved by Congress on this day. I remember that from Mr. Falion's class.

BEN: The Bill of Rights! Are you sure?

BILLY SWEETSER: I got an A.

MR. FALION: The Bill of Rights. Strange, I never thought of that.

BEN: We never thought of that.

HARMON: What has the Bill of Rights got to do with us?

MRS. NATHAN: Yes. How can this be the reason we're here . . . me in my apron . . .

MATTY: And the storm . . .

MRS. NATHAN: And the storm . . .

DR. SLATTERY: Maybe because we forgot about it yesterday.

BEN: And many yesterdays . . .

MR. NATHAN: And here in this room . . .

SYBIL HUNT: How did we forget about it yesterday?

BEN: We attacked a man for speaking his mind.

SYBIL HUNT: I was home.

BEN: You were there. Every man and woman was there.

MR. WILKINSON: He said evil, dangerous things.

BEN: No. He only said unpopular things.

DR. SLATTERY: It's his right to say them.

MR. NATHAN: There is room here for unpopular opinions, and this is our strength.

DR. SLATTERY: Yet we punish as though we were the law . . . and the crime is not a crime but the way a man thinks.

MR. NATHAN: And we offer no counsel, no trial, no jury.

BEN: What's happened to us? Where have our freedoms gone? This is the anniversary of the Bill of Rights! One hundred and sixty-five years of freedom. Doesn't that mean something to you?

MR. WILKINSON: We shouldn't have to be prisoners here.

BEN: Something had to make us stop and think. Look what we've done!

MR. FALION: We've spat on the rights of another human being.

BEN: We're afraid.

DR. SLATTERY: We're afraid to allow our neighbors to be free.

MR. FALION: And where one man is not free, then no man in all the world is free.

MR. NATHAN: That's very true. Very true.

BEN: This country was born free, out of the blood of the oppressed. They wrote our Bill of Rights. It guarantees the liberty and dignity of man. Who in this room knows what it says?

MR. NATHAN: Freedom of speech, it says . . .

SYBIL HUNT: . . . And freedom of religion, freedom of the press. All guaranteed to everybody.

BEN: Guaranteed! What else? Speak up or hold your tongue and be ashamed.

DR. SLATTERY: Each man is secure in his person, his home and his effects against search without cause and without sworn warrant.

BEN: Right! And there's more.

MR. NEARY: The people can assemble peaceably for any purpose whatsoever!

BEN: Go on! Let's hear it loud!

BILLY SWEETSER: They can't take away what a man owns without just compensation.

BEN: And how they can't!

MR. FALION: They can't deprive us of life, liberty or property, without due process of law.

BEN: Life, liberty or property! You said it, brother. What else?

MAC HUNT: No man can be compelled to testify against himself.

BEN: No man, no matter what! Come on, speak out!

TED FRANKLIN: They can't try a man twice for the same crime. Right?

BEN: Right, they can't . . . and that's not all! Let's shout it out!

HARMON: They've got to let a man face his accuser!

BEN: Every time!

HANK LE SEUER: And they've gotta tell you what you're being tried for!

BEN: Yes sir!

MATTY: Every accused man must have a lawyer to defend him.

BEN: That's a must!

MRS. CHURCH: And a fast trial by jury!

BEN: And a fast trial by jury!

OTTILIE: They can't ask for excessive bail, and they can't make you pay excessive fines!

BEN: You said a mouthful.

MR. WILKINSON: And no man has to submit to cruel and inhuman punishment.

BEN: No man, Mr. Wilkinson. No man! (*To all*) Those are our rights, bought and paid for with the bones of our fathers. Do you hear me? They're what make us free!

DR. SLATTERY: They're what make us strong!

MR. FALION: They're what make us men!

BEN: And as long as we've got those rights we don't have to be afraid. But when we start destroying liberty in the name of liberty, then we'd better run and hide, each man from his neighbor and each father from his son. Because no one will be safe and no one will be free. We've got this Bill of Rights. It's written in blood and pain on a little scrap of paper. Don't let anyone destroy it. Not anyone! Now hear what I tell you. Pledge your lives and your fortunes and your sacred honor to let every man and woman and child walk erect and free until the day they die. Because that's our right, and if we stand firm . . . then it's indestructible!

And everyone stands transfixed, looking at Ben, and then we see Horace Sweetser turning away from the window where he has been standing through all of this. The tears stream down his face. He looks at them and they look back.

HORACE (*Low*): I pledge . . .

And Ottilie and Billy walk to him and stand next to him. Cut to John Carter, who stands alone in front of the lectern. They all look at him now and he at them. Cut back to the crowd. We do not see John Carter, but only the faces of the people. And now they are calm, and they understand why they have come. Suddenly, in the silence, there is a gasp from all of them and their eyes widen. Cut back to the lectern. John Carter is gone from the room. They look at each other in silence, then suddenly we hear the honking of a horn and we hear a car riding down the street. They stand and look around the room, and no one quite knows what to do. Then, one by one, they begin to look up at the clock. It reads 10:25 and the second hand is moving around it. And now Susie and Mike begin to skip toward the door. They open it and the sunlight streams in.

MIKE: Race you to the corner!

And they run out gleefully. Now the others soberly begin to follow and Mr. Neary watches them till they leave. Then he takes his duster and slowly begins to dust the lectern as we fade out.

AUTHOR'S COMMENTARY ON

An Almanac of Liberty

Supreme Court Justice William O. Douglas has been in recent years one of the few strong voices in the wilderness which plead for a return to the concepts of liberty and democracy intended for us by the founders of this country. One of his most brilliant contributions toward this end was the thoughtfully written, and very moving book, An Almanac of Liberty, published in November 1954.

An Almanac of Liberty is, as its name implies, an almanac with an entry for each day of the year. The entries describe, in simple, unadorned language, events in history both large and small which have contributed vitally to the concept of freedom we somehow take for granted today. The book includes stories of the struggles which resulted in such human enlightenments as the signing of the Magna Charta, the enactment of Child Labor laws, the establishment of the concept that no man may be forced to bear witness against himself, the abolition of slavery, and so on. The parts of the book make fascinating reading, but the whole of it is the story of man's incredibly difficult, bloodstained battle to be free, and is at once a tribute to humanity for the progress it has made and a scathing denunciation of humanity for the obstacles it has placed in its own path.

The idea of adapting this book for television belongs to Felix Jackson and Florence Britton of "Studio One." They brought it to me and I took it home to read. The more I read, the more I realized that a literal adaptation of An Almanac of Liberty would be impossible to attempt, so vast is the scope of this book. Each of the events depicted in the book would make an hour play in itself. Therefore, I decided to use only the title and something a little bit more elusive—the spirit of the book—and try to make a television drama out of those elements alone.

Actually, the spirit of the book is the spirit behind the Bill of Rights, and it was for this reason alone that I selected the Bill of Rights as the moving force of the play and the violation of these rights as the plot-generating element. The protagonist of An Almanac of Liberty is the force for good and its antagonist is the force for evil. The people in the play are merely instruments to stir these forces into movement and, as such, were intended simply to be representatives of the various walks of life in a small town, rather than whole people with individual problems of their own.

The plot I constructed for An Almanac of Liberty is actually quite simple, although it may seem to be complex. There is an element of science fiction in it, the stoppage of time, which was injected for several reasons. First, it effectively symbolized, I believe, what happens basically when something impedes man's unending struggle to be free. Second, it lent a mystical quality to the play which made the revelations arrived at by the assemblage in Act III more realistic within the context of the play, and a good deal easier to verbalize. Third, it produced almost immediately the element of suspense and lent a workable foundation upon which to create a series of small, interpersonal dramas within the room.

The first act of An Almanac of Liberty has a great deal in common with the first act of The Remarkable Incident at Carson Corners in that both depict a group of small-town people gathering at a public hall for an unknown reason, and then discovering that something quite awful in which they are all personally involved is in progress. The difference between the two is this: The opening of The Remarkable Incident at Carson Corners is completely real, quite gay and full of excitement, and the people are happy, friendly and anticipating a good time. The opening of An Almanac of Liberty is strange, mystical, almost dreamlike in quality from the moment at which the old janitor, alone in the room, sits down without reason and stares blankly at the podium. I realized that in part, at least, I was duplicating the general dramatic set-up of a previous play in writing An Almanac of Liberty, but there was no other way I could find to tell a story in which a roomful of people are meant to symbolize a world full of people.

The immediate response to An Almanac of Liberty was large and vigorous. After phone calls, telegrams and letters had been tabulated, it was found that between eighty-five and ninety per cent were strongly in favor of An Almanac of Liberty and felt that it had something valid to say which would bear repeating from time to time. I sampled some of the comments of the dissenters, and although I realized what the temper of the times was in November 1954, I was shocked nevertheless at some of the things I read and heard. Sample: A few minutes after air time I answered one of three studio phones which had been ringing constantly. A man who refused to give his name shouted the following over the phone, "I'm a college graduate, so you can't fool me with that stuff. Why don't you 'Studio One' Commies go back to Russia?" This for a play which had a few kind words to say about a basic American heritage, the Bill of Rights!

Paul Nickell directed this one with skill and understanding in the face of the difficult problem a mob scene always presents to a television director, and an extremely good cast of relatively unfamiliar faces was so emotionally caught up in the play that they managed to finish it nearly three minutes ahead of schedule. The display of credits at show-end was minutes longer than usual, and eminently satisfying to all concerned.

I'd like to point out here that An Almanac of Liberty is one of the few dramas that might be classified in certain quarters as "controversial" which has appeared on a national television show, and for this I would like to offer my appreciation here and now to the advertising agency and sponsor of "Studio One" and to the network on which it appears.

Crime in the Streets

—— MARCH 8, 1955 ——————————

PRODUCER	Herbert Brodkin
DIRECTOR	Sidney Lumet
ASSOCIATE PRODUCER	Philip Barry, Jr.
SET DESIGNER	Fred Stover
TECHNICAL DIRECTOR	John Broderick
ASSOCIATE DIRECTOR	James Walsh
PRODUCTION ASSISTANT	Edith Hamlin

CAST

FRANKIE DANE
    John Cassavetes

LOU MACKLIN
    Mark Rydell

ANGELO "BABY" GIOIA
    Ivan Cury

RICHIE DANE
    Van Dyke Parks

MRS. DANE
    Glenda Farrell

MR. GIOIA
    Will Kuluva

BEN WAGNER
    Robert Preston

GLASSES
    David Winters

BLOCKBUSTER
    Jerry Wynne

THE FIGHTER
    Bobby Brivic

BENNY
    Tony Mitchell

MR. MCALLISTER
    William Hawley

DRUNK
    Tom Gorman

VOICE FROM STREET
    Ralph Friar

ACT I

Fade in on a fire escape on the second story of a run-down tenement house. It is early evening. Crouched uncomfortably on the fire escape are Frankie Dane, Lou Macklin and Angelo "Baby" Gioia. The three boys wear jackets with the word "Hornets" lettered on the backs. Frankie, eighteen, is cold, arrogant, hostile—a bitter, intense kid who long ago has squared off at society and invited it to come get him if it can. He is quick, bright, a powerful and magnetic leader whose word is law to the boys around him, who has ever been unopposed by his contemporaries simply because he is Frankie Dane. And he has an almost psychopathic quirk, respected meticulously by his flock. He cannot stand being touched by anyone. Physical contact, unless accidental, sends Frankie into a savage rage. And if the physical contact is accidental, if another body or a hand touches his, he moves away uncomfortably. Lou Macklin, also eighteen, is big, heavily muscled and bop-crazy. He lives in this tenement house, two floors above Frankie, and is proud and glad to be Frankie's strong right arm. Angelo Gioia is fifteen and Frankie is his god, a god he fears more than respects. He lives behind the Gioia candy store, which is next to the tenement house, separated from it by the alley. He is called "Baby" by everyone because he is what the name implies, a baby trying to be a tough, cold gangster, and he despises the name. Between Baby and Frankie there is a strange kind of affection. It is as if Frankie is leading Baby to manhood, and if manhood is arrived at along with death, then this is all right with Baby. The three boys crouch there on the fire escape. Behind them is the window opening into the mean and shabby little apartment in which Frankie lives with his mother and his ten-year-old brother Richie. Inside, we see Richie sitting on an unmade bed doing his homework. He is a quiet, small, sensitive boy who somehow, in spite of Frankie's makeup, loves Frankie, knowing as he does so that Frankie cannot understand the meaning of the word "love." Within the boys on the fire escape there is a wild elation, controlled but threatening to burst forth. Lou smokes a cigarette. We see them first in a long shot. Frankie is talking, using strong, incisive gestures, but we cannot hear him. He stops. Lou, who was sitting leaning against the rail, suddenly goes forward onto his knees. He kneels in front of Frankie. Baby sits up straight. Frankie has obviously shocked them.

Cut close to them as Lou makes his move.

LOU: And . . . Come on, willya? Don't stop there!

FRANKIE (*Quietly*): . . . and we're gonna kill him.

LOU (*Amazed*): No!

FRANKIE: That's what I said.

LOU: Crazy! (*He looks up at window above Frankie's*) Mr. McAllister! How about that!

    He laughs nervously.

FRANKIE: It's not funny.

BABY (*Awed*): No, it ain't funny. Frankie, you kiddin' us?

FRANKIE: You want me to be?

BABY (*Trying to be tough*): No!

    Frankie tousles Baby's hair.

FRANKIE (*To Baby*): Is your heart bumpin'?

BABY (*Lying*): No.

FRANKIE: Y' sweatin'?

BABY: No.

FRANKIE (*Grinning*): You're lying.

BABY: No!

FRANKIE: It don't matter. You'll get used to it. Okay, that's the deal. We're gonna kill him. (*Pointing*) You, you and me.

BABY (*Looking up*): His window's open.

FRANKIE: He's out.

LOU: Yeah, but you said it so loud. Your brother's inside.

FRANKIE: He's doing arithmetic. That's all he knows. Forget my brother.

BABY: Listen, Frankie . . . We never did anything like this before.

FRANKIE: That's right. So?

BABY: No . . . I'm just askin' like . . . y'know like . . . what do we do?

    Baby stands up nervously.

FRANKIE: Baby, what are you standin' up for?

BABY: I gotta. My leg's asleep. (*He turns to Frankie*) Listen, why do you have to call me Baby? Why don'tcha call me Angelo? My name's Angelo.

FRANKIE: You're fifteen. When you're eighteen I'll call you Angelo. Come on, sit down.

> *Baby squats in front of him. Frankie looks at Baby and Lou.*

FRANKIE (*Slowly*): I surprised you with this, right?

LOU (*Low*): And how.

FRANKIE: First I was gonna take him and open up his head for him all by myself. (*He smacks his fist into his leg*) How did he know it?

BABY: What's the difference?

FRANKIE: Nobody knew Lenny had a gun except me. And Mr. McAllister sicked a cop on him. For nothin'! Lenny was just standin' there on the corner. What did he have to do it for?

BABY: Frankie . . .

FRANKIE: And then he smiled like a fat little pussycat when he heard they sent Lenny away for two to five. I saw him! Listen, we know Lenny all our lives. Since we're little kids. And Mr. McAllister sent him up! He didn't even know him! Well . . . we're gettin' even. I'm tellin' ya . . . first I was gonna—(*He stops and makes a violent stabbing gesture*) All right. Forget that. We're doin' it together. That's smarter. It takes three.

BABY: What about the other guys?

FRANKIE: They're all gonna be part of it. Every one. They're gonna be havin' a great big stag party at someone's house, and they're gonna swear we were there if we need it.

BABY: You told them yet?

FRANKIE: Later. First us.

LOU (*To Baby*): Stop askin' questions, willya? Let Frankie talk. (*To Frank*) C'mon, tell it to us.

FRANKIE: Okay. Three of us. Right? One brings him where we want him. One holds him still and quiet. One gives it to him.

LOU (*Excited*): Go, go, go!

FRANKIE: It takes ten seconds and we're outa there.

LOU: The end! (*Laughing*) Frankie, you kill me!

He reaches over and slaps Frankie playfully several
times on the cheek. Frankie stiffens. Instantly Lou
shrinks back against the railing and covers his head with
his arms, rolling his body into a ball. Frankie leaps to
his feet and stands over Lou in a savage fury. His whole
body trembles. Baby stands up and tries to push Frankie
back.

BABY: Frankie . . . don't . . .

Frankie sweeps Baby back into the railing, knocking
him down. Baby stares at him. Frankie reaches down
and picks Lou up by the shoulders. His hands go
around Lou's neck. Lou stares into his face and Frankie
stares back, his features dark with rage. Inside the room
we see Richie watching, terrified.

LOU: Please . . . please . . . I forgot. I swear I forgot.
Frankie! On my mother's grave I swear. Please . . . let me
go! Look at me! I'm begging you, boy. . . .

MALE VOICE FROM STREET: Hey, look up there! No . . . up
there on the fire escape!

Frankie's hands tighten around Lou's throat.

LOU (Begging): Frankie . . . don't . . .

Frankie stops suddenly. He sits down.

MALE VOICE FROM STREET: Did you see that? He was choking
him!

BABY (Shouting back): They're just kiddin' around. Take a
breeze, willya!

Lou stands over Frankie.

LOU: I'm sorry. It's the first time I ever forgot about you,
Frankie. I never touched you before, did I? (Frankie looks
up at him blankly) Did I?

BABY: He never did, Frank.

FRANKIE (Low): This morning on the stoop I started to tell
Mr. McAllister off and he called me a dirty little bug and
he slapped me across the face. (Richie starts walking toward

the window) There were some people there. For a minute
I couldn't see. D'ya know that? That's how I was. I couldn't
see. Then he walked away.

> *Richie opens the window and pokes his head out,
> timed perfectly with Frankie's last line.*

RICHIE: Frankie . . .

FRANKIE (*Simultaneously*): We're gonna kill him!

> *They all turn to face Richie. He has heard Frankie's
> last line. There is a pause.*

BABY (*Loud*): And how we're gonna kill him. When that
cigar goes off in his puss, he'll drop dead. Bo-o-o-o-om!

> *He drops dead on the fire escape. From a prone posi-
> tion he looks up.*

BABY: Right, Frankie?

FRANKIE (*To Richie*): Get back inside before I break your
arm.

> *Richie stares at Frankie, frightened, knowing that Baby
> was just trying to cover. He closes the window and
> goes over to the bed. They watch him. He picks up a
> book.*

FRANKIE: He don't know. Forget him. (*To Baby and Lou*)
Okay, let's get done. I'm gonna tell you who does what
so you can think about it. (*To Baby*) Are you ready? (*Baby
nods*) You're gonna bring him to us.

BABY: Okay.

FRANKIE (*To Lou*): You're gonna hold him.

LOU: I'm gonna hold him.

FRANKIE: And I'm gonna slice him.

LOU: Frankie, I'm telling you, it's the end!

> *Frankie pauses for a moment, thinking about it. The
> door to his apartment opens and we see, through the
> window, his mother enter. Mrs. Dane is middle-aged,
> poorly dressed—a sad, defeated woman who has all but
> lost hope. She works as a waitress. We see her kiss*

Richie and begin to take off her coat. Every move she makes is fraught with weariness. And a great deal of this weariness is Frankie. She doesn't understand him, nor he her, and between them there is nothing but a cold and loveless truce. Baby sees her enter.

BABY: Hey, your old lady just came in.

Frankie turns, looks at her. She sees him. They stare at each other for a moment and then she turns away.

FRANKIE: Take off.

LOU: When are we gonna do it, Frankie?

FRANKIE: I don't know. Soon. I'll see you later.

He opens the window and starts to climb in. He closes the window. While it is open we hear Mrs. Dane from inside.

MRS. DANE: Tired? Richie, I never been so tired in my life. I don't know what was so special about today, but you'da thought it was the only restaurant in New York. . . .

Baby and Lou look at each other and the excitement shows in Baby's face.

BABY (Low): Can y'imagine? Hey, Lou, can y'imagine?

LOU (Annoyed): Ah, grow up, will ya?

But Lou is excited too, and we can see it. They begin to climb down the fire escape.

Cut to inside of Frankie's living room. Mrs. Dane has hung up her coat and hat. Through the following lines Frankie looks hard at Richie. Richie is listening to Mrs. Dane, who is sitting in a battered arm chair, but he keeps looking at Frankie, trying to smile.

MRS. DANE (Tired): . . . from twelve to two and then from five to eight they never stopped coming. My feet are ready to scream. And they most of them want ham and eggs. I don't think they know there is anything else. We got nice salads on the menu. I didn't see one salad all day. Richie, honey, I'm so sick of looking fried eggs in the eye. If I could maybe get a job in one of those French-type restaurants. They got the eggs all covered up with sauce. You don't have to look at them. (*She sighs*) Would you make me some tea, honey?

RICHIE: Okay, Mom.

> *He gets up and goes through the business of putting a pot of water on the hot plate. Frankie watches him. Mrs. Dane studies Frankie.*

MRS. DANE: Hello, Frankie.

FRANKIE: Hello.

MRS. DANE: I thought maybe you'd say hello first for once. (*He looks at her*) I ought to know better. (*To Richie*) Nice and strong. (*He nods*) (*To Frankie*) Well, what did you accomplish today?

FRANKIE: Same as anybody.

> *He watches Richie.*

MRS. DANE: Did you look for a job?

FRANKIE: All day.

MRS. DANE: And?

FRANKIE: And nothin'.

MRS. DANE: You didn't look.

> *Frankie walks over to the hot plate where Richie stands.*

MRS. DANE: You hung around on the corner with the neighborhood punks. Rotten kids!

FRANKIE (*Looking at her*): That's what their mothers say about me.

MRS. DANE: Do you ever have an answer that isn't smart? Sometimes I almost wish your father was back here.

FRANKIE: And you're the only one.

MRS. DANE (*Sadly*): I'll tell you, Frank. I don't know where you get the strength to fight me like you do. I haven't got it. I don't know what to say to you any more. I find myself just . . . saying nothing. I don't know. How am I supposed to be? I don't feel like a mother. I can't tell you to do anything. It's like telling a rock. Maybe I'm too old. I don't know. It's my fault, I s'pose. How much can a person think about?

> *Frankie looks at her, no emotion showing on his face. Then she turns away and looks out the window.*

MRS. DANE (*Embarrassed*): It's muggy for this time of year.

> *Frankie looks at Richie.*

RICHIE (*Smiling*): Hiya, Frank. Listen, I'm sorry about before. (*He waits*) You want some tea?

FRANKIE: I want to tell you something. You open the window when I'm out there again and I'll belt you around the block, Richie honey.

> *Mrs. Dane gets up quickly.*

MRS. DANE: Don't talk to him like that!

RICHIE: Gee, I only wanted to ask you something, Frankie.

FRANKIE: Don't ask me!

> *Richie looks at him, troubled, as Mrs. Dane walks over to him.*

MRS. DANE: Now listen, Mr. Frankie Dane, you're not talking to the garbage in the streets now. You're talking to your brother.

FRANKIE (*Ignoring her*): Do you hear me?

> *Richie nods. Frankie looks at his mother, opens the front door and exits fast. Mrs. Dane looks at Richie. Then she kisses him on the forehead gently and looks at the door.*
>
> *Cut to the street in front of Gioia's candy store. We hear the honking of autos and the many sounds of the street. Gioia's is a tiny store in a shabby building, separated from Frankie's house by a deep, high-walled, trash-filled alley. No windows in either building face the alley. Standing in front of Gioia's are Lou Macklin and four other boys, all wearing "Hornets" jackets. They are Glasses, Blockbuster, The Fighter and Benny.*

They laugh raucously as a girl walks by ignoring their catcalls and whistles.

THE FIGHTER (*Calling*): Hey, lady, yer motor's runnin'.

BENNY: Moron! Hey, Blockbuster, dig the tomato!

GLASSES (*Squinting*): Man, is that stacked!

BLOCKBUSTER: How would you know? You can't see that far.

GLASSES: That I can see that far.

BENNY: Hey, Glasses, I'll flip you quarters against the wall.

GLASSES: Listen to him. Quarters! You crazy nut, you ain't got no quarters. (*Still looking off*) What a jelly apple!

BENNY: So I'll owe!

GLASSES (*Turning to him*): Get lost!

Glasses pushes Benny in the face.

BENNY (*Angrily*): C'mon! Keep your hands off, ya big slob.

Glasses bristles at Benny.

LOU: Hey, here comes Frankie!

Frankie enters to a chorus of "Hiya Frank," "Hey Frankie," etc. He looks around the group without returning their hellos.

FRANKIE: Where's Baby?

THE FIGHTER (*Pointing at store*): Helpin' his old man with the five cents plain.

BLOCKBUSTER: Hey, where you been, Frankie? We been waiting around here for an hour.

FRANKIE: I'll send you a letter of apology. Now listen, I got something to tell you and I don't wanta be interrupted. Come here.

They group around him closely.

GLASSES: Something big, right, Frankie?

LOU: The biggest.

FRANKIE: Shut up. Now let me give it to you fast and plain. Don't nobody fall down. We're bumping a guy!

They look at each other, suddenly silent, awed. He studies them.

FRANKIE: Everybody all of a sudden got cold. Don't pass out on me, boys. Lou, me 'n Baby are doing the job. All you got to do is set up the alibi. The mark is Mr. McAllister.

The group widens as they all, except for Lou, back away from the very idea of murder.

FRANKIE: What's wrong? Well, come on. Talk up. You're walkin' away from me, Benny.

BENNY: I'm not gettin' into no murder, Frankie.

FRANKIE (*Pointing at store*): There's a fifteen-year-old kid inside didn't say that. What'sa matter with you?

BLOCKBUSTER: Me either, Frankie. Anything else, but no killings. I ain't nuts!

GLASSES: Ditto.

FRANKIE (*To the Fighter*): Fighter?

THE FIGHTER: I'm with them, Frank.

Frankie stares at them, amazed.

LOU: I'll knock your dumb heads together.

He advances on The Fighter, who swiftly reaches into his pocket and makes as if to draw a knife. Lou stops.

FRANKIE: Cut it! (*To the others*) Get outa here.

BENNY: Listen, Frankie . . .

FRANKIE: Nothing to listen. Take off.

LOU: Frankie, you're crazy. You're the head man. Tell 'em.

BLOCKBUSTER (*Softly*): You feel like sockin' me, Frank?

FRANKIE (*To all, loud*): Beat it!

They back away, then turn and walk off. Lou looks at Frankie as Ben Wagner enters. Ben is thirtyish—big, rugged, yet sensitive-looking. He is one of the new school of social workers, men who know how to reach tough kids on their own level without being patronizing. Ben is new in this neighborhood, but he knows Frankie and the other boys by name and is trying to win their confidence. This is slow, painstaking, delicate work, and he is treading carefully. He wears a wind-

breaker, smokes a cigarette and talks the language of the streets. *Perhaps once he was a tough, angry kid himself.*

BEN (*To Lou*): Hiya, Lou. Hello, Frankie.
> *Neither of them answers. Frankie looks off at the departing gang and Lou looks at Frankie.*

BEN: If you've got a private war going, I'll keep walking.

LOU (*Turning*): No. Nothing like that.
> *Lou seems to like Ben, if not to trust him.*

BEN: You owe me a buck.

LOU: What for?

BEN: Mays went three for four this afternoon.

LOU: So I owe you a buck. (*To Frankie, who is lost in thought*) I'm gonna talk to 'em, Frankie.

FRANKIE: Don't talk to 'em.

LOU: I don't dig ya, Frankie. What are you tryin' to do?

FRANKIE: Leave me alone.

LOU (*Disturbed*): Okay, call me, willya?

BEN: So long, muscles.

LOU: What a riot you are!
> *Lou exits. Ben walks over to Frankie, who stares off, thinking, figuring, looking for an angle.*

BEN: Is he good for the buck?
> *Frankie turns and looks at him. He speaks quietly now, without viciousness.*

FRANKIE: Why don't you stop suckin' around? What are ya—in love with us or something?

BEN: No. Suckin' around's my job.

FRANKIE: Well, why don't you and your two-bit welfare agency work somebody else's block once. We're doin' okay on this one.

BEN: Are you? What's the box score this week? One kid in jail for two to five years. One gang fight. One mashed nose, one broken arm. Nobody dead. You're right, you're doing okay here. Maybe I'll try in front of the Waldorf.

FRANKIE: You do that. They got plenty of juvenile delinquents there for you to practice on.

BEN: What's new, Frankie?

FRANKIE (*Snapping*): Look, what d'ya want out of me?

BEN: You're eighteen. I want to see you live till you're twenty-one.

FRANKIE (*Hard*): Why?

BEN (*Hard*): So you can vote!

> *Ben turns and walks into Gioia's candy store. Frankie watches him.*
>
> *Cut to inside of store. Mr. Gioia, an old-world Italian, is busy behind the soda fountain, waiting on a small girl. There are some empty soda bottles on counter. Baby is there, opening a carton of cigar boxes and stacking them on the shelf. We hear Mr. Gioia's voice, heavily accented, in background.*

MR. GIOIA: That's six cents, Miss America.

BEN (*To Baby*): Hello, Angelo.

> *Baby looks up, pleased.*

BABY: Hiya.

> *He bends to his job.*

BEN: Good evening, Mr. Gioia.

MR. GIOIA (*Looking up. Pleased*): Oh . . . *buona sera*, Mr Wagner.

BEN: How goes it? Busy?

MR. GIOIA (*Shrugging*): I don't know. It depends on what you call busy. What I mean, I'm doin' big business in one-cent candies. I gotta sell hundreds to make one dollar. If that's busy, I'm busy. (*To small girl*) I hope your momma's not gonna be sore you spent her bottle deposit on jelly beans. (*The small girl smiles and exits*) Hey, guess what happens to the dollar, Mr. Wagner? (*Pointing at Baby*) This one he jump out of his diapers and spend it in the poolroom.

BABY: Ah, Pop, cut it out!

MR. GIOIA: What cut it out? Listen, Mr. Wagner, you workin' with kids. Maybe you tell my Baby what gonna happen to him from hangin' out with bums on the street.

BABY (*Loud*): Pop! Now listen . . .

BEN: Take it easy, Angelo.

The door opens and Frankie stands in the doorway.

BABY: What's he gotta pick me apart all the time?

MR. GIOIA: You see how fresh? No respect!

FRANKIE (*To Baby*): Baby, I want to see you when you're done.

Mr. Gioia turns and sees Frankie.

MR. GIOIA (*Angrily*): You get out of here! (*He advances around the counter*) How many times I told you to stay out of the store! Listen, I'm gonna throw you out!

Frankie ignores Mr. Gioia completely.

FRANKIE (*To Baby*): When you're done.

MR. GIOIA (*To Ben*): Look at him! (*To Frankie*) I'm talking to you, lousy bum! Trash! Get out of here!

BABY: Pop, shut up!

MR. GIOIA (*Turning*): You tell me to shut up? I'm gonna smack your behind.

He advances on Baby.

FRANKIE (*Quietly*): I'll be outside.

MR. GIOIA (*To Frankie. Shouting*): You keep away from my boy!

Frankie winks at Baby and exits, but as always he is hurt deep within him at another of the countless rejections he suffers.

MR. GIOIA (*To Baby*): Get in the back. I'll show you shut up!

He walks over to Baby and slaps him across the face. Baby stares at him.

BEN (*Loud*): Mr. Gioia!

MR. GIOIA (*Turning*): What do you want?

BEN (*Low*): A malted.

MR. GIOIA (*To Baby*): Get in the back.

> *Slowly Baby turns. Mr. Gioia, trembling, goes behind the counter as Baby goes through the curtain which leads to the Gioia living quarters. Mr. Gioia begins to make a malted milk.*

MR. GIOIA: Shut up, he said. Shut up. I'm his father.

BEN: Don't hit him, Mr. Gioia.

MR. GIOIA (*Saddened*): Why not? You gotta hit 'em, all of 'em, else they gonna be no good. To hit. That's all they know. Look at my boy. Fifteen years old. Ask him what he wants to be when he grows up. You know what he says? Doctor? Lawyer? Teacher? No! Big Wheel! So I say how you be a big wheel, Baby? And he says, be tough. Tough! That's all he wants. So you gotta hit. You gotta punish. And for that one (*Pointing at door*) you gotta put him in jail, else he's gonna kill somebody.

BEN: Maybe.

MR. GIOIA: I'm tell you. (*Handing Ben malted*) That's seventeen cents.

BEN: Look, Mr. Gioia, you're not talking about wild animals. These are just tough, angry kids. You beat them, they get tougher and angrier. You put them in jail, maybe you destroy them for good. Those aren't the answers.

MR. GIOIA: So what are the answers?

BEN: We don't know. We try to understand them. Everybody expects it to happen all at once. They expect a kid who's been bumped on the head all his life to become a respectable ribbon clerk tomorrow, just because they say he ought to. That's not the way it happens. Look, it takes a long time to straighten out one bad kid, the way we work, Mr. Gioia. But if it's your kid, it's worth it.

MR. GIOIA (*Shaking his head*): You don't understand, Mr. Wagner. I'm tell you. You're a good man, but you don't understand.

He walks to the back of the store and through the curtains. Ben watches him for a moment and then he walks toward the door.

Cut to street as he comes out. Frankie stands there at the curb. When he sees Ben, he turns his back. Ben looks at him and then walks away. Frankie turns, as he hears Ben's footsteps, and watches Ben walking. The streets are empty now. Frankie walks into the alley and looks around. Carefully he examines the alley, pacing off the distance from wall to wall. He goes out into the street, looks into the alley and now seems satisfied. Lou comes down the street and walks over to Frankie. Frankie looks into the alley.

LOU: Hiya, Pops. (*Frankie doesn't answer*) What're ya lookin' at?

FRANKIE: The alley.

LOU: What for? (*Frankie doesn't answer*) C'mon, let's get some beer or something.

FRANKIE: This is the place, Lou.

LOU: What place?

FRANKIE: This is where we're gonna kill him.

LOU (*Amazed*): You're kidding!

FRANKIE: I'm not kidding!

LOU: This is where we live! The three of us. You and me in this house, and Baby in the store. Frankie, what's happening to you?

FRANKIE: This is the place. I don't know when we're gonna do it, but it's gonna be here. Nobody'll believe we worked in our own back yard.

LOU: Frankie, you're buggin' me! This is wild.

FRANKIE (*Hard*): Do you want to figure it?

LOU (*Backing down*): Not me. You're the one, Frank. Listen, what about the other guys?

Frankie looks steadily at Lou.

FRANKIE: We don't need them. It's gonna work. It can't miss. Just do what I say, Lou. Just do what I say.

LOU (Low): Okay, Frankie.

> *They look into the blackness of the alley for a moment.*

FRANKIE: It's our first. How do you feel?

LOU: My skin is crawling.

FRANKIE: I feel loose. I could fall asleep standing up. I never been so loose in my life. It's like I was made for it. Getting even. Go home, Lou. I'll see ya.

> *Lou looks at him strangely for a moment.*

LOU: So long.

> *He turns and walks away. Frankie stands in the street for a moment and then slowly moves into the alley. The street is silent, deserted. He stands there in the darkness looking around. Then he hears footsteps tapping down the street. Slowly he walks to the lip of the alley and stands there. A middle-aged man comes walking by—a quiet, plain, tired-looking man. He walks in front of Frankie.*

FRANKIE: Hello, Mr. McAllister.

> *The man turns, looks at Frankie and walks on. Frankie watches him. He turns into Frankie's house. Frankie takes a deep breath and lets it out. He closes his eyes. Fade out.*

―――― **ACT II** ――――――――――――――

> *Fade in on a long shot of the fire escape. It is early the following evening. Frankie and Baby are seated on it. Frankie is talking, and, as in the opening of the first act, we cannot hear him.*
>
> *Cut close to them now. We see Richie inside the room, lying on a bed reading a book.*

FRANKIE: What time is it?

BABY: About eight.

Frankie gets up and looks over the fire escape railing nervously.

BABY: Listen, Frank, I gotta go help in the store.

He gets up.

FRANKIE: Wait a minute. (*He opens the window*) Richie! (*Richie looks up from his book*) Come 'ere.

Richie walks slowly over to the window and stops just short of it.

FRANKIE: Well, come 'ere. What are you afraid of?

RICHIE (*Softly*): You, Frankie.

Frankie looks at him for a moment and we can see that this has hurt him. Frankie reaches into his pocket for a quarter.

FRANKIE (*Softly*): Here. Get me some cigarettes, willya?

Richie takes the quarter and nods, backing away from the window. Frankie watches as he turns and walks out the door.

FRANKIE: Listen, Richie . . .

But Richie is gone. Frankie looks after him for a moment and then slams down the window. He turns to Baby.

BABY: What'sa matter with him?

FRANKIE: Nothin' . . . nothin' . . .

BABY: I gotta go. I'll see you tomorrow.

He turns and makes as if to leave.

FRANKIE: We're doing it tonight, Bambino.

BABY (*Amazed*): You're kiddin'!

FRANKIE: Never.

BABY: Wow! It's so fast. . . . We only decided last night.

FRANKIE: That's right. We got any reason to wait?

Baby shakes his head and stares off over the fire escape,

gritting his teeth as Frankie talks, and we know that he is afraid.

FRANKIE: Look, Mr. McAllister's going bowling tonight. He'll get home around two. We'll be waitin' for him. D'ya hear me, Baby?

BABY: I hear.

FRANKIE: We're gonna plan it move for move. I'm meetin' you and Lou in the alley at ten. (*He looks at Baby closely*) What are you grindin' your teeth for?

BABY (*Looking at him*): I'm not.

FRANKIE (*Smiling*): Go ahead. I'll see you at ten . . . Angelo.

Baby looks at him. Frankie climbs into the window and closes it. Baby looks at him for a minute and then begins to climb down the fire escape.

Cut to the stoop of the house. Richie is climbing up the steps holding a pack of cigarettes. We hear Ben's voice, off.

BEN (*Calling*): Richie.

Richie turns as Ben walks up the stoop beside him.

RICHIE (*Smiling*): Hi, Mr. Wagner.

BEN: Ben.

RICHIE: Ben.

BEN: Whenever somebody calls me Mr. Wagner, I think they mean my father. (*Richie laughs*) How's everything?

RICHIE: Okay.

BEN: Gettin' ready for Easter vacation?

RICHIE: And how!

BEN: No more pencils. No more books.

RICHIE: No more teacher's sassy looks.

BEN (*Laughing*): As the saying goes. (*Seeing cigarettes*) Hey, are you taking up smoking?

RICHIE (*Smiling*): No. These are for Frankie.

BEN: How is Frankie?

RICHIE (*Suddenly frowning*): Okay.

BEN: What's the matter—is he giving you a hard time?

RICHIE: No.

BEN: He's a strange guy, your brother. . . .

> *Richie looks at Ben for a long moment and then he speaks quietly.*

RICHIE: I think he's gonna kill somebody.

> *Ben tries not to react.*

BEN: What makes you say that?

RICHIE: I heard him talking.

BEN: When?

RICHIE: Last night.

BEN: Who was he talking about?

RICHIE: I don't know. I don't know anything else. I shouldn't have said it. (*Frightened*) Listen, if you tell him I said—

BEN: I wouldn't do that, Richie.

RICHIE: Maybe I'm wrong. I don't know. I mean he's not . . . such a terrible guy. Like sometimes he buys me a soda. (*He looks up at Ben*) I'm scared. Please don't say—

> *Ben puts his hands on Richie's shoulders.*

BEN: Don't be scared. Is he home? (*Richie nods*) Stay out here for a while.

RICHIE: Listen . . .

BEN: It's gonna be okay.

> *He pats Richie's shoulder and starts into the house, as Mr. McAllister comes out carrying a bowling ball. Mr. McAllister nods at Ben and exits. Ben enters the house. Richie stands on the stoop, frightened now, holding the cigarettes, waiting.*
>
> *Cut to Frankie in the room. He sits on the bed with a book on his lap and a piece of paper on the book. On the paper is drawn a diagram of the alley. He studies it. There is a knock on the door. Frankie picks up the dia-*

gram, *folds it, puts it into his pocket and opens the
door.*

FRANKIE: Okay, Richie . . . (*Then he sees Ben*) What do
you want?

Ben enters. Frankie looks him over.

BEN: I just want to say hello.

FRANKIE: Nobody asked you up here. What'd you come for?

Ben sits down on the bed.

BEN: No reason. I was downstairs. I've never seen your place.

FRANKIE: Well, feast your eyes. It's straight outa the movies.

BEN: It's a pretty lousy place. You want a cigarette?

*He holds out the pack. Frankie looks at it and takes
one. He looks closely at Ben, wondering what he wants.*

BEN: What are you doin' with yourself?

FRANKIE: Nothing. Why don't you take off?

BEN: Why don't you get a job? Nothing's for when you're six.
You're eighteen.

FRANKIE: How much do you make saving souls?

BEN: Seventy-five.

FRANKIE: I don't want a job.

BEN: I'm living, boy! I make a lot more than your mother
makes and I haven't got a soul to worry about but myself.

FRANKIE: You trying to get me sore?

BEN: That's right. I figure maybe you'll belt me one—and then
I'll lay you out and then we can shake hands and start even.

FRANKIE: If I ever belted you . . .

BEN: Maybe. What's the matter, Frankie? You're chewin'
yourself to pieces. Let me earn some of that seventy-five.
Tell me your troubles. I won't open my mouth.

*Frankie looks at him for a long moment. Then he walks
over to the window.*

FRANKIE: Who made you so dumb? Tell you my troubles.
(*Turning*) You're sittin' in my troubles! Take a look around
you, dumb! Take a sniff. Anywhere. Go in the corner and

sniff. Go ahead! Tell me what it smells like. Look at the place. Open your eyes and look at this dirty, filthy, rotten, stinkin' hole! It's where I live. (*He walks angrily over to Ben*) What do you want outa me—a case history? You buckin' for a raise? Okay! Take this! I got a hole in my shirt and my brother's wearing my underwear and my mother's stickin' her thumb in some slob's soup! That what you want? Okay, you got it! Now lemme ask you something. Who did it to me? Who put the stink into my room? Who told me I gotta squat on a fire escape if I want to be alone? Who told me if I stop littering the streets I'll go to heaven? C'mon, tell me! Cause I'm waiting to get even, and when I find him I'm gonna spill his brains in the gutter, and lemme tell you something—I can't be stopped! There's your report. Now take it down to your fat-belly committee. And tell me how many old ladies pass out!

EN (*Quietly*): Nobody'll pass out, Frankie.

FRANKIE: No? Listen, brother, I know you people. I know why you're comin' up here to let the kids cry on your shoulders. It's not because you want to help us. (*Loud*) It's because you're scared to death of us! It's because you shake in your pants every time you pass us on the street! It's because we're gettin' our pictures in the papers! If you weren't scared of what we might do to you, you wouldn't be here. You'd be sendin' doughnuts and old furniture!

BEN: You're all wrong, Frankie.

FRANKIE (*Loud*): Am I? Well, I'll tell you something. You got a right to be scared of me, brother! Now get up on your feet and get out of my house!

> Ben looks at him for a long while and he knows that right now Frankie is an impenetrable rock. Ben gets up and goes over to Frankie.

BEN (*Quietly*): You sound like you're gonna kill somebody, Frankie. Just for fun.

Frankie turns to him, furious. Ben puts his hand on Frankie's arm.

BEN: Listen . . .

Frankie flings Ben's hand away.

FRANKIE (*Shouting*): Get your hands off me! Get out of here! *Ben looks at him and then exits. Frankie stands alone in the room, sick at having stripped himself naked. He closes his eyes, grits his teeth and stands there, trying not to cry.*

Fade out.

Fade in on the street in front of Gioia's candy store a moment later. Glasses, Blockbuster, The Fighter and Benny are there. Blockbuster is smoking a cigarette. The Fighter and Benny are sparring. They cuff each other with open hands.

BLOCKBUSTER: Anybody see Frankie today?

GLASSES: Yeah, this morning. He gave me a look like I was a disease or something.

BENNY: Okay. Knock it off. (*They stop fighting*) So I got no left. Could a guy have everything?

THE FIGHTER: You got nothin'.

They join Blockbuster and Glasses, panting slightly.

THE FIGHTER (*To Glasses*): You saw Frankie?

GLASSES: Yeah. What d'ya think of that guy?

THE FIGHTER: He's off his nut.

BLOCKBUSTER: What about Lou and Baby?

THE FIGHTER: Them, too. It's the craziest. What're they gonna get out of it?

We hear footsteps off. Then we see Ben approaching from Frankie's house.

BENNY: The absolute most they can get is nothin'. Whyn't they scramble the guy's face for him if they wanta teach him a lesson? Killin's for nuts.

Ben enters and Benny changes his tone and subject

matter without losing a beat.

BENNY: You don't kill the ball; you just meet it. Look at Robinson. He don't hit a flock o' homers, but he can bust you apart with singles and doubles. That's all. Just meet it. (*Turning to Ben*) Right?

BEN: Well, it depends on your style. You wouldn't say Duke Snider just meets it.

But Ben has heard what went on before and knows the subject has been changed.

BENNY: My style is I just meet it.

BEN: What d'ya hit?

BENNY: I'm not sayin' how often I meet it, am I? I hit what I hit, and I field great. Right?

THE FIGHTER: Fair.

BENNY: Aaaah . . .

Benny makes as if to hit The Fighter, then turns away.

BEN: Anybody seen Frankie?

BLOCKBUSTER: No.

BEN: How come he's not hanging around?

BENNY (*Cold*): Who knows? Ask him. Hey, I'm going to the movies. Anybody coming?

BLOCKBUSTER: I'm with you.

GLASSES: You got money?

BENNY: For you, any time.

THE FIGHTER: And away we go. (*To Ben*) See ya around.

They move off. Ben watches them for a moment and then walks over to the candy store. He opens the door. Cut to inside. Baby and Mr. Gioia are arguing. Baby is holding his "Hornets" jacket, ready to put it on and go out. Ben stands unnoticed in the doorway. Mr. Gioia is extremely emotional. Baby is sullen, defiant. As the door opens, we hear Mr. Gioia in the middle of a sentence.

MR. GIOIA: . . . Why? Tell me why. I don't understand. Why

you gotta go out? What's out? Run in the streets. Make trouble. Make people afraid. Baby, I'm beggin' you. Stay home! Just one time! Talk to me. I don't know you 'cause we don't talk no more. Only yell. (*Baby turns away from him*) Please . . . don't turn your back.

BABY: What d'you want outa me?

MR. GIOIA (*Loud*): Talk nice to me!

BABY: Leave me alone!

Mr. Gioia comes over to him and turns him around.

MR. GIOIA (*Low*): Your momma's in the back. She's afraid to come out because we yell. You take a look at her sometime. Skin's like paper, wrinkled. Feet hurt. Hair's change color. Used to be shiny black. She's stand up at the counter all day long, work to buy you a gangster jacket.

He rips it out of Baby's hand and looks at it.

BABY: Gimme that.

Mr. Gioia looks at him, tears the jacket suddenly and flings it to the floor. Baby looks at him, frightened and annoyed.

MR. GIOIA (*Shouting*): Hornets! Stand on the street corner and talk dirty when a girl walks by. Fight! Steal! Yell! Hate! Against everything! No respect! Just tough! What good's tough? I'm not tough. I'm a quiet man. All my life. And I got a lot. I got a store. 'Sfor you. I make it for you. (*Suddenly tender*) Look . . . you're my son. Used to be a fat little baby, all the time laugh. I like to kiss you, make you giggle. You growin' up all wrong.

BABY: Pop . . .

MR. GIOIA: No. It's all wrong. I don't know how to talk to you. You don't understand. I'm your father. I kiss you! Let me kiss you!

He puts his arms around Baby. Baby turns around. Mr. Gioia, tears in his eyes, speaks to Baby's back.

MR. GIOIA: You not listen. Baby, I'm tell you to be good. You the only baby we got. I can't hit you no more. I'm begging you. Be a good boy. Please . . .

Baby is stirred by these lines and his voice trembles.

BABY: Papa . . . let me grow up.

He breaks away and runs to the door. Ben stands aside. Baby exits. Mr. Gioia turns his back on Ben and wipes his eyes. Ben stands there helplessly. Then Mr. Gioia turns around and tries to smile.

MR. GIOIA (*With an effort*): You wanta malted?

BEN: No, thanks.

Mr. Gioia turns suddenly and goes through the curtain into the back of the store. Ben looks after him for a moment and then goes out of the store.

Cut to the street. He stands in the front of the alley and looks up and down the street. Several people walk by. Suddenly Ben cups his hand to his mouth.

BEN (*Calling*): Angelo! Angelo! (*The passers-by look at him curiously*) Angelo!

He looks up and down but doesn't see Baby.

Cut to the back of the alley. There, in the darkness, seated on the ground and leaning against a wall, is Baby. He looks at Ben, hears him calling and doesn't respond. Ben finally walks away. Baby sits in the alley and he suffers as he thinks of the argument with his father. He would like to go back, perhaps, and put his arms around his father, but there is a murder to commit and this is Baby's private rebellion against a father who has always refused to think of him as anything but a baby. He sits in the alley and he stares at the wall, and he wonders what is to become of him. Fade out to indicate a lapse of time.

Fade in on the alley. Baby still sits there, but now he hears footsteps entering the alley and he stands up. It is Frankie and Lou.

LOU (*Hissing*): Baby.

BABY (*Whispering*): Here.

> *They walk to the back of the alley, Lou in the lead. He sees Baby, grabs him by the shoulders. All of the conversation in this scene is held in whispers.*

LOU (*Excited*): Baby—we're doin' it tonight.

BABY: I know.

LOU: No kidding around! Tonight!

FRANKIE: Shut up, Lou!

> *They turn to look at him. His face is fierce.*

FRANKIE: Sit down!

> *They sit down, arranging themselves against the wall. They cannot be seen from the street.*

FRANKIE: Now listen to me and get this into your skulls. Here's the plan.

LOU: Take it slow, Frankie.

FRANKIE: Okay. He's out bowling. It's ten o'clock now. He won't get home till about two. Here's how it goes. When we finish talkin' here, we each go straight home. By twelve o'clock we're in the sack. We lie in bed like we're asleep until one-thirty on the nose. At one-thirty we get up, and we stuff pillows into the beds to make 'em look like we're still in 'em, and we go out. Now get this straight. Nobody can see you go out. If somebody sees you, go home and forget it. We'll try it again another time. If nobody sees you, come straight to the alley. Got it?

> *They nod.*

FRANKIE: We meet right here by twenty to two at the latest. If one of us don't show up, the other two'll go home and we'll know that somebody saw that one guy. If all three of us get here, we're safe. Then we wait here for Mr. McAllister. When he walks by, if there's anyone else on the street, we let him go. If not, (*Pointing at Baby*) you go out after him. You're gonna be cryin', and you're gonna tell him your father's out and your mother's sick and you need help. You're gonna lead him by the alley real close. Then (*Pointing at Lou*) you're gonna grab him after he goes by that wall, one arm around the throat so he can't yell, and one arm around the chest. You're gonna swing him around into the alley and . . . I'm gonna give it to him.

LOU (*Breathlessly*): With what?

FRANKIE: With this. (*He pulls a switch-knife out of his pocket and flicks it open*) Nobody's gonna hear a sound. We're gonna leave him here and go home, and crawl into our sacks without being seen. We'd better! Ya hear me? Anybody wants to know where we were when Mr. McAllister got it, we were home in our beds dreamin' up a storm. Our families'll guarantee it.

LOU: Crazy!

FRANKIE: Any questions?

> *There is no answer. Baby and Lou stare at Frankie. Lou is trembling with excitement. Baby is numb. Frankie looks at his watch.*

FRANKIE: It's seven minutes after ten. Set your watches.

> *They do so and then Frankie stands up. They follow suit.*

FRANKIE: Okay. We're going home.

> *He turns to Baby and lifts Baby's face up to his. He looks into Baby's eyes.*

FRANKIE: You okay?

> *Baby nods, frightened.*

FRANKIE: You're gonna be a man tonight.

> *They start to walk out of the alley. The streets are empty as they reach the edge of the alley. Frankie steps into the street first and then suddenly jumps back.*

FRANKIE (*Hissing*): Look at this!

> *They watch the street and from the direction of the candy store comes a drunk, weaving and giggling to*

himself. He moves past the alley and stops at the stoop of Frankie's house, leaning against it, close to falling down. Frankie gathers Baby and Lou around him. He looks at them for a moment.

FRANKIE: We're gonna try it on for size. Get over here. (He flattens them against the wall) He's stoned. He won't know what's happening.

LOU (Frightened): You're not gonna knife him!

FRANKIE (To Baby): Get him. (Baby looks at Frankie) I said get him.

Baby slides out of the alley and walks slowly toward the drunk. The drunk hums to himself. Baby reaches him. The drunk throws out his arms to Baby.

DRUNK: Sonny boy! (Singing) Climb upon my knee, sonny boy. . . .

BABY (Hesitantly): Come here a minute, willya?

He takes the drunk by the arm. The drunk follows, grinning and singing.

DRUNK (Singing): You are only three hunnert and thirty-three, sonny boy . . . Where we going?

BABY: Over here.

DRUNK (Singing): You've no stinkin' way of knowing . . .

And swiftly, as the drunk passes the alley, Lou's arms are around him, from behind, throttling him, pinning his arms to his sides. He goggles in fear. Swiftly in the dark, Lou swings the drunk's body around to Frankie, presents his belly to Frankie's waiting knife.

Frankie draws back his arm, plunges it forward. Baby gasps. Frankie stops an inch short of the drunk's belly. They hold their positions in absolute silence. The drunk's eyes are wide with horror. Lou holds him immobile. Frankie looks him over. Baby stares, terrified.

FRANKIE: Let him go.

Lou lets the drunk go. Frankie grabs him, spins him

around and shoves him out of the alley into the street.

FRANKIE: Beat it!

The drunk, weaving, terrified, turns to look at them. They stand in the shadows. Then, slowly, the drunk begins to giggle. And he turns and staggers crazily down the street. Frankie smiles and then suddenly the smile freezes on his lips. There at the edge of the alley, stepping out of a shadow, is Richie, carrying two newspapers. Eyes wide with fear, he walks over to Frankie, stands in front of him. The knife is still in Frankie's hand.

RICHIE (Whispering): Frankie . . . what're you doing? You were gonna kill him. You were gonna ki—

And Frankie, dropping the knife, reaches out for Richie, grasps him by the shoulders and snaps him roughly to him. He grabs Richie's face and looks into it, and when he speaks it is with an awful, controlled viciousness.

FRANKIE: What you saw . . . if you ever tell it, I'll cut you up and throw away the pieces.

Richie closes his eyes. Frankie shakes him violently.

FRANKIE: Open your eyes.

Richie does so. He hangs limply in Frankie's grasp.

FRANKIE: I'll kill you, Richie. Believe what I say. I'll kill you!

RICHIE (Whispering): Frankie . . .

FRANKIE: D'ya hear me?

RICHIE (Sobbing): I hear.

Frankie shoves him away violently. Richie falls. Frankie and the others watch as he gets up, looks at them with the tears streaming down his face and then, sobbing, turns and runs home. Baby and Lou look at Frankie.

BABY (Softly): Frank . . .

FRANKIE (Hard): What?

He turns and looks at Baby, who has been shaken by

the rehearsal and the scene with Richie. Baby silently
shakes his head. Frankie looks at him for a long moment and he can see Baby mutely pleading to be released from his part in the murder.

FRANKIE: One-thirty.

Baby turns and leaves. Frankie looks at Lou. Lou tries
to grin, but his lips are trembling.

LOU: One-thirty, Frankie.

Frankie watches him as he leaves, and now again
Frankie is alone in the alley. He looks around it for the
last time, then walks out of it and toward his house.
He goes past the front entrance, and as he starts to turn
around the far side of the house, we see Ben walking
toward the alley from the direction of the candy store.
He has not seen any of this. But he stops as he reaches
the alley, seeing Frankie round the corner of the house,
and then he looks into the alley, puzzled, wondering
what is going on.

Fade out.

───────── *ACT III* ─────────

Fade in on the fire escape, a moment later. Frankie
climbs up onto it from the street and stands there in
the darkness for a moment. Then he bends down and
looks into the window. His mother stands in the middle of the room, holding Richie tightly to her, com-
forting him. Richie still cries. Frankie throws open the
window and leaps into the room. As soon as the window opens, we hear Mrs. Dane's voice.

MRS. DANE (*Softly*): . . . No, it's all right, sweetie, it's all
over. No. Don't cry, baby. Don't cry. Tell me what it is.

Frankie is in the room and he knows now that Richie

has not told. He stands watching his mother and she,
speaking to Richie, stares back at Frankie as she talks.

MRS. DANE: It's all right. It's all right, baby. I'm holding you.
Don't cry. There. (*Slowly Richie stops sobbing*) There.
That's better. What is it? Tell me, sweetie.

Richie looks up at her. Frankie watches.

RICHIE: Nothing.

MRS. DANE: You don't cry for nothing. What happened?

RICHIE: I fell.

She looks at Frankie and steps away from Richie.

MRS. DANE (*To Frankie*): What did you do to him? (*Frankie looks at her silently*) I said, what did you do to your brother?
(*Frankie doesn't answer*) Look at him!

RICHIE (*Pleading*): Mom, he didn't do anything.

She advances on Frankie slowly.

MRS. DANE: Look at him. I could feel his heart pounding
against me. What did you do to him? Answer me!

FRANKIE: Lower your voice!

MRS. DANE (*Shouting*): Lower my voice! Do you know who
I am? I'm your mother! You've got to respect me.

FRANKIE (*Roaring*): Shut up!

She raises her hand to strike him across the face. His
eyes go wide and she swings at him. Violently, he
catches her hand and holds it. For a moment he loses
all control at the thought of being struck. He holds
her arm and twists her close to him, and his rage is
fierce to see.

RICHIE: Frankie!

FRANKIE (*Trembling*): Don't touch me!

She stares at him. He lets her arm go.

FRANKIE (*Shouting*): Don't ever touch me!

She steps back. He stares at her, trembling.

MRS. DANE (*Whispering*): I'm your mother. (*She looks at him*
for a moment) God help me, when I say it, the word feels

dirty in my mouth. Don't touch me, Mother. Well, listen to me! I touched you once. I gave birth to you. That's touching you! You're part of my body and every time I think of it I want to wash. You're garbage, Frankie Dane! (*Shouting*) I give you up!

> *She stands firm, looking at him strongly. He turns away, shocked. Then slowly he walks toward the window and climbs out. He stands on the fire escape for a moment and then he closes the window. Mrs. Dane turns her back on him. Richie goes to her and looks up at her.*

RICHIE: Mom . . .

> *Her arms go around him and she rocks back and forth.*

MRS. DANE: What did he do to you, baby? What did he do?

> *And Richie, his face a mask of fear, lets her hug him. They stand together this way, soundlessly. Cut to fire escape. Frankie—whipped, numbed—stands there looking out over the city. A few drops of rain begin to fall. He doesn't notice them at first and then, finally, he does, and he sits down on the fire escape, huddled in a corner, as the rain beats down a bit harder. For a few moments he sits there, then we hear footsteps coming up the ladder and Ben climbs onto the fire escape. He stands there and looks down at Frankie, and Frankie is too numb to react. Ben sits down near him.*

FRANKIE: What do you want?

BEN: I want to talk.

FRANKIE: We talked.

BEN: You talked. I listened. I'm asking for the same deal.

FRANKIE: Get lost.

> *Ben gets up.*

BEN: It's your fire escape.

> *He stands, looking at Frankie huddled against the railing. He turns to go. Frankie looks up at him.*

FRANKIE: Wait. (*Ben turns*) What do you get out of it? Do you get kicks?

BEN: I told you. I get paid.

FRANKIE: Time and a half?

BEN: No.

FRANKIE: So what're ya knockin' yourself out for? It's afta six.

BEN (*Softly*): I think you're worth it.

> Frankie sits up fast.

FRANKIE (*Hard*): You're full of ——

BEN (*Interrupting*): I wouldn't lie to you, Frankie. You wanta hear it?

> Frankie looks at the window. Mrs. Dane walks over to it and pulls down the shade, looking right through Frankie.

FRANKIE (*Slowly*): All right. Go ahead. It don't make no difference. They're only words. Whatever anyone says . . . they're only words.

BEN: Okay, I'm gonna lay you bare, Frankie Dane, so brace yourself. It goes like this. You're eight years old and your father walks out of the house one day without kissing you good-by and you never see him again. Then all of a sudden, there's another kid. Richie. And you haven't got a mother any more. You're big enough to take care of yourself, she tells you, and she sits there nursing the baby, in front of you, and you run out of the house, and you cry for the last time in your life. You're eight years old and you've lived a century. And then you learn a very sad thing. The only time anybody pays attention to you is when they're lumping you on the head. You gotta have attention. Everybody does. So you get it by being the toughest, wildest, angriest kid on the block. If you can't be loved, be hated. Be feared. At least they know you're there. That's how you figure it. Plenty of kids up here are like that. If they're good, they're neglected. If they're bad, they're noticed. So they run the streets fighting and busting things. It's like they're yelling, "Hey, look at me, I'm somebody too!" Some of them get hurt. But most of them grow up. You didn't. You look like you're eighteen, but you're still only eight. And you're still hating and being hated. It's the only way you know who you are. You think you're a big man, but you're not. You're just a little kid yelling, "Pay attention to me, everybody. I'm the worst thing that ever happened. (*Ben moves to touch Frankie's arm and Frankie shrinks from him*) Look, I'm so bad I'm untouchable!" But you can't admit you're just being bad to be noticed. So you call it something else. You call it getting even. Getting even for having to live in the filth of a slum. And that's what makes me sick to my stomach about you. The way you beat your breast and scream about how rotten everything is. Sure it's rotten, but who says you're the only one who knows it? There are thousands more just like you right here under your nose, butting their heads against these walls like goats trying to make it better! And you know what? You could lead them, because you're a leader, one of those rare ones, Frankie, but that would be too hard. That would be creating something new instead of crying about what's busted. That would be growing up.

Ben looks at Frankie for a long moment. Frankie stares off into the night.

BEN: Frankie, you make me want to weep. You're eighteen years old and you're preparing yourself to die. Sooner or later it'll happen. Maybe tonight, maybe next week. You'll kill and you'll be killed. That's the only way it can end, and it's such a waste! Nobody'll even turn around to look at you. I'm sorry for you, Frankie, and pity is the worst thing I can give you, I guess, because it means I like you.

Frankie looks at him in an agony of pain.

BEN: You want attention? Let somebody love you, Frankie— or you're nothin'.

Then he gets up and climbs down the fire escape.
Frankie sits there on the fire escape for a long while.
Then, as if in a dream, he gets up, opens the window
and climbs in. The room is dark. There are two studio
beds against opposite walls. Richie is in one bed asleep.
Mrs. Dane is in another room. Frankie sits down on
the other bed in the dark and drops his head into his
hands. Then finally he gets up, pulls the covers down,
takes off his shoes and, looking to see if Richie is asleep,
gets into the bed with his clothes on. He lies there on
his back, staring at the ceiling. Finally he looks at his
watch. It is five after eleven. He stares at the ceiling.
And now we cut to a head shot of Lou, in his bed, staring at the wall. And we cut to a head shot of Baby, in
his bed, staring at his trembling hands. And we cut
back to Frankie, whose eyes never blink in the darkness. Through all of this we hear the ticking of a clock—
loud, insistent, frightening. Suddenly the ticking becomes louder and louder, and it speeds up, and Frankie
still stares at the ceiling. Then he looks at his watch
again. It is one-thirty. Slowly now, soundlessly, he gets
out of bed. He puts on his shoes. Then he stuffs the
bed with pillows and pulls the covers over it. It looks
as if he is sleeping there. He starts slowly for the door
now and the floor squeaks horribly. He freezes, looks at
Richie. Richie, eyes closed, doesn't move. Frankie
moves to the door, opens it and slides out. We see him
in the hall for a moment, flattened against the door.
Then he slithers away.
Cut back to Frankie's room. Richie is sitting up in bed,
staring at the door.
Cut to street as Frankie comes out of the house. He
looks carefully up and down the street. It is empty.
Then he scoots for the alley, reaches it and flattens him-

self against the wall. He waits in the darkness, alone.
Finally there is a scuttling of footsteps and Lou plunges
into the alley breathlessly. He stands next to Frankie
and they wait in silence for Baby. The wait is long, but
at last they hear footsteps, and Baby runs into the
alley and stands next to the wall with Frankie and Lou.
And they wait, almost unable to bear the suspense.
There is a silence, broken only by the sound of their
breathing. Baby's lip trembles. The sweat pours down
Lou's forehead. Frankie grinds his teeth and his face is
a mask of hatred. They wait. A car goes by with a roar
that makes Baby jump. Frankie clutches his arm. There
is silence again. They wait. And finally, very faintly,
they hear slow footsteps. Agonized, they listen. The
footsteps come closer and closer and then, suddenly, as
the three of them turn their heads to the street, Mr.
McAllister comes into view, walking slowly, carrying
the bowling ball, obviously tired. He smiles to himself
as he passes the alley and then he is gone. Baby looks
at Frankie—he is close to tears and his lips frame the
word "please"—and Frankie shoves him violently out
into the street. Terrified, he looks up and down. The
only person in sight is Mr. McAllister, trudging wearily
toward the stoop. Baby looks pleadingly at Frankie in
the alley and Frankie, with a violent gesture, urges him
on. He looks at Mr. McAllister, then finally he runs
toward him and there are tears on his face.

BABY (Calling): Mr. McAllister! Mr. McAllister!

Mr. McAllister turns to look at him. Baby reaches him.
Mr. McAllister is startled. Baby grabs his arm.

BABY (Breathlessly, between sobs): You gotta help me! My
mother's sick! In the store! Please, Mr. McAllister . . .
please . . .

He pulls at Mr. McAllister's arm and Mr. McAllister

follows him, ready to help. Baby trots, holding Mr. McAllister's arm, and he leads him close to the lip of the alley. They reach the alley, Baby in the lead. Baby runs ahead and suddenly Lou takes one step out of the alley and his arm encircles Mr. McAllister's neck. His other arm pins Mr. McAllister's arms to his sides and he scoops him into the alley. Mr. McAllister struggles soundlessly, but Lou holds him firm. He swings him around to Frankie now. Frankie stands with the knife ready, pointed at Mr. McAllister's belly. And Frankie stares. Baby gasps. Mr. McAllister goggles. Lou grunts fiercely.

LOU (Hissing): Go, Frankie, go!

And Frankie draws his arm back to stab. Suddenly there is a blur of sound and a small form hurls itself into the alley. Richie. He flings himself at Frankie, and strikes Frankie in the face with all his force. The sound is shocking in the stillness. Frankie stares at Richie. Richie stands there, pitifully small, white with fear. The knife glitters in Frankie's hand as Frankie, with a rage more violent than he had displayed toward Mr. McAllister, suddenly turns on Richie. He seizes him fiercely. Richie stares up into his face. Baby flattens himself against the wall. Lou holds the struggling Mr. McAllister.

LOU: Frankie! Frankie! Now!

And Frankie, clutching Richie by the shoulders, staring with hatred into Richie's face, his knife cold against Richie's neck, speaks in a low voice.

FRANKIE: Get out of here.

No one moves.

FRANKIE (Louder): Get out of here.

No one moves.

FRANKIE (Shouting): Get out of here!

Baby moves away from the wall and scoots out of the

alley. Lou slowly lets Mr. McAllister go. Mr. Mc-
Allister begins to sag to the ground, then catches himself. Lou turns him around and propels him out of the
alley. He staggers down the street. Then Lou, taking a
last frightened look at Frankie, walks out of the alley.
Through all of this, Frankie has stared into Richie's
face, his features working violently. Richie looks up at
him and waits to die. Frankie stares into the white,
frightened, tear-stained face, and his grip tightens and
he draws Richie closer. The knife glitters at Richie's
throat.

RICHIE (Whispering): Frankie . . .

Frankie's features contort and his anger seems to spray
about the alley.

RICHIE (Softly): You're my brother.

Frankie stares and suddenly a shudder passes through
his body. He looks at Richie and suddenly the anger,
the hatred, the violence are gone from him. His arms
go around Richie, and Richie's go around him, and they
stand this way for a long time. Then Frankie gently
kisses Richie on the brow and looks into his eyes for a
moment. And when he speaks, his voice is soft.

FRANKIE: Go home, Richie.

And Richie turns and walks out of the alley. Frankie
turns his back on the street and stands alone, and as
Richie moves slowly into the street we see Ben standing there, watching Frankie. We do not know how
much of this episode he has seen. Frankie stands in the
alley, the knife in his hand, his whole body sagging.
Then, suddenly, with one last burst of rage and hostility
and frustration, he turns to the wall and stabs at it
ferociously with the knife. The blade snaps off and
tumbles to the ground. He drops the handle and, head
down now, walks to the street. At the lip of the alley

he stops. Ben stands there watching him. He and Ben look at each other for a long moment and then Ben smiles.

BEN (Low): Let's get some coffee, boy.

And then he walks over to Frankie and lightly puts his arm around Frankie's shoulders. Frankie tenses and begins to shake the arm off, but Ben, firm and strong, tightens his grip, pulling Frankie to him hard. And they walk that way, Ben's arm strong around Frankie's shoulders, down the empty street, and the broken knife glitters in the alley. Fade out.

AUTHOR'S COMMENTARY ON

Crime in the Streets

Crime in the Streets *was turned down by the sponsors or advertising agencies of three major network shows for precisely the same reason. It dealt sympathetically with juvenile delinquency at a time when juvenile delinquents were considered to be eminently unpopular. This kind of predetermination of what an audience's reaction to "controversial" material might be is obviously infuriating to an author. But how infuriating it might be to a public, which is sometimes denied controversial entertainment without being aware of it, is almost impossible to measure.*

What runs through the agency mind, when it is faced with the prospect of doing a controversial show, is sometimes difficult to understand. I assume it is felt that antagonizing even a small minority of the audience would relate immediately to the sale of the sponsor's product, diminishing same to the point where it hurts. This kind of reasoning is pretty maddening and leads me to believe that agency men have no faith in either the product they try to sell or the advertising they have created for it. The function of a television show, it seems to me, is simply to garner as many viewers as possible and stimulate them to the point at which they will tune in the following week and forever after, to be alternately entertained by the show and at the same time subtly induced to try the sponsor's product. This is all well and good and is a system with which I happen to be in agreement. But I also happen to take issue with a point of view popular on Madison Avenue which, I believe, distorts the function of the entertainment portion of the show. That function is simply to keep viewers at their sets spellbound, or a reasonable facsimile thereof, so that they will be available to see and hear the advertising pitch. The distorted point of view holds that the entertainment itself should also be geared to create a favorable selling atmosphere for the product. This is where the problem spreads out to areas which include sponsors' responsibilities to the public and is where, I feel, so many agencies and sponsors fall down. In trying to create what they consider orthodox and inoffensive entertainment, they are creating pap and managing to offend a good many potential customers who, it is true, do not write angry letters but merely turn off their television sets.

Perhaps I may pose this twister to the agencies. Take, for instance, two plays. One is "controversial" enough to stir up an audience into taking sides quite passionately. The other is a good "family" show which entertains pleasantly for an hour, bothers no one and then slides away into history, leaving a sort of rosy indifference. What has the sponsor got going for his product with each of these?

With the "family" show he may have as many as twenty million people peacefully watching, and then vaguely remembering, a free hour of entertainment for a day or so, and just as vaguely interested in what they'll be seeing at the same time next week. With the "controversial" show he may have ten million people violently agreeing with a point of view and ten million violently opposing it. But at least all twenty million have been stimulated to think about the show, to talk about it, to be interested in it. Of course it would be just as unfair to assume that those agreeing with the point of view of the show will be favorably inclined toward the sponsor's product as it would be to assume that those opposed will boycott the product, but in raising a controversy it seems to me that the sponsor may very well raise the pitch of interest in his television show for a long while to come.

The entire point is this: Simply because a particular show is "controversial"—and agencies have some pretty unusual ideas about what is and what is not controversial—it does not necessarily follow that sales of the sponsor's product will drop. They may very well increase.

This is not an argument in favor of "controversial" shows in general or of Crime in the Streets in particular. It is simply an argument against an alarmingly prevalent attitude which seems to have arisen out of a somewhat exaggerated fear of what relatively puny minorities can do to the sales of giant corporations. I sometimes wonder why people who are in a creative field—and the ad-agency business must be classified as creative—will tend to steer clear of anything that hints of the unorthodox, when the business which gives them sustenance has made its most giant strides using the unorthodox.

As for Crime in the Streets, I couldn't for the life of me see what was controversial about it to begin with, and still don't. It concerns an enormously serious problem whose implications are growing more serious day by day, and whose impact upon our social structure will be fully felt only when the ever-expanding numbers of delinquent children begin to reach adulthood and take their places in society. This is not to imply that the play solved anything or even offered any solution, but I felt that it might present a large block of viewers with at least an insight into some of the motivations behind this strange, self-destructive, antisocial drive. Since juvenile delinquency seems to be a segment of our culture about which all thinking people should be vitally concerned, I think it only reasonable that a mass medium such as television should be obligated now and again at least to expose viewers to a treatment of this problem. The claim was made by one network that Crime in the Streets was too violent a show for the public to swallow. This is strange to hear, when we can see every day that the networks are not afraid to dose the public with violence and murder as long as there is no reference to "controversial" social problems. Therefore, it must follow that what they were afraid of was the social problem presented here—a problem which can thrive and grow outside their doors, but somehow cannot make its way into their studios.

To talk for a moment about Crime in the Streets, it might be interesting to note here that the original title of it was The Alley. This was changed to the present title by "The Elgin Hour," the show which finally bought the script, on the grounds that The Alley was not an exciting enough title and would not be inclined to titillate an action-hungry viewer into tuning in. Go figure these fellows!

The story itself employed a technique that I believe is eminently adaptable to the time limitations of television. Crime in the Streets is actually the ending of a story rather than a whole story. Events which are an integral part of the story are only referred to briefly in dialogue and have taken place before the story actually begins. Events such as the arrest of Lenny, the reasons behind his display of a gun in public, the slapping of Frankie Dane by Mr. McAllister—all of these are part of this story but could not be shown, since they would leave no room for the more important events.

The opening scene on the fire escape, which set the mood and action of the play, will appear in the motion-picture version of Crime in the Streets approximately one third of the way into the picture. About thirty minutes of story will precede the fire-escape scene and the events which inexorably lead to the introduction of the murder plan by Frankie will be shown in entirety. Thus when Frankie says, "We're gonna kill him," the audience will know why and will also know what kind of person Frankie is and why he needs to kill.

The television performance of Crime in the Streets, I think, was notable for two reasons. First, Sidney Lumet's direction was absolutely electric and lent a relentless drive to the script which never let up for a moment. Second, there were some really remarkable performances given, notably those of John

Cassavetes and Mark Rydell as Frankie Dane and Lou Mack-lin. These two roles came alive beyond my most hopeful ex-pectations, but I didn't really realize how authentic and grip-ping both portrayals were until a month later when I attended a kinescope showing of Crime in the Streets at a New York settlement house.

There were a good many requests for kinescopes of this show by settlement houses and organizations whose job it is to deal with juvenile delinquents. It was the hope of social workers at these places that they could stimulate group discussions among members of neighborhood gangs if they showed them the kine-scope. I watched a showing given in a dilapidated building for a group of fourteen-, fifteen- and sixteen-year-old boys, and I listened to a small part of the discussion which followed. During the kinescope, I watched the reactions of these boys to characters and events with which they are all too familiar, and, incredibly, I saw them—each and every one—become Frankie Dane and Lou Macklin. Their faces mirrored the emo-tions these two characters displayed and they seemed actually to be living these roles. During the highly emotional scenes be-tween Frankie and his mother, and Baby Gioia and his father, the boys made pointless jokes and began violent horseplay in the room. Later, their social worker told me that this reaction came about because they identified so strongly with the char-acters that they were unable to face scenes which reminded them of the sometimes agonizing problems in their own homes.

Particularly shocking to me, however, was the following. During the scene in which the boys rehearse the murder, using a drunk as the victim, one boy in the audience stood up, stretched, exclaimed in a bored voice, "Christ, who can sit through this crap!" and walked out of the room, snickering. Feeling slightly wounded, I questioned the social worker about him after the meeting and was told that this boy, just sixteen, had returned home the previous week from a four-year term in a reform school. He had been sent there when he was twelve years old for participating in a murder! The murder scene was so terribly painful to him that he had to leave the room and he covered his retreat, as so many problem children do, with a pungent remark and a swagger.

On the way home that night I found myself wondering about Crime in the Streets. I had tried my best to make it real, and a few moments before had found that I was successful, yet the reality of it had given a great deal of pain to at least one person and possibly more. This kind of thing gives one pause to think now and again of the incredible power of the written word and the responsibility that befalls the man who decides to write.

The Incredible World of Horace Ford

—— JUNE 13, 1955 ——

PRODUCER	Felix Jackson
DIRECTOR	Franklin Schaffner
SET DESIGNER	Willard Levitas
ASSOCIATE PRODUCER	William Markham Altman
STORY EDITOR	Florence Britton
ASSOCIATE DIRECTOR	Joseph Dackow
PROGRAM ASSISTANT	Bette Stein

CAST

HORACE MAXWELL FORD
    Art Carney
LAURA FORD
    Leora Dana
MRS. FORD
    Jane Seymour
LEONARD O'BRIEN
    Jason Robards
MR. JUDSON
    House Jameson
OLD MAN
    Joseph Leberman
YOUNG MAN
    Tom Troupe
GIRL
    Carolyn King

CHILD
    Bruce Marshall
FIRST KID
    Billy Harris
SECOND KID
    Tommy White
THIRD KID
    Joey Fallon
HERMY BRANDT
    Kenneth Sharpe
OFFICE BOY
    Buzzy Martin
BETTY O'BRIEN
    Bettye Ackerman
YOUNG HORACE FORD
    Raymond Duke

WOMAN
Lucie Lancaster

ACT I

Fade in on the office of Horace Maxwell Ford. It is late afternoon of a fine spring day. The office is quite small and cramped, and one of a long row of similar offices occupied by minor executives of the Educational Toy Company of New York, Inc. The office contains a small desk and a drafting table. On the desk are a number of mechanical toys and a small nameplate reading "Horace Maxwell Ford." A series of blueprints lies scattered about on the drafting table. More toys sit on a row of shelves on one wall of the office. Seated at the desk, daydreaming, is Horace. He is approaching thirty-five and growing paunchy. Horace is a bulky man with an elusive, almost boyish quality. His clothes never seem to fit. His shirt blouses out of his trousers. His socks are always down around his ankles. And his thinning hair cannot stay combed at all. He is a mild man, an apologetic man, except when he is discussing his beloved childhood memories. Then he seems to find a strange vitality, which somehow doesn't fit him. Horace is the kind of man who would naturally become the butt of endless jokes, would the jokers not feel instinctively sorry for him without quite knowing why. Were they wise enough, they would understand that the tragic quality of Horace Ford is based in the fact that he is not an inadequate man but really an inadequate grown-up boy. He sits at his desk, staring at the wall, and a tiny mechanical mouse buzzes around his desk, unnoticed by him. Then the door of his office opens, and Leonard O'Brien enters. He occupies the office next to Horace and has been Horace's friend for many years. If anyone understands Horace, and this is doubtful, Leonard comes closest. He is perhaps thirty-five years old and has, like Horace, been employed by the Educational Toy Co. for about twelve years. Leonard is mature, dependable, well adjusted. He looks at Horace for a moment. Horace doesn't seem to notice him.

LEONARD: Listen, Horace . . .

Horace suddenly lunges for his desk drawer, rips it open, pulls out a cap pistol and fires it five or six times at Leonard. Leonard stands there looking at him almost pityingly.

LEONARD: Look, Horace, why'd you do that?

HORACE: Do what?

LEONARD: You know, with the cap pistol.

HORACE (Smiling): Scared the pants off you, right?

LEONARD: Come on, Horace. Listen, you do it almost every day.

HORACE: I get a kick out of it. I love cap pistols. They have a great smell. (*He holds it toward Leonard*) Smell it.

LEONARD: I know what it smells like.

HORACE: Boy, when I was a kid I always had a cap pistol. Listen, d'ya remember Ken Maynard in the movies? Everybody on the block was Tom Mix, except me. I was Ken Maynard. Me and my horse Tarzan. (*Laughs*)

LEONARD (*Annoyed*): I want to talk to you about the design for that new robot toy. There's something out of whack . . .

HORACE: Tarzan! Boy, we used to run out of the theater and shoot up the whole neighborhood.

And he acts out the parts of two kids while sitting at his desk.

HORACE (*First kid*): Pow! Gotcha right in the heart! (*Second kid*) You're coo-coo! You missed me a mile! Bam! Bam! (*Dropping his pose*) Aren't kids the greatest?

LEONARD: Horace . . .

HORACE: What's the matter?

LEONARD: Do you know how loud you were yelling? (*Horace shrugs*) I'll bet you could hear it all the way down to Mr. Judson's office.

HORACE: How much? I'll betcha my ball of silver paper. Hey, Leonard, remember that? Remember when you used to collect tin foil from old cigarette packs and roll it into a great big ball? I had one that must've weighed five pounds. Boy!

He smiles.

LEONARD: Horace, look I came in here to talk to you about the new robot toy. I've been in the office next to you for twelve years. I know all about how you used to collect tin foil. Now, will you listen to me for a second?

HORACE: You must have had a miserable time when you were a kid.

LEONARD: Right. I couldn't wait till I grew up.

HORACE (*Subdued*): What do you want, Leonard?

Leonard takes a blueprint off the drafting table and

spreads *it in front of* Horace.

LEONARD: There's something wrong with this.

HORACE: There is not. I designed that toy. There's nothing wrong with it. The kids'll go crazy about it. Do you know what it does?

LEONARD: I know what it does. Look, Horace, I'm trying to help you.

HORACE: I mean a toy, where the eyes light up and it talks and everything . . .

LEONARD: Listen, I'm just a designer here like you.

HORACE: It's a good toy.

LEONARD: It is a good toy. But it can't be turned out at the price Mr. Judson wants. Look here. (*Pointing at plan*) When he sees it, he's gonna blow his stack. (*Horace looks it over*) It's got too many parts. Believe me.

HORACE: You think it's wrong?

LEONARD: I know it is.

Horace, *suddenly depressed, turns away from the blueprint and stares out the window.*

LEONARD: Horace, all you have to do is work it over.

HORACE (*Low*): How's Betty?

LEONARD: What?

HORACE: Betty.

LEONARD: What has Betty got to do with—

HORACE: Thanks a lot. I'll look it over.

Leonard *looks at* Horace's *back.* Horace *doesn't turn.* Leonard *exits.* Horace *stares out the window. Then, swiftly, he moves to the drafting table and takes a sheet of paper from it. He makes several hurried folds and suddenly he has a paper airplane in his hands. He looks at it. Then he walks over to the window and sails it out. He leans way out after it and begins to smile. Cut to* Leonard's *office, which is right next door and exactly the same as* Horace's. *He looks out the window, rumi-*

nating, and then he sees the plane. He follows it down
with his eyes and there is deep concern in his face. We
hear a knock on the door.

LEONARD: Come in.

The door opens and Horace's wife, Laura Ford, enters.
She is about thirty-two years old and pretty in a brittle
sort of way. She is quite a bit more aggressive than
Horace, and although she genuinely loves him, she re-
sents the fact that he is not more successful than he is.
She pushes him gently, knowing all the while that he is
not capable of going much higher. Laura carries a large,
gift-wrapped package and has a conspiratorial air about
her.

LEONARD (*Pleased*): Laura!

She puts her finger to her lips.

LEONARD (*Whispering*): What's the matter?

LAURA (*Smiling*): I don't want Horace to see this. (*Pointing
at package*) It's his birthday present.

Leonard closes the door.

LEONARD: Well, how are you?

LAURA: Exhausted. Shopping kills me.

He takes the package from her and shakes it as she sits
down.

LEONARD: What'd you get him?

LAURA: A smoking jacket.

LEONARD (*Grinning*): Well, that proves he's going to be thirty-
five. Betty and I got him one of those sets with a tie bar and
cuff links and everything. We got him a yo-yo, too. To
give him first as a gag.

LAURA: That'll probably be his favorite present.

Leonard laughs. Laura takes off her shoe and rubs her
foot.

LAURA: I must be the only woman in the city of New York
who hates shopping.

Leonard laughs.

LEONARD: Listen, the surprise party's all set for Friday night, isn't it?

LAURA (*Rubbing foot*): All set.

LEONARD: What's the plan?

LAURA: Well, everybody's meeting at your house at seven-thirty and you're all coming over to our place together at eight. Horace thinks the two of us are going to a movie after dinner. I'll make him answer the door when you ring. Sing "Happy Birthday" or something.

LEONARD: He'll go right through the floor.

LAURA: Probably. (*She puts on her shoe*) Len, would you take that home with you? I don't want Horace to see it around the house.

LEONARD: Check. I'll bring it along Friday night.

LAURA: Thanks. (*She gets up and looks at her watch*) Is he busy?

LEONARD: Pretty.

LAURA: Well, I'm taking him home. It's almost six, anyway. See you Friday.

LEONARD: So long, honey.

She opens the door, just as we hear the door of Horace's office open. A sharp voice sounds out. Laura and Leonard listen.

MR. JUDSON (*Off*): Horace!

HORACE (*Off, as if surprised*): Oh, Mr. Judson . . . I . . .

MR. JUDSON (*Nettled*): What are you doing at the window?

HORACE (*Nervously*): Nothing. Well, I mean, just thinking.

MR. JUDSON: Thinking! What about?

HORACE (*Confused*): I don't know. Business.

Laura looks at Leonard. During Mr. Judson's next line she closes the door of Leonard's office and she and Leonard stand there. Mr. Judson's voice is much fainter, but still discernible.

MR. JUDSON: Whose business? You don't seem to have done very much thinking about ours. Take a look at this.

> *Cut to Horace's office. Mr. Judson, a pleasant-looking man in his mid-fifties, stands at Horace's desk holding a blueprint. Horace stands rather helplessly, looking at him. Mr. Judson is not a menace, not raging mad, but he is annoyed. He does not shout, but his low, even voice carries a great deal of strength.*

MR. JUDSON: Well, look at it.

HORACE: I know what it is.

MR. JUDSON: Well, what happened?

HORACE: I don't know, Mr. Judson.

MR. JUDSON: Do you know how much we could lose if we ever put this toy into production the way it is?

HORACE: It's a good toy.

MR. JUDSON: Very good. But that has nothing to do with it. Look, Horace, you've been here for a long while. It's about time you learned that we're in business to make a profit. This robot toy is too complicated. It's got too many parts and I want it simplified.

HORACE (*Sullenly*): What do you want to simplify?

> *He turns away as a child might turn away from a teacher who has scolded him.*

MR. JUDSON: The eyes don't have to light up.

HORACE (*Turning*) (*Passionately*): Sure they have to light up! You want to ruin the whole thing? The eyes lighting up— that's the beauty part. It's a terrific thing. You could play the greatest games with a toy like that.

> *Mr. Judson looks at him peculiarly throughout this.*

MR. JUDSON (*Quietly*): What's the matter, Horace?

HORACE (*Loud*): Nothing! You're talking about—

MR. JUDSON (*Quietly*): Look, Horace, I don't want to argue about it. Just do the design over. I need it pretty quickly.

> *Cut to Leonard's office. Laura and Leonard listen.*

HORACE: Listen, don't you remember when you used to play soldiers? This robot thing—

> *We hear a door slam and footsteps go down the hall. Laura looks at Leonard with a pained expression. Then she moves toward the door.*

LAURA: Good night, Len.

> *She opens the door.*

LEONARD: Laura . . .

> *But she goes out. Cut to Horace's office. He stands over his desk. Then suddenly he picks up the blueprint, crumples it up and flings it out of the window. The door opens and Laura enters. She tries to behave as though she has not heard the argument with Mr. Judson.*

LAURA (*Smiling*): Is this the office of Horace Maxwell Ford?

> *He looks up at her.*

HORACE: Hello, Laura.

> *She goes to him and kisses him heartily.*

LAURA: Well, aren't you a little surprised that I'm here?

HORACE: Yes, I am. What time is it?

> *Horace takes out a large, ornate gold pocket watch and looks at it during Laura's next lines.*

LAURA: Almost six. Horace, I've never been so exhausted in all my life. I've been shopping all afternoon. (*He looks at her*) Well, how about taking me home?

> *He puts the watch back after winding it.*

HORACE: Okay.

> *He puts on his jacket and gets his hat. Laura watches him carefully.*

LAURA: I'm just going to fall into bed tonight. Literally fall into bed.

HORACE (*Putting on hat*): I have some homework to do.

LAURA: Oh, not again. What is it?

> *He puts out the light and they exit.*

HORACE (*Closing door*): The robot toy. I'm telling you, that nutty Mr. Judson's trying to ruin it. That toy has no meaning unless the eyes light up. . . .

> *Cut to the living room of their apartment. The apartment is in a low-rental project in New York City and is furnished inexpensively. The Fords have bought some new pieces, but there is some furniture there which obviously belonged to Horace's mother and is many years old. The room is overly neat, but not without warmth. Mrs. Ford, Horace's mother, a woman in her late fifties, is setting a table for dinner at one end of living room. She hums a tune as she lays out the dishes. Mrs. Ford is a very plain, simple woman, not overly bright, and she plays an unimportant part in the Ford household. She is content merely to be comfortable after a long and difficult life spent running a fruit store with her late husband. Horace supports her now and this is enough to make her happy, this and the fact that she has risen above the lower East Side neighborhood where the Fords lived when Horace was a boy. She looks up pleased as the door opens and Horace and Laura enter.*

MRS. FORD (*Singing out*): Hello, children.

> *She continues to set the table as Horace comes over to her and gives her an automatic kiss.*

MRS. FORD: How's my boy?

HORACE (*Dully*): Fine.

MRS. FORD: That's good. Are you hungry?

HORACE: A little.

> *Laura walks into kitchen.*

MRS. FORD: Dinner's almost ready. (*Calling*) Listen, Laura, there's something wrong with the chicken. It's like leather. (*To Horace*) These birds they give you nowadays . . . like people don't know what chickens are any more.

Laura comes in from kitchen.

LAURA: It looks all right to me.

Horace sits down on the couch. Laura begins to help with the table.

MRS. FORD: Well, how was the office today?

HORACE (*Dully*): It was okay.

His mother finds something disturbing in his voice.

MRS. FORD (*Looking up*): What's the matter?

HORACE: Nothing's the matter.

MRS. FORD: No, I can tell. Just from your voice. What is it?

LAURA: Nothing. Everything's fine. Let's eat dinner.

HORACE (*Softly*): I'm telling you, that Mr. Judson is just plain nuts. (*He thinks for a moment*) He reminds me of Corey. (*A bit louder*) Hey, Mom, remember Mr. Corey? (*He chuckles*) Corey! I had him in Five-B. What a character! (*Imitating Corey in a precise nasal tone*) You take the least com-mon de-nom-in-a-tor, the *least* common denominator, and you multi-ply . . .

He laughs, suddenly alive again. Now he talks animatedly, roaming about the room.

HORACE: You know what we used to call him? Guess. (*A pause*) I wouldn't even tell you. Boy, I'll never forget the time he caught me with one of those candy balls in my mouth—you know, the kind that change colors while you suck them.

He laughs.

LAURA: Horace . . .

HORACE (*Wound up now*): So he made me stand up and every minute he'd point that pointer at me and say, "Mr. Ford, what color is it?" And I'd have to take it out of my mouth and tell him. I swear I thought Hermy Brandt would bust trying not to laugh. (*He laughs*) Hey, Mom, remember Hermy? Laura, this Hermy was the greatest kid. He absolutely killed me. One time he wrote on Corey's blackboard—

real big, you know—"Mr. Corey has cooties," and just as he finished old Corey walked in. (*Horace laughs almost hysterically. Laura is disturbed*) Cooties! Listen, Laura, do you remember cooties? So what'd Corey do? He wouldn't let him be window-pole monitor any more. (*He bursts out laughing again*) What a dumb punishment!

LAURA: Horace!

HORACE (*Reverently*): Hermy Brandt! The greatest stickball player in the whole world. Listen, one time during a fire drill—

LAURA: Let's have dinner.

> She sits down at the table. Mrs. Ford goes into the kitchen. Horace walks over to the table.

HORACE (*Softly*): What great times. I was ten. What great, great times.

LAURA: Horace, why don't you stop it? Nobody cares about when you were ten any more.

HORACE (*Sitting down*): I care.

LAURA: You're almost thirty-five.

HORACE (*Annoyed*): So what?

LAURA (*Pouring water*): You don't act thirty-five sometimes.

HORACE (*Louder*): So what?

LAURA: That's what I mean. So what. What kind of an answer is So what?

HORACE (*Standing*): Listen, Laura . . .

> Mrs. Ford enters from the kitchen, carrying a roast chicken on a platter.

MRS. FORD: I'm telling you, it's dry. No matter how much I basted it, it's still dry. That's a pretty annoying thing.

LAURA (*To Horace*): Why do you have to keep talking about when you were a kid. I mean all the time. People get tired of it.

HORACE (*Exploding*): Oh, be quiet for once, will you!

MRS. FORD: Horace . . .

> *Horace gets up angrily and stalks off into the bedroom.
> Mrs. Ford looks at Laura and sets the chicken down on
> the table. She turns toward the bedroom.*

LAURA: Let him go.

> *But Mrs. Ford goes into the bedroom. Horace is lying
> on the bed, looking up at the ceiling.*

MRS. FORD: Horace. (*No answer*) Horace, the chicken'll get
cold. (*No answer*) Come on, eat a little. (*No answer*) Listen, Laura's probably tired from shopping. She didn't mean
to yell. (*No answer*) I'll cut you a leg and a second joint.
Your favorites.

> *He lies there staring at the ceiling.*

HORACE: You remember Hermy Brandt?

MRS. FORD: No.

HORACE: Listen, how come you never remember anything
about Randolph Street? We lived there eleven years. I was
born there. Why don't you ever talk about it? The swell
times and all.

MRS. FORD: Swell times. There were no swell times.

HORACE (*Sitting up*): Sure there were! Mom, you don't know
what you're talking about.

MRS. FORD: That was a terrible street. I want to forget it.
Horace, we're in a good neighborhood now. In a nice house.
Why do you have to—

HORACE: What was terrible? Listen, I had the best times there.
Like, remember when Pop used to give me an Indian burn?

MRS. FORD: Why do you always talk, remember when you
were a kid? Why don't you have kids of your own? Talk
about them.

HORACE: I don't make enough money to have kids of my own.

MRS. FORD: You make a lot more than your father used to make
on Randolph Street.

> *Horace gets up.*

HORACE: Randolph Street. Do you know what I'm gonna do? I'm going back there. Right now.

MRS. FORD (*Upset*): Horace, have supper.

HORACE: I haven't been there since I was eleven. I don't know why. Why shouldn't I?

> *He strides out of the room. Laura sits alone, eating dinner. Mrs. Ford follows Horace. He gets his hat.*

MRS. FORD: Horace, it's a dirty old street. What are you going to see? Stay home.

LAURA: Where's he going?

HORACE: So long.

MRS. FORD: Horace, listen . . . (*He goes out, closing the door*) Why does he want to remember the dirt?

LAURA (*Getting up*): Where's he going?

MRS. FORD: Randolph Street.

LAURA: What for?

MRS. FORD: I don't know.

LAURA: All right. Maybe it's good for him. Let him get it out of his system. Come on, eat. He'll be back. He's got homework.

> *Fade out on them. Fade in on Randolph Street. It is a slum street—dirty, old, decrepit, lined with old brownstones, littered with refuse, teeming with life. People sit on the stoops, people walk the streets, kids play under the street lights. After a moment we see Horace round the corner and stop. He stares down the street, surveying it, smiling with excitement, almost trembling in his eagerness to revive old memories. He does not notice that the styles of the people's clothes are slightly out of date. The boys we see, for instance, wear knickers. Horace stands for a moment and then, smiling, wanting to drink it all in, he walks slowly down the street. He passes a frankfurter cart. An old man thrusts a frankfurter at him.*

OLD MAN: Frank on a roll, three cents.

> *He walks by the cart. A young man and a girl, lovers, arm in arm, walk toward him and split as they go by him. He walks between them.*

YOUNG MAN: Bread and butter.

GIRL: Bread and butter.

> *A big man walks by him, bumping Horace's shoulder.*

BIG MAN: Watch where you're goin', huh?

> *Horace smiles all the more and walks on. A ball rolls toward him and he picks it up and throws it at someone off camera. We hear a woman shriek from a window.*

WOMAN: Davy, you come home or you're gonna get smacked!

> *An elderly lady walks by him, drops a package and nods when he picks it up for her. We hear a child's voice shouting.*

CHILD: Ringolevio! Caught, caught, caught!

> *He takes out his gold pocket watch and, still smiling, looks at the time. And suddenly a group of four boys come racing down a stoop right in front of him.*

FIRST KID: Fins! Listen, I yelled fins, didn't I? Waddyewant?

> *They are all between the ages of ten and twelve. They run by Horace, knocking into him, spinning him around. He drops his watch and stares after them, amazed, shocked, terrified. One of them—a small, dark, intense-looking boy—stares at Horace for a moment. Then they run up the block and Horace watches them. Then he hears a shout.*

FIRST KID (*To dark, intense kid*): Hey, wait up, Hermy! Hey, Hermy Brandt! Hermy Brandt! Wait up!

> *And Horace turns, terrified, and runs off in the direction from whence he came. He disappears around the corner, leaving his watch on the sidewalk. Fade out. Fade in on his living room. Laura sits on the couch, reading. Mrs. Ford has gone to bed. Laura looks up as*

the door opens, determined to give Horace hell for running out. Horace enters and on his face there is still fear. Laura stands, looks at him.

LAURA: Well, it's nice of you to come back.

HORACE: Laura . . .

LAURA: Where were you? Why didn't you tell me you were going?

HORACE (*Scared*): Listen, Laura . . . I was down on Randolph Street.

LAURA: What's the matter?

HORACE: I don't know. Laura, I want to tell you something.

LAURA: Take off your hat.

HORACE (*Doing so*): I am. Listen, I saw some kids on the block. Little kids, maybe ten or eleven years old. Laura, they were the kids I played with when I was ten . . . the same kids.

LAURA: You're perspiring.

HORACE: I'm not. You're not listening to me.

LAURA: I heard you. I think you're catching cold or something. Wipe off your face. They couldn't have been the same kids, dear. That's nonsense.

HORACE: They were. . . . I saw them.

She begins to wipe him off with his handkerchief.

LAURA: Maybe they looked like some kids you used to know.

HORACE: I'm telling you . . .

LAURA (*Sharply*): Horace, you're talking like a child!

He looks at her, and then turns and walks into the bedroom. She watches him, disturbed. Then she starts toward his door. We hear the doorbell ring. She turns and opens the door. Hermy Brandt stands there, dark and quiet. He speaks softly.

HERMY: He dropped this.

He hands her Horace's gold watch. She takes it, wonderingly, and Hermy swiftly walks down the hall and

out of sight. Laura looks at the watch and then at the
closed bedroom door, and her face is puzzled. Fade out.

———————— **ACT II** ————————

Fade in on Horace's office, the following day. He stands
at his drafting board, bending over a design he is working on, but he does not put pencil to paper. He stares
at the design and then slams his pencil down.

HORACE (*Softly*): Ringolevio! Caught, caught, caught!

The door opens on his line and a teen-age office boy
enters with a mail basket.

OFFICE BOY: What'd you say, Mr. Ford?

HORACE: Ringolevio. What d'you think I said. You never
heard that?

OFFICE BOY: No, sir.

HORACE (*Fast*): Did you ever play saloogie?

OFFICE BOY: No, Mr. Ford.

HORACE (*Angry*): Make a little hole in the old man's back?

OFFICE BOY (*Backing out*): No, sir.

HORACE (*Fast*): One two three four five six seven eight nine
ten red light!

The office boy closes the door fast.

HORACE (*To closed door*): Where were you ever brought up?
He turns away angrily and pulls out his watch. He
looks at it for a long time. The phone rings. He picks
it up.

HORACE: Mr. Ford speaking. (*Pause*) It's not finished yet.
(*Pause*) Well, I don't know when it'll be ready. (*Pause*)
I can't help it if Mr. Judson wants to know. (*Pause*) No.
(*Pause*) Listen, you can't turn these things out like dough-
nuts. (*The door opens and Leonard enters*) (*Pause*) You
tell him I am rushing it. (*Pause*) Well, what does he think

I am? (*Pause*) Then let him do it! (*Pause*) Sure you can tell him that! (*He slams the phone down and looks up at Leonard*) What does he want out of me?

LEONARD: Judson? (*Horace nods*) They want to get that toy into production in time for Christmas.

HORACE: He's got six months. What's he nagging me for?

LEONARD (*Sitting down*): Take it easy, Horace. Look, he's a pretty nice guy. But he's in business. You've got to remember that. It's nothing personal. (*Horace turns away and looks out the window*) How ya doin' on it?

HORACE: Now don't you start on me.

LEONARD (*Gently*): What's wrong, Horace?

> *Horace stands with his back to Leonard for a moment, wondering whether to accept Leonard's offer to hear his troubles. Then he turns.*

HORACE: I don't know. Listen, I'm very nervous.

> *Leonard waits. Horace sits down at his desk and picks up a gyroscope top which he toys with and spins throughout the following lines.*

HORACE: I saw a kid last night. Listen, were you ever on Randolph Street? No. You never were. Well, that doesn't make any difference. Randolph is my old street when I was a kid. He wore knickers. This kid I saw. Remember when you wore knickers? With the buckles and all. They were all the time slipping down. Kids never wear knickers any more. I'm telling you. Never. So he wore these knickers—you're not going to believe this, but I swear to God it's true. I was walking on the street and all of a sudden I heard a kid yell "Ringolevio." That's a game we used to play. Ringolevio. You know how it could make you feel, hearing that? I was a very good Ringolevio player. You have to be fast and you need a lot of stamina. Boy, the running you have to do. Look, first we used to choose up sides. (*He begins to smile*) One potato, two potato, three potato, four.

Remember that? Then one side has to hide. So once I was hiding behind the grocery, in the back where they keep like the cartons and all . . .

LEONARD: Horace . . .

HORACE: . . . And I fell asleep. Is that ridiculous? (*He laughs*) So when I woke up I took one look at my Mickey Mouse watch and I . . . Mickey Mouse watch? My God, I haven't thought of that in twenty years. (*Excited*) Listen, remember when you had a Mickey Mouse watch? What a deal that was! (*He stops*) Oh, I was telling you about last night. (*Seriously*) Look, this is a very serious thing. I was on Randolph Street last night for the first time in twenty-four years. . . .

LEONARD: Horace, look, I've got some work on my desk. I just dropped in to say hello.

HORACE: Well, I only wanted to tell you . . .

LEONARD: I'll see you later.

> Horace spins the gyroscope. Leonard looks at him peculiarly and then exits. Horace watches the top spin. Then he takes the designs from the drafting table and scribbles on them for a moment. The door opens and Mr. Judson enters. He stands watching Horace scribble, not able to see what he is drawing.

MR. JUDSON: Horace. (*Horace turns*) I want to ask you something. What was the point of shouting at my secretary over the telephone.

HORACE (*Too loud*): Well, she was shouting at me!

MR. JUDSON: I was sitting in the same room with her. She spoke in a normal voice.

> Horace bends over the drafting board again. Mr. Judson looks at him for a moment.

MR. JUDSON (*Softly*): Aren't you happy with your work here?

HORACE (*Low*): Yes.

MR. JUDSON: Look, Horace, you're a fine designer. You have

value to this company, and for our good as well as yours I don't want to see it dissipated. You've been behaving . . . badly. Is there something wrong . . . maybe at home?

Horace shoots Mr. Judson a suddenly angry look.

HORACE: I'm trying to get this thing done here.

MR. JUDSON (*Hardening*): And I'm not speaking just to hear the sound of my voice!

They look at each other for a moment and then Horace stalks out of the office. Mr. Judson watches him go and then, after a moment, walks over to the drafting board. On it is a sheet of paper—Horace's design. And drawn boldly on it is a cross-eyed face such as a child might draw as a prank in school. But instead of being labeled "Teacher," this one is labeled "Mr. Judson." Mr. Judson looks at it for a moment and then puts it down and exits. Fade out.

Fade in on Horace's living room, same evening. Horace's mother is setting the table again and Laura is sitting at the table eating a stalk of celery.

MRS. FORD: How did he look this morning when he left?

LAURA: All right. A little nervous.

MRS. FORD: I couldn't get up. I don't know, lately all I want to do is sleep.

She busies herself with the table for a moment. Then she turns to Laura.

MRS. FORD: Answer me something. Why does he have to go back to Randolph Street?

LAURA: Do I know?

MRS. FORD: I never want to see that place again if I live to be a hundred. It's all tenements. The day we got out of it I thanked God on my knees. Why does he want to go there?

LAURA: He's always talking about when he was a kid. I guess he just wanted to see it again. He won't go back.

Mrs. Ford busies herself at table.

MRS. FORD: I think he's getting a virus.

LAURA: Maybe.

MRS. FORD: Otherwise, why should he act so peculiar? I hear sometimes a virus can affect the brain.

Laura gets up, gives Mrs. Ford a despairing look and goes over to the couch. She flops on it. Mrs. Ford watches her.

MRS. FORD: All right, you're so smart, why should he act funny?

LAURA (*Annoyed*): How do I know? He saw some kids and he thought they looked like kids he used to know. So he got upset.

MRS. FORD: What about that boy who was here?

LAURA: Well, he didn't do anything. He just returned Horace's watch. He said he dropped it. What's so special about that?

MRS. FORD: Nothing. (*She eats a piece of celery*) I don't know why he looks so pasty lately. He should get some color in his cheeks.

LAURA: Oh, for heaven's sakes, color in his cheeks! He's going to be thirty-five tomorrow!

The door opens and Horace enters slowly. He looks tired.

LAURA (*Singing out*): Hello.

Horace closes the door and goes over to Laura, who still sits on the couch. He bends over and kisses her lightly.

HORACE: Sorry I'm late. The subway was tied up for about twenty minutes.

MRS. FORD: Somebody jumped?

HORACE (*Annoyed*): Nobody jumped. (*Mrs. Ford shows disappointment*) Why do you have to think of that right out?

MRS. FORD: It happens. If you read the papers . . .

HORACE: Something broke down.

Mrs. Ford comes over and kisses him.

MRS. FORD: You can't kiss your mother hello any more?

He takes off his hat and coat as Mrs. Ford goes into the kitchen.

LAURA: Tired?

HORACE: Yeah.

LAURA: How was the office?

HORACE: The same.

LAURA: Did you finish the design?

HORACE: No.

LAURA: Why not?

HORACE: I don't know. I'll finish it tomorrow.

LAURA: Well, do you have to work tonight?

HORACE: No.

LAURA: Good! Listen, there's a swell double bill at the Regent. Two British pictures . . .

HORACE: I'm going back there tonight.

LAURA: Where?

HORACE: Randolph Street.

LAURA: What for?

HORACE: I feel like it.

LAURA (Concerned): Listen, when you came home last night you were scared to death. What are you trying to do to yourself?

HORACE: I want to see those kids.

LAURA: Why?

HORACE: Because I want to.

LAURA: You say it like it's something big. Like it's important in your life. Since when did you—

HORACE (Angrily): It is important!

The kitchen door opens and Mrs. Ford enters, carrying a platter of meat.

MRS. FORD: Hot veal!

She puts it on the table and goes back into the kitchen. Laura and Horace silently take their seats. The kitchen

door opens again and Mrs. Ford enters, carrying a bowl
of vegetables and a bowl of mashed potatoes.

MRS. FORD: Succotash. (*She begins to sit down*) It's canned,
but you can hardly tell it from fresh. (*To Horace*) Help
yourself to meat, Horace. If it's stringy, blame it on the
subway. (*She ladles out potatoes*) You sure nobody jumped?

LAURA (*Exasperated*): Mother!

HORACE: What's so great about disasters?

MRS. FORD: What?

HORACE: You know, I remember you from the block. Every
time there was an accident or something you were right in
front, watching.

MRS. FORD: Horace!

HORACE: Well, it's true. What about the time Harvey Bender
got his arm caught in the fire hydrant and we all figured
they were gonna have to bust it to get it out? You never
moved out of the front row.

MRS. FORD: Harvey Bender? Who's Harvey Bender? What are
you talking about?

HORACE (*Softening*): If that wasn't the dopiest thing.

MRS. FORD (To Laura): What's he talking about?

HORACE: The hottest day of the summer he picks to clog up
the hydrant. (*To Mrs. Ford*) What do you mean you don't
remember Harvey? (*To Laura*) We were playing immies,
you know, on the manhole cover, and I'm cleaning up. I
remember it like it was this morning. I've got this big, fat
purey (*He pretends to shoot a marble on the table*) and
I'm belting them out, cleaning up, when all of a sudden
this nut says let's turn on the hydrant. (*He laughs, happy
for the first time since he's been home*) I swear, he was the
gooniest kid . . . his favorite thing was shake . . . spear,
sock in the ear . . . (*He demonstrates*)

Laura, who has slowly been reaching a boiling point,
slams down her napkin.

LAURA (*Sharply*): Horace, stop it!

HORACE (*Fast*): What's the matter with you?

LAURA: Just stop it!

HORACE: He was one of the kids last night.

LAURA (*Loud*): Who was one of the kids?

HORACE: Harvey Bender.

LAURA (*Standing*): What are you talking about?

HORACE: I saw him last night.

LAURA (*Slowly*): Don't you know that's impossible?

HORACE: I know what I see.

LAURA: He was ten years old when you were ten years old. He's as old as you are.

HORACE: I saw him.

LAURA: He's a grown-up man!

HORACE: You think so? I'm telling you I saw him last night on Randolph Street. And I saw George Langbart and Sy Wright. They're still kids.

MRS. FORD: Horace! What are you saying? (*To Laura*) Feel him. He's got a fever. I can tell.

HORACE (*Standing up*): I have not got a fever!

LAURA: Mother, be quiet! (*To Horace, quietly*) Horace, sit down.

> *He looks at her for a minute, then sits down.*

MRS. FORD (*Softly*): Feel his head.

HORACE: Let me alone!

MRS. FORD: What?

LAURA (*Sharply*): Mother! (*To Horace*) Listen, darling . . . I'd like to talk to you quietly for a minute. I don't know what's happening at your office, but I've been seeing the way you come home. You're tired. I mean, overwork can some- times . . . I'd like you to see a doctor.

HORACE (*Standing*): What for?

LAURA: Just to let him check you.

HORACE: You think I'm imagining this thing with the kids.

LAURA: No, I don't.

HORACE: Yes, you do!

LAURA: Listen, Horace . . . (*But he turns quickly and moves toward the door*) Where are you going?

He takes his hat on the way and opens the door. Laura follows.

LAURA: Horace! Please . . .

But he is gone. Laura and Mrs. Ford look helplessly at each other as we fade out. Fade in on Randolph Street. It looks exactly the same as it had the night before, down to the last detail. The people on the street are doing exactly what they had been doing at fade-in in the first act. And this entire scene will now be duplicated move for move, exactly as it happened in Act I. The only thing different about it will be Horace's attitude. He will recognize the duplication quickly and be stunned by it, but powerless to change it. He turns the corner now, and stands for a moment looking down the street, smiling. Then he begins to walk slowly down the street. He passes a frankfurter cart. An old man thrusts a frankfurter at him.

OLD MAN: Frank on a roll, three cents.

He walks by the cart. A young man and a girl, lovers, arm in arm, walk toward him and split as they go by him. He walks between them.

YOUNG MAN: Bread and butter.

GIRL: Bread and butter.

A big man walks by him, bumping Horace's shoulder.

BIG MAN: Watch where you're goin', huh?

Horace walks on. A ball rolls toward him and he picks it up and throws it at someone off camera. We hear a woman shriek from a window.

WOMAN: Davy, you come home or you're gonna get smacked.

An elderly lady walks by him, drops a package and nods

when he picks it up for her. We hear a child's voice shouting.

CHILD: Ringolevio! Caught, caught, caught!

He takes out his gold pocket watch and looks at the time. And suddenly the group of four boys come racing down a stoop right in front of him.

FIRST KID: Fins! Listen, I yelled fins, didn't I? Waddyewant?

They run by Horace, knocking into him, spinning him around. He drops his watch and stares after them, amazed, shocked, terrified. The small, dark, intense-looking boy stares at Horace for a moment. Then they run up the block and Horace watches them.

FIRST KID (*To dark kid*): Hey, wait up, Hermy! Hey, Hermy Brandt! Hermy Brandt, wait up!

And now, instead of turning and running off, Horace finds himself following the kids. They stop in front of a fruit store. He stops, panting, watching them.

HERMY: Let's swipe some apples.

FIRST KID: Hey, Nitsy!

HERMY: We each grab one.

SECOND KID (*Very fast*): Larry.

THIRD KID (*Instantly*): Nexta Larry.

SECOND KID (*Instantly*): Nexta nexta Larry.

They all look at Hermy. Boldly, he walks over to the fruit stand, takes an apple and whips it into his jacket. Then in order, the first kid, the third kid and the second kid each takes an apple. As the second kid takes one, the four of them dash off down the block again, bouncing off Horace. He turns, frightened and confused. He goes after them.

HORACE (*Calling*): Wait.

They run into a tiny alley. Horace follows them to the alley and stands just outside of it as they bite into their apples.

HERMY: Boy!

FIRST KID (*Grimacing*): Sour, huh?

> *They all chew the apples silently for a moment.*

SECOND KID: Hey, can y'imagine not being invited to the birthday party? Can y'imagine?

HERMY (*Chewing*): Yeah, and I'm s'posed to be his best friend.

THIRD KID: He stinks.

FIRST KID: We oughta mobilize him, right, Hermy?

> *Horace stares in silent horror at what he hears.*

SECOND KID: Boy! and how!

> *Horace turns suddenly and begins to run down the block. The kids have not noticed him at all. They chew on their apples. Fade out. Fade in on Horace's living room. Laura is waiting up for him. Mrs. Ford has gone to bed. Laura lights a cigarette, a feat she performs awkwardly. She puffs on it for a moment, coughs, puffs on it again. She stands as she hears a key in the door. The door opens and Horace enters. He looks frightened. He pants heavily. Laura goes to him, startled.*

LAURA: Horace. (*He doesn't answer her*) Horace. (*Still no answer*) Horace, are you all right? (*He looks at her blankly*) Why don't you say something?

HORACE (*Slowly*): The same thing happened all over again.

LAURA: Sit down over here.

> *She leads him to the couch. He sits down.*

LAURA: I'm glad you're home. I was worried. I mean, the way you walked out of here . . .

HORACE: Nothing changed. Same man wanted me to buy a hot dog . . . Those people said bread and butter . . . This big guy bunked into me. . . .

LAURA: What are you talking about?

HORACE: I'm telling you, nothing changed, Laura. It's some kind of a pattern and I'm in it. The kids . . . I mean, they swiped some apples, and they ran into an alley, and I heard them talking and I almost died. I'm in it! I remember being in it from twenty-five years ago, but I don't remember how. . . .

LAURA: Oh, God, Horace, stop! Listen, I'm going to call a doctor.

HORACE (*Standing*): You're not! I don't need a doctor. I'm not sick. I saw this!

LAURA (*Standing*): Please. You have to listen to me. You've got to have some help with this thing, Horace.

HORACE: Let me alone!

He walks away from her and into the bedroom. While he is walking, Laura speaks.

LAURA: You could get into bed for a few days. Stay home from the office. You don't have to go in.

The door slams. She looks at the door for a moment and then she sits down in front of the telephone. She stares at the phone. The doorbell rings. She jumps. Then she gets up and opens the door. Hermy Brandt stands there quietly.

HERMY (*Softly*): He dropped this.

He hands her Horace's gold watch. She takes it and Hermy swiftly walks down the hall. Laura looks at the watch.

LAURA: Wait!

But Hermy is gone. She turns toward the bedroom, clutching the watch. Fade out.

───────── **ACT III** ─────────

Fade in on Horace's office the following day. The room is empty and quite disorderly. The door opens and Laura enters. She looks distraught. She looks around

*the room briefly, then closes the door. She begins to
look through the papers on the drafting table. The
door opens and she turns, almost guiltily.*

LEONARD: Horace? (*Leonard enters now, sees Laura and
smiles*) Laura. I didn't know you were here. Where's
Horace?

LAURA: I don't know. I just this second walked in.

LEONARD: Aren't you supposed to be home baking a birthday
cake, or something? (*He walks over to her and kisses her on
the cheek*) Don't tell me it's gonna be store-bought. A
woman with your talents?

LAURA: Listen, before he comes back, I have to tell you something. I don't know how he got into the office this morning.
I begged him to stay home. Leonard, I've got to get him to
a doctor.

LEONARD (*Concerned*): What do you mean?

LAURA: Something's happening to him. It's this thing with
kids. It's like it's eating him alive.

LEONARD: Now look, Laura, he's had that ever since I've
known him. I mean, I can always snap him out of it.

LAURA: Not now. Listen, he's been going back to his old street.

LEONARD: He started to tell me.

LAURA: He comes home in a cold sweat. I've never seen him
like this. He tells me he sees kids that he grew up with . . .
and they're still kids. I don't know what to say to him, Len.
He's got to have help. (*Near tears*) Look, I'm not saying
I'm the best wife in the world, or anything, but I try. I try
hard. I make a home for his mother and that's not easy.
Listen, I love Horace. Sometimes I don't know what to say
to him, but I love him. I don't know what to do.

LEONARD: Do you want me to talk to him?

LAURA: If you could get him to go to a doctor . . . I'm afraid.
I'm afraid about his job, and how he is, and everything.
Leonard, if you . . .

LEONARD: I will. I'll talk to him. (*He looks at his watch*) Look, it's after four now and tonight's his surprise party. Why don't I hold off till tomorrow. I mean, I hate to get him all upset just before the party.

LAURA: He's so upset now.

LEONARD: Well, let's not make it any worse.

Laura turns away for a moment.

LAURA (*Suddenly near tears*): He's seeing things that aren't so . . . and we're standing here talking about him so calmly. He's my husband. . . .

LEONARD: Laura. (*She tries not to cry*) I think he's just . . . overtired, maybe. Look! I don't think he ought to see you here.

LAURA: No. Len, will you help me get him to a doctor tomorrow?

LEONARD: I'll talk to him. (*Laura nods and goes to the door*) See you at eight sharp.

She nods again and exits. Leonard looks around the office for a moment. He picks up a few papers from the drafting table and looks through them. Then he starts out of the office. As he gets to the door, Horace opens it from the outside, almost hitting Leonard with it.

LEONARD (*Smiling*): Boing! Just like a Laurel and Hardy movie. Hiya, Horace.

Horace enters the office.

LEONARD: Where were you?

Horace, who carries a face towel, puts it into his desk drawer.

LEONARD: Oh.

Leonard lights a cigarette and sits on Horace's desk as Horace sits down.

LEONARD: I just finished the designs for that kangaroo toy. Mr. Hop-Hop, they're gonna call it. I came in here to kill some time. (*Laughs*) I wonder who thought of that name, Mr. Hop-Hop.

HORACE: I did.

LEONARD: No kidding! When?

HORACE: Last week.

LEONARD: It's a real good name. Catchy.

HORACE: Do you remember this thing? Step on a crack and you break your mother's back. There's another part to it. I been trying to remember it all day and I can't.

LEONARD: I never heard it. (*There is silence for a moment*) Y'know, you started to tell me a story yesterday about your old block and you never did finish it, Horace.

HORACE: Step on a crack . . .

LEONARD: What happened the other night?

HORACE: I don't want to tell you. You'll give me a blank look and you'll tell me I'm crazy or something.

LEONARD: What are you talking about?

HORACE: I don't want to tell you.

> *The door opens and Mr. Judson enters. Leonard gets off the desk quickly.*

MR. JUDSON: Hello, Leonard. I'd like to talk to Horace alone for a minute, if you don't mind.

> *Leonard looks at Horace.*

LEONARD: Uh, Mr. Judson, I was just gonna ask you to go over that Mr. Hop-Hop toy with me.

MR. JUDSON: In a little while. I'll see you in your office.

LEONARD: The designs are all finished.

MR. JUDSON (*Firmly*): In a little while, Leonard.

> *Leonard looks at Horace helplessly and exits. Horace sits stolidly at his desk. Mr. Judson looks at him for a moment.*

MR. JUDSON: How are you, Horace?

HORACE (*Sullenly*): Okay.

MR. JUDSON: You look a little tired.

HORACE: I'm not tired.

> Mr. Judson looks at Horace for a moment. Horace turns away.

MR. JUDSON: I thought maybe you'd have the robot toy designs finished by now. I'd like to see them.

HORACE: I haven't got them.

MR. JUDSON: Why not?

HORACE: Well, I don't know, I just haven't gotten to them.

MR. JUDSON: Oh? Well, what have you been doing?

HORACE: What have I been doing? Well, listen, I've been . . . What d'you mean, what have I been doing?

MR. JUDSON (*Softly*): Well, Horace, you haven't been very helpful here for quite a while. . . .

HORACE (*Angry*): Helpful! I don't see how you can—

MR. JUDSON (*Interrupting*): That toy has to get into production. Maybe you ought to start on something else and let Leonard finish up the—

HORACE (*Loud*): Listen, that's my design! Nobody else is touching it.

MR. JUDSON (*Mildly*): I still run this firm, Horace.

HORACE (*Loud*): Well, you're not gonna start taking my stuff—

MR. JUDSON (*Sharply*): Lower your voice! (*Horace shuts up*) Horace, I'm trying to be decent to you because I think something's wrong. I think maybe you're sick.

HORACE (*Low*): Whatever you say for me goes double for you!

> Mr. Judson looks at him and shakes his head.

MR. JUDSON: I'm going to suggest something to you and I want you to listen. I'd like you to take a leave of absence. And I want you to see a psychiatrist. Horace, I think you're approaching a nervous breakdown.

HORACE (*Loud*): I am not approaching a nervous breakdown! Who do you think you are to tell me that?

MR. JUDSON: I'm trying to help you.

HORACE (*Angry*): There's nothing wrong with me!

MR. JUDSON: Maybe. But if there is, it's nothing to be ashamed of, Horace. I want you to take a leave of absence to find out.

HORACE (*Loud*): I'm not taking any leave of absence.

MR. JUDSON (*Quietly*): Then I'm afraid, with the way things are, that you can't work here any more.

HORACE: All right, then I can't work here any more!

MR. JUDSON: I'm sorry, Horace. I wish you'd think about it. You can change your mind at any time.

HORACE: Would you please get out of here? (*He turns away from Mr. Judson.*) Would you please?

> Mr. Judson gives him a pitying look and exits. Horace stares at the door for a long moment. Then he sits down at his desk, suddenly terrified. Fade out. Fade in on his living room. Mrs. Ford carries a large birthday cake out from the kitchen. The cake is lettered "Happy Birthday Horace." Laura is on the telephone.

LAURA: No, three quarts. One chocolate, one vanilla and one butter pecan.

MRS. FORD: Laura . . .

LAURA (*Shushing her*): All right, chocolate chip. (*Pause*) Five forty-three Dayton Street. Apartment One-D. One-D as in David. Right. Ten o'clock tonight. Thank you.

> She hangs up.

MRS. FORD: Laura, do you think I bought enough potato chips?

> Laura nods. Mrs. Ford carries cake over to Laura.

MRS. FORD: Where can I put this so Horace won't see it?

LAURA (*Nervously*): I don't know. Maybe in the bedroom somewhere. (*Annoyed and worried*) Where is he?

MRS. FORD: What time is it?

LAURA: Twenty to eight. I'm getting worried about him. He should have been home an hour ago.

MRS. FORD: He probably got stuck in the office.

LAURA: I'm going to call there.

She goes to phone.

MRS. FORD (*Walking to bedroom with cake*): The lettering is all uneven. "Birthday" is like all squeezed in. You'd think for four and a half dollars you could get good lettering.

She goes into bedroom and closes door just as front door opens and Horace enters. Laura stands up and looks at him, putting phone down.

LAURA (*Hesitantly*): Hello. (*He enters*) How come you're so late?

HORACE: I didn't know what time it is.

LAURA: It's twenty to eight.

Mrs. Ford enters living room, giving Laura a secret, conspiratorial look. She has hidden the cake.

MRS. FORD: Hello, dear . . .

HORACE: I'm fired.

LAURA: You're what?

HORACE: I'm fired.

MRS. FORD: What are you talking about?

LAURA: Mother . . .

HORACE: I went and had a hamburger in a drugstore. That's why I'm late.

MRS. FORD (*Goes to Horace*): You're fired from your job?

LAURA: Mother, will you for heaven's sakes? . . .

MRS. FORD (*To Horace*): Horace, I'm asking you something.

LAURA (*To Mrs. Ford*): Will you stop?

MRS. FORD: What are you yelling at me for? I want to know from Horace. (*To Horace*) You're trying to be funny.

HORACE: No.

LAURA (*Gently*): Why were you fired?

HORACE: I was inadequate.

LAURA: That's not so.

HORACE: I was inadequate in my work.

MRS. FORD: Who said that?

LAURA: What does it matter?

> *Horace walks over to the couch, his hat still on. Mrs. Ford follows him. He sits down. Laura walks over and takes his hat off. She leans over him.*

LAURA: It doesn't matter, Horace.

MRS. FORD: What doesn't matter? A man loses a job he's had twelve years, and it doesn't matter? (*She stands over Horace*) What do they mean, inadequate? A man like you! A top designer of toys. Don't they know what they've got? I'll tell you. Pure gold! They've got pure gold.

LAURA: Mother . . .

MRS. FORD (*To Horace*): Listen, maybe they don't know, but I know what you did for them in twelve years. They have to be told. Your life's blood is in that place. Look, I want you to call whoever it is at that firm. Mr. Johnson or whatever his name is. Get him on the wire and let him know what's what.

HORACE: I'm not calling anybody!

MRS. FORD (*Slowly*): But you're fired! A hundred and ten dollars a week! Do you think you can find a hundred and ten dollars a week on the street?

> *Horace doesn't react as Laura snaps at Mrs. Ford.*

LAURA: Will you please stop it!

MRS. FORD: What's going to happen to us?

HORACE: I don't know.

MRS. FORD: Because all of a sudden my whole life is going before me. I don't know why. I couldn't tell you what it is. (*She begins to cry, and cries all through this*) But it's been ups and downs, ups and downs. I'm sixty-one years old. Sixty-one! It's time I didn't have to be afraid any more. Why don't you look at me when I talk to you? What's going to happen to me?

LAURA (*Shouting*): Shut up!

*There is silence for a moment. Mrs. Ford weeps and
Horace looks at Laura silently. Laura goes to Mrs. Ford,
stands her up and begins to walk her toward the kitchen.*

LAURA (*Firmly*): I'm going to talk to Horace, alone.

MRS. FORD (*Softly*): What did I do wrong? Ever, in my whole
life? If somebody could tell me . . .

*She goes into the kitchen. Laura goes back to Horace.
She stands looking at him.*

HORACE: I couldn't help it.

She sits down next to him.

LAURA: It's only a job. There are other jobs. You were stagnat-
ing there, Horace.

HORACE: I never had another job.

LAURA: What are you going to do?

HORACE: Why did she have to cry?

LAURA: She's an old woman, Horace.

Laura kisses him gently.

HORACE: I mean, it's unfair for her to cry.

LAURA: That's always her first reaction to trouble. Crying.
She'll be all right. Did you get any severance pay?

HORACE: I don't know what I got. I walked out of there.

LAURA: Well, let's forget about it now. We've got the week
end to think about it. Monday, you can start looking. We'll
make a list of places.

HORACE: She's scared to death.

LAURA: She'll get over it.

HORACE: I've got to support her. (*Laura looks at him questioningly*) And you.

LAURA (*Looking at watch*): I want to tell you something.

HORACE: And me. That's three people. You think that's easy?
(*He stands up*) You know what that Mr. Corey said? He
said that I—

LAURA (*Strong*): Mr. Corey was your teacher in Five-B!

HORACE: Mr. Judson! You know what that Mr. Judson said? He said that I was having a nervous breakdown! He's out of his mind! Listen, I'm telling you I saw those kids and I know who they are!

LAURA: Horace!

HORACE: They were running up and down the street, swiping apples, and yelling and having fun. That's all they were doing, having fun. They yelled "fins!" Did you ever yell "fins?"

LAURA: That's not what we were talking about!

HORACE: That *is* what we were talking about! Me making a living for three people while they're swiping apples and running in the streets!

LAURA: Well, you're a grown-up man! What do you think you're supposed to do?

HORACE: And they were sore because they weren't invited to some kid's birthday party. That's the biggest problem in their whole life!

LAURA (*Shouting*): Horace, you've got to stop this!
>*Mrs. Ford comes out of the kitchen. Horace looks at her. She is blowing her nose softly and Laura stands in front of him, close to tears herself now.*

HORACE (*Softly*): You don't have to yell.
>*He turns and walks toward the front door.*

LAURA (*Screaming*): Horace!
>*He opens the door.*

MRS. FORD: Horace, where are you going?

LAURA: You can't go out now! You can't! (*He exits, slamming the door. Laura opens it and screams into the hall*) Horace!
>*But his footsteps recede into the distance. She closes the door and turns to face Mrs. Ford. They look at each other for a moment and then Laura suddenly races for the telephone book.*

MRS. FORD: What's wrong with him? Laura, tell me! Laura!

(*Laura riffles through the phone book*) What are you doing? Who are you going to call? Laura, for heaven's sakes, I have to know what's going on here. Who are you calling?

LAURA (*Sobbing*): I don't know. That's the whole thing. I don't know who I'm going to call. What's the name of a doctor? Will you tell me the name of a doctor?

The doorbell rings. Laura jumps up.

LAURA: Horace . . .

She runs to the door and opens it. Eight people are outside. Clustered around the door, grinning and holding gift-wrapped packages. Leonard is in the foreground with his wife, Betty. As the door opens, they shout.

ALL: Surprise!

Laura looks at them, watches their grins fade.

BETTY: Hey, where's the birthday boy?

LEONARD: Laura, what's wrong?

But Laura can't answer. She is close to tears. They look at each other.

BETTY: Well, maybe we'd better go.

LAURA: No. Please come in. He'll be back.

And silently they file in as we fade out. Fade in on Randolph Street. And again we duplicate the scenes played in Acts I and II, move for move. Horace turns the corner now and stands for a moment looking down the street. Then he begins to walk slowly. He passes a frankfurter cart. An old man thrusts a frankfurter at him.

OLD MAN: Frank on a roll, three cents.

He walks by the cart. A young man and a girl, lovers, arm in arm, walk toward him and split as they go by him. He walks between them.

YOUNG MAN: Bread and butter.

GIRL: Bread and butter.

A big man walks by him, bumping Horace's shoulder.

BIG MAN: Watch where you're goin', huh?

> *Horace walks on. A ball rolls toward him and he picks it up and throws it at someone off camera. We hear a woman shriek from a window.*

WOMAN: Davy, you come home or you're gonna get smacked.

> *An elderly lady walks by him, drops a package and nods when he picks it up for her. We hear a child's voice shouting.*

CHILD: Ringolevio! Caught, caught, caught!

> *He takes out his gold pocket watch and looks at the time. And suddenly the group of four boys comes racing down a stoop right in front of him.*

FIRST KID: Fins! Listen, I yelled fins, didn't I? Waddyewant?

> *They run by Horace, knocking into him, spinning him around. He drops his watch and stares after them, amazed, shocked, terrified. The small, dark, intense-looking boy stares at Horace for a moment. Then they run up the block and Horace watches them.*

FIRST KID (*To dark kid*): Hey, wait up, Hermy! Hey, Hermy Brandt! Hermy Brandt, wait up!

> *And now Horace finds himself following the kids. They stop in front of a fruit store. He stops, panting, watching them.*

HERMY: Let's swipe some apples.

FIRST KID: Hey, Nitsy!

HERMY: We each grab one.

SECOND KID (*Very fast*): Larry.

THIRD KID (*Instantly*): Nexta Larry.

FIRST KID (*Instantly*): Nexta nexta Larry.

> *They all look at Hermy. Boldly, he walks over to the fruit stand, takes an apple and whips it into his jacket. Then, in order, the first kid, the third kid and the second kid each takes an apple. As the second kid takes one, the four of them dash off down the block again,*

bouncing off Horace. He turns, frightened and confused. He goes after them.

HORACE (Calling): Wait!

They run into a tiny alley. Horace follows them to the
alley and stands just outside of it as they bite into their
apples.

HERMY: Boy!

FIRST KID (Grimacing): Sour, huh?

They all chew the apples silently for a moment.

SECOND KID: Hey, can y'imagine not being invited to the birthday party? Can y'imagine?

HERMY (Chewing): Yeah, and I'm s'posed to be his best
friend.

THIRD KID: He stinks.

FIRST KID: We oughta mobilize him, right, Hermy?

Horace stares in silent horror at what he hears.

SECOND KID: Boy! And how!

The kids chew on their apples. Horace stands near
them, trembling, completely unnoticed by them.

THIRD KID: Why don't we bust in on the party?

HORACE: Fellers . . .

They behave as if they do not hear him or see him.

FIRST KID: Ah, what for?

HORACE: Listen to me, fellers. I gotta tell you something.

SECOND KID: He'd probly bawl, or something.

HORACE: Now you've got to listen to me! I want to tell you!

The first kid playfully pushes the second kid and then
points down to his shoe.

FIRST KID (Grinning): Step on a line and you bust your
father's spine!

SECOND KID: Cut it out!

The boys ad-lib now, but we hear no sound save the
sound of Horace's agonized voice. Camera moves close
in on the boys. Their lips move soundlessly as they

chew their apples and talk. We no longer see Horace.

HORACE: Please look at me. I'm standing right here. Hermy! Hermy, are you my buddy? Why don't you listen to me? Fellers, please. I've got to tell you something. Please! You think I don't know I've got some apologies to make to you guys? Georgie, Sy, come on, what're ya giving me the treatment for? I have to tell you something. Willya listen? Willya please listen to me? I couldn't help it! (*And suddenly, without losing a beat, we hear a child's voice, shrilling*) Willya listen? Willya please listen to me? I couldn't help it!

Camera pulls back and we no longer see the adult Horace, but in his place is Horace the boy, pleading with the other boys.

HORACE: I'm telling you, you hafta give me a chance, fellers. Hermy, I'm your best friend! Please listen to me for a minute!

The boys turn and look at him now.

HERMY: Well, if it ain't Horace Maxwell Ford!

FIRST KID: The birthday boy.

SECOND KID: Why didn't ya invite us to your party, Horace Maxwell Ford, you dopey nut?

They advance on him menacingly.

FIRST KID: We're gonna mobilize you!

HORACE (*Screaming*): No! No, please. No . . . don't . . . don't . . . don't . . .

But they pile on him, beat him up and leave him sobbing on the sidewalk. They scamper away, giggling. Fade out. Fade in on Horace's living room. The guests sit and stand about the room quietly, waiting. Laura and Mrs. Ford sit on the couch. Three or four people are grouped about the upright piano, talking softly among themselves and looking at their watches from time to time. Betty walks over to Laura.

BETTY: Laura, honey, I'm awfully sorry about his job. But he'll have another one in no time. He's really a wonderful designer.

LAURA: Thank you.

BETTY: I guess he must be pretty depressed, and all, but this party'll perk him up. Best thing in the world for him right now. Listen, we got him a yo-yo.

LAURA (*Trying to smile*): I know.

The doorbell rings. Everyone turns. Laura stands, Betty tiptoes over to the light switch and turns out the light. She puts her fingers to her lips. Everyone tiptoes over to one corner of the room, everyone but Laura and Mrs. Ford. They wait expectantly, hushed. The bell rings again. Betty waves Laura to the door. But Mrs. Ford walks to the door instead and opens it. Hermy Brandt stands there, an odd smile on his face. He holds up a nickel-plated pocket watch to Mrs. Ford.

HERMY: He dropped this.

Mrs. Ford takes the watch and Laura, rushing to her, takes it from her with trembling fingers. Hermy pads silently away. Laura looks at the watch and then she raises a hand to her face and begins to sob. Cut to close-up of watch. It is a Mickey Mouse watch.

Fade out.

AUTHOR'S COMMENTARY ON

The Incredible World of Horace Ford

One of the first letters I received concerning this show came from a man in North Dakota and was addressed as follows:

> Reginald Rose
> Section 8 Ward
> CBS Television
> New York City

This may give you a general idea of the passionate reaction to The Incredible World of Horace Ford. At this writing, some eight months later, I am still receiving and answering letters. These letters alternate between violent denunciation of the script and unqualified praise. Letters from six psychiatrists in different parts of the country claimed that, for various reasons, Horace Ford was among the best television shows they had ever seen, while letters from as many housewives announced that if they ever catch me they'll claw me bald. No one, it seems, was neutral about this play. One New York newspaper columnist mentioned it five days in a row in his column, certainly some kind of record. He hated it. Yet The New York Times critic called it moving, provocative, sensitive, insightful, etc. A mystified English class in a Southern university sent a plea, signed by all thirty-five students in the class, begging for a complete explanation of the play, and a man in Buffalo sent a brief note which stated bluntly, "Anyone didn't like Horace Ford is a Goddamn nitwit."

In pondering this diverse reaction, I find it difficult to pin down the reasons for the violent feelings on both sides. Since most of the letters denouncing the play indicated that the writers were unable to understand the ending, it would seem that the abrupt and perhaps puzzling final curtain was the cause of most of the furor. Somehow, though, I can't get myself fully to believe this. I think that perhaps the angry, anti-Horace Ford feelings were inspired by something more personal.

As for the letters of praise, many of them, peculiarly enough, sounded defensive, perhaps as though the writers needed to express their feelings in order to convince themselves they were valid.

In trying to define the vigorous reaction expressed in these letters and in reviews, conversations, etc., I offer the following:

Horace Ford, the problem-ridden grown man who relishes esoteric little memories of his childhood and articulates them over and over again for the benefit of anyone who will listen, is a type familiar to most of us. We see Horace Fords wherever we go, among our friends, our families, and even sometimes in ourselves. Reminiscing about one's childhood can be a pleasant, satisfying thing now and again. As an opening conversational gambit the line, "Hey, remember when we used to swipe pomegranates from Ippolito's grocery, Charlie?" can often lead to an hour or so of funny, earthy, enjoyable conversation. It is only when childhood memories begin to invade too large an area of our adult lives and become a means of escape that we begin to consider them a problem. As always with neuroses, it is a question of degree. For instance, all of us at one time or another have had the paranoiac feeling that we are being persecuted. It is simply the degree to which we suffer from this feeling which classifies us as normal, neurotic or psychotic. Horace Ford had obviously allowed his fantasies to become a dominant factor in his life and was just beginning to have trouble functioning as an adult at the curtain-rise. He was immediately recognized by many members of the audience as someone familiar to them, perhaps as themselves, and although the degree of his problem was reasonably severe, the basic problem was still the same, and so he became a character with whom many identified. Once having identified with Horace, they watched, uncomfortably perhaps, as the pressures on him began to mount, but, as is the custom in television drama, they expected that the ending would contain a solution to a problem which was now a bit too personal and too frightening to be comfortable. What finally happened to Horace was so unexpected and so shocking to them that they simply refused to accept it and instead found it more reassuring not to understand it.

Perhaps this theory is completely invalid, but it makes for interesting speculation at any rate. I have discussed Horace Ford with a good many people who found it difficult to understand the ending, and it is the claim of most of them that the sudden leap from reality to fantasy was simply too difficult to bridge. This may well be so, but I had originally felt, in writing this play, that it was quite clear that the story, although it revolved about a very real character, was sheer fantasy from the middle of Act I straight through to the end. From the moment at which Horace arrives on his old street, finds the people dressed as they were when he was a boy and sees frankfurters being sold at three cents apiece, I felt that an audience would have no doubt that he had moved backward in time and that this play was a fantasy, or a piece of science fiction, if you will.

Perhaps what was confusing was this: The audience may have recognized the fact that the play dealt in fantasy but was not able to distinguish whose fantasy it was. Some people felt that the fantasy was Horace's own and a prelude to a complete nervous collapse. Actually this is not the way it was intended. The entire story was a fantasy about real people and I felt that this was clearly proven when Hermy Brandt, Horace's little

childhood friend, broke out of what many thought to be
Horace's private fantasy, appeared at Horace's home, and was
seen and spoken to by Horace's wife and mother.

What I meant to do with The Incredible World of Horace
Ford was to tell a simple horror story about an everyday man
with a somewhat exaggerated but everyday kind of problem
and, in so doing, point out that the funny, tender childhood
memories we cling to are often distorted and unreal. What
happened to Horace when he finally made it back to his childhood was typical of what actually happened to so many of us
again and again when we were children. He was ridiculed, re-
jected, beaten up. These are all familiar experiences to us, yet
somehow we tend only to remember, as Horace did, the joys
of swiping pomegranates from Ippolito's.

What made The Incredible World of Horace Ford memo-
rable for me was the brilliant, compelling performance of Art
Carney as Horace Ford. His portrayal was as fine as any I've
ever seen on television; the shadings and insights he brought
to the childlike, tormented character he played were nothing
short of incredible. As a matter of fact, I must admit here and
now that, when I heard him describe the game of Ringolevio
in Act II, I wished to hell I was playing it again!

About the Author

REGINALD ROSE was born in New York City and has lived there all his life—that is, for thirty-five years. He attended City College but did not graduate (and never will, he says). He has been a camp counselor, three kinds of clerk (file, receiving and stock), publicist for Warner Brothers pictures, and advertising account executive and copy chief.

From 1942 to 1946 he served in the Air Force Quartermaster Corps as enlisted man and then officer. He has been married for eleven years and is the father of four boys, including baby twins.

His first TV play was written in 1951—"The Bus to Nowhere"— and since then he has written six "Studio One" adaptations, five half-hour originals, four pilot films, and thirteen hour-long originals, six of which make up this book. Two of these plays—"Crime in the Streets" and "Twelve Angry Men"—are being made into movies.